To Jane

Whatever you can conceive
& believe you can achieve

CAN DO!

Kevin
Jan 2023

Making the
impossible
POSSIBLE!

First published in South Africa in 2020 by Print Matters,
6 Opal Way, San Michel, Noordhoek 7979, Western Cape, South Africa
www.printmatters.co.za / info@printmatters.co.za

ISBN: 978-0-9870428-1-1

Publisher: Robin Stuart-Clark
Editorial Panel: Biddy Greene, Robert Meintjies, Toby Shenker, Robin Stuart-Clark
Formatting for Press: Michelle de Almeida, The Design Drawer, Johannesburg.

Printing: Novus Print Solutions, Cape Town

TOBY SHENKER
Memoir & Speech Writer
+27 83 949 5579
tshenker@iafrica.com | www.tellyourstory.co.za

print
matters
business

The author and the publisher
thank the following sponsor for their support:

A FAMILY OF BRANDS

DRIVEN BY SERVICE

TTC.COM

Dedication

For humanity

Our deepest fear is not that we are inadequate.
Our deepest fear is that we are powerful beyond measure.
It is our light, not our darkness that most frightens us.
We ask ourselves, Who am I to be brilliant, gorgeous, talented,
fabulous? Actually, who are you not to be?
You are a child of God.
Your playing small does not serve the world.
There is nothing enlightened about shrinking
so that other people won't feel insecure around you.
We are all meant to shine, as children do.
We were born to make manifest the glory of God that is within us.
It's not just in some of us; it's in everyone.
And as we let our own light shine, we unconsciously give
other people permission to do the same.
As we are liberated from our own fear,
our presence automatically liberates others.

Nelson Mandela from his Inauguration Speech, 1994.

Contents

Foreword

What ultimately matters in life is not where we come from in the world, how much money we have in the bank, what language we speak, the size of our muscles or how we identify ourselves with respect to our gender, sexuality, ethnicity, culture or spiritual beliefs.

What matters is our humanity, and our ability to recognise the humanity in others. What sets us apart from all other known species of life are our abilities to be compassionate, generous and humble; to love, to forgive – and to understand the vulnerabilities we all share.

We are made for each other. In Southern Africa we refer to this human inter-dependence as Ubuntu. We say, I am because you are. That which I say and do matters not only to me but also to you.

I believe that we are all related, literally. We are God-carriers, all of us. Were it possible to trace our ancestry enough steps back in history we'd discover that at the end of the rainbow we are actually sisters and brothers in one family, the human family, God's family.

We were made for goodness. When we set out together to reach a righteous destination we become an unstoppable

Kevin and Archbishop Emeritus Desmond Tutu share a light moment together.

force. Conversely, history has taught us that errant members of the family who have believed they have acquired sufficient earthly power to render themselves invulnerable and unaccountable generally fall off their horse.

Many of us support the principles of reaching out across our differences of race, class and culture, but either don't know how to go about it or are too busy focusing on making a living to support families and pay the rent – or building our wealth. Few forfeit a hard-fought pole position in the race for earthly riches to focus on our collective, family wellbeing.

When I was first introduced to Kevin Chaplin, he was a banker with good intentions of changing the world for the better. Since that meeting 20-odd years ago, he has given up banking to focus on the rest of us. Today he heads a pair of complementary foundations, the SA Ubuntu Foundation and the Amy Foundation, the latter named after Amy Biehl, the US student tragically murdered in Gugulethu, Cape Town, on the cusp of our democracy.

In this motivational memoir, Kevin shares the experiences he has gained on the road less travelled, from the be-suited boardroom to the tatty hardships of South African township life. Through it all runs a rich seam of love for his immediate family, and relatively rare insights into the lifestyle and culture of Jewish members of our South African family.

Kevin's journey is deeply inspirational, and I commend it to you. God bless you.

Archbishop Emeritus Desmond Tutu
Hermanus, South Africa

Preface

Despite all the political and socio-economic problems besieging our beloved South Africa and the rest of the world, I'm of the firm belief that with the right mindset, we as individuals, on a personal level, can be resilient enough to change the stories we tell ourselves, to reshape our lives and ensure that we succeed beyond all expectations. This has largely been my own experience, as recounted herein. I invite you to sit tight, grab your oars, and join me in paddling through some turbulent waters as I share the adventure of my personal journey in making the impossible possible. Hopefully, this will provide you with the necessary insights and skills to configure new ways to row with or against the current, making clearly determined choices about how to best reach your desired destination.

So let's take a ride on the wild side that will enable you to navigate the inevitable rapids of life, to create the reality and future of your dreams.

> It all seems impossible until it's done.
> NELSON MANDELA

In 1994, South Africa's new democracy was born, and along with it came a sense of optimism and hope. As a country and nation reborn, we chose to embrace equality, freedom of choice, and opportunity – yet despite these bold commitments written into our constitution, many of us remain shackled by our own mindset, inherently burdened by an unhappy past, heavily weighted with yesterday's misfortunes and mistakes. Now, twenty-five years later, with much water having flowed under the bridge and a disastrous Zuma era, I believe that we still have the power to bring about a major paradigm shift that will change the course of our lives. Along with millions of people around the globe living in such turbulent, uncertain times, now is the time for us to change our perspectives and re-direct the flow of our personal and inter-personal narratives, creating new tributaries and fresh opportunities. In so doing, we will make a difference to our own lives and hopefully in turn, to the well-being of our fellow travellers on this journey. The election of South Africa's new president, Cyril Ramaphosa, heralds a new era of cautious optimism promising much needed transformation and regeneration. Let us not miss this exciting opportunity to channel our efforts – individually and collectively, into a surging river of hope, possibility, and positivity. I invite you to join me on a collective quest for Ubuntu, in which we work together towards achieving a compassionate and benevolent world, with a warm generosity of spirit. By believing in ourselves and one another, we will nurture and feed off this new energy, enabling us all to flourish as individuals and as a nation.

This memoir is intended to illustrate that we don't have to 'take life the way it comes' and live a stagnant existence that is not of our choosing, fraught with misery or undesirable consequences. There is so much we can do to convert our dreams into goals, our goals into plans, and our plans into reality. We can design a life that will come to us, the way we want to live it, with meaning, purpose, and fulfilment. Nothing is impossible – the difference between the impossible and possible lies in your determination to tell a new, invigorating and inspiring story. And it's only impossible until it's done. In short, by reading this book, I believe you will find the tools to turn every perceived 'can't' into 'can do'! ■

1

My early childhood

Little Lorraine Tramontino presents a bouquet to Princess Elizabeth on the first Royal visit to South Africa in 1947, while King George VI and the Queen Mother look on.

Overcoming disability

My mother, Lorraine Ann, née Tramontino, was born in Durban in 1940 with spina bifida – a disorder caused by the incomplete closing of the embryonic neural tube. This potentially crippling condition often results from some vertebrae overlying the spinal cord not being fully formed and remaining un-fused and open. If the opening is large enough, a portion of the spinal cord protrudes through the opening

CAN DO! ✓

in the bones. Spina bifida can be surgically closed after birth, but this does not restore normal function to the affected part of the spinal cord. There are various forms of spina bifida, with mild to severe symptoms and complications.

Doctors said that my mother would not live beyond the age of seven. Although medical knowledge was relatively unsophisticated in those days, she courageously endured ongoing surgery to her legs and feet, virtually every year from ages five to 16, which necessitated tedious three to four-month stays in hospital. My grandmother had to catch two buses to visit her, with parental access being allowed only three times per week. In her usual accepting way, mom bravely whiled away the hours by reading, doing puzzles and chatting with the nurses and fellow patients. Statistics show that babies can be severely affected, and in fact mom's family was cautioned that she was unlikely to live beyond the age of 14, yet she survived and went on to produce three children, against all odds.

Lorraine Ann Tramontino.

Interestingly, when Princess Margaret and Princess Elizabeth (the future queen) made their first royal visit to South Africa in 1947, my mother, then a somewhat nervous seven-year-old wearing calipers, was given the honour of presenting flowers to the young princess on behalf of the children of KwaZulu-Natal. To everyone's amazement, my mother was blessed with another seven years, and much more! While in her late teens, Lorraine was courted by my father, Maurice. It did not take him long to become besotted and request

From left: Cecil Henry Chaplin, Hilda Eliza Chaplin, Maurice Henry Chaplin, Lorraine Ann Chaplin née Tramontino, Thora Catherine Tramontino, Seconde Albert Tramontino – March 1961.

her hand in marriage. Because by now it was expected that she would die by the age of 21, two of her aunts refused to go to the wedding in the belief that Maurice would be left a widower at a young age. Isn't it sad how readily people give up on something or someone so important? Having survived into her twenties, doctors told my mother that she would never be able to bear children. Many years later, I was able to use this story to save another child's life – as explained in the following narrative.

Doctors are not always right

While working for First National Bank (FNB), my secretary let me know that Dave Eastment, our Adderley Street branch manager, was most distressed and desperate to see me. A doctor had done an ultrasound scan on his pregnant wife, Nicki, and suspected the baby had spina bifida. He had advised them to consider aborting the pregnancy. They

CAN DO! ✓

were understandably distraught. Not knowing what to make of this, they felt helpless and unable to make such a critical decision. I advised Dave to put the matter in God's hands with prayer and also shared my mother's story. On the basis of my mother's experience, Dave and his wife decided not to abort, and to everyone's relief, the baby, Hayley, was born 100 per cent healthy. I met with him some years later, and tears welled up in his eyes when I reminded him of this story.

> **Know that in uncertain times, despite the dark cloud hovering overhead, there are always options. There's hope out there.**
> **It's also best not to panic, because making an impulsive decision is often not to your advantage. Seek advice from people whose opinions you trust and respect, and pray.**

Life happens while one is busy making other plans: Two years after her marriage, against all the odds, mom fell pregnant with me, and later, my brother Ashley, followed by a third son, Dale. Despite the odds, all three sons were born healthy and normal. I'm told that I made a boisterous arrival on 7 April 1963. Mom was naturally overjoyed, but this unexpected turn of events would prove to be most problematic for dad. As I grew up, he became increasingly jealous, particularly since I enjoyed the lion's share of his adored wife's love and attention.

Unlike me, my father was an extreme introvert. In fact he was socially dysfunctional, to the point of disliking most of the people he knew – and even those he didn't! Besides being rude and abusive, dad was generally uninterested in the well-being of other people, including his siblings. The hard truth is that the arrival of his three sons hindered his hitherto exclusive access to his beloved wife Lorraine, who adored us.

As far as I can recall, my existence started to become problematic to dad when I was about seven. Driven by his unhealthy obsession with mom, he abused me emotionally and physically by beating me virtually every day. Some years later, one of our neighbours – who vividly recalled the constant howling emanating from our home –

confessed that they had often contemplated reporting him for child abuse. Lance Mindry, one of my best friends at school, recently said he would never forget me leaping into the car to escape my father while the latter was angrily hurling coat hangers at me! How well I recall this all-too familiar scene: All three of us lined up at the back door waiting to come in, terrified at the prospect of having to make our way past him to enter the kitchen. Being the eldest, I was always in front, and destined to bear the brunt of his fury, since I was clobbered the hardest. Today, my uncle and aunt often marvel at the fact that I did so well in life, despite the appalling treatment at the hands of my father.

Mom wisely countered this abuse by ensuring that I had other more appropriate male role models to emulate. Always loving, selfless and generous by nature, my mom taught me so much about so many important things, too numerous to mention. Despite dad's glaring inability to connect, empathise, or express love, Lorraine's warmth and affection more than compensated for his deficiencies.

Moving past your past

I believe that tough experiences in life often come our way as an opportunity to learn, and we should avoid blaming our past as the primary obstacle to future growth. Very often, one hears of people who perpetuate a cycle of abusive parenting, resulting in their own relationships with their children becoming dysfunctional. In exoneration of my father's inadequacies and dreadful behaviour, I must add that according to my grandmother, my dad's father – Cecil Henry but known to all as Charlie – no relation to the inimitable Charlie Chaplin – was impossibly stern and autocratic. My grandmother often felt terribly sorry for Maurice. I suspect that because my uncles were good at sport and Maurice, Charlie's eldest son, was somewhat lacking in that regard, Charlie sorely mistreated him while being kind to his brothers. Such a scenario can only result in

> 'We define ourselves by the best that is in us, not the worst that has been done to us.'
> EDWARD LEWIS

CAN DO!

bitterness, anger, and loss of self-confidence. In some ways my dad was a very clever man, endowed with an extremely high IQ. This may to some extent explain his anti-social behaviour! Nevertheless, I believe that his irrational behaviour enabled, and possibly even empowered me, to become a better person and parent.

Find good role models

I was raised in a household where I was loved by one parent, and loathed by another – and this bizarre phenomenon lasted throughout my mother's lifetime. About six years ago my father acknowledged this, saying, 'The worst thing that ever happened in my life was when you were born. The minute I heard you crying in the hospital, I knew you were going to be a problem.' No child ever wants to hear a parent utter such dreadful words. Although dad only voiced this harsh sentiment in my adulthood, it manifested in his mistreatment of me throughout my formative years, in more ways than I care to remember. Fortunately, my mother's unreserved love and level-headed approach balanced the scales and enabled me to work through this pain. Of particular significance is the fact that I never bought into his irrational judgment of me. What really matters is that I've been able to make some meaningful and coherent sense out of what has happened.

Many people continue throughout their lives to deflect responsibility for their misfortunes onto an unhappy childhood or dysfunctional upbringing.

While it is not easy to change the architecture of our thinking, there comes a time when one has to unlock oneself from the emotional cages of one's past, and move on with resilience, to find a workable way forward. This involves making a conscious decision not to dwell on all that was wrong in the past, for it will most certainly sabotage one's future. At some point, sooner rather than later, we all must take full responsibility for the choices we make as an adult.

Fortunately for me, my mother in her wisdom ensured that we had good male role models: We spent a lot of time with dad's two brothers, my uncles Colin and Neville Chaplin, and mom's brothers,

Lorraine Ann Chaplin, née Tramontino.

my uncles Rowland and Lionel Tramontino, who were all extroverted, well balanced, and gentlemanly as well as exceptional sportsmen who proved to be excellent role models for me. In addition, we also spent quality time with her father, Seconde Albert Tramontino. Even at 15 or 16, if I was out with friends and my grandfather was coming to visit, I would be sure to return home in time to chat, since I hugely valued his input, advice and time, as well as that of my uncles. Having this diverse group of role models to some degree compensated for the gaps and paved my way to a well balanced, successful life. I cannot stress strongly enough the importance of suitable role models for one's children.

I realised early on that my father was the problem and not me. I still vividly recollect my aunt explaining, 'Don't worry Kevin, your father is just jealous of you.' Much like a petulant child who doesn't get his way, he constantly lashed out angrily, sometimes violently. When I was older, I always felt sorry for him, with his damaged relationships and the miserable lifestyle he created for himself. Fortunately, my siblings and I were raised in a close, supportive neighbourhood where the company of our neighbours took precedence and became like family. What warm memories I have of the fun and friendship I enjoyed with wholesome people like the Basels, Esselens, and Breeds! I can still hear Aunty Dawn singing while she prepares a mouth-watering Lebanese feast for the family and neighbours. When I think about it now, these were formative relationships, which I've subconsciously emulated in my own family life, and the person I chose to become. Interestingly, I'm still in touch with most of them, even though we've

CAN DO!

From left: Colin Noel Chaplin, Neville Ernest Chaplin and Maurice Henry Chaplin, 1960.

Kevin, 1963.

Ashley, Kevin & Dale Chaplin, 1968.

Kevin with his uncles and grandfather – From left: Lionel Tramontino, Kevin, Colin and Neville Chaplin, Rowland Tramontino and Grandpa Tramontino, 1989.

Making the impossible possible

all long since moved away. Today, it's a depressing fact that most of us haven't even met our neighbours, since we all lead such busy, parallel lives which rarely seem to interlink or coincide. The Ubuntu culture advises one to make an effort to connect. For starters, we can at least wave at the familiar faces driving down our street, and maybe we can build on this by having a street party!

A rather curious turnaround occurred in my father after my mother passed away in January 2016 at the age of 75. In an inexplicable change in human behaviour, his overall demeanour improved dramatically – almost as if he'd undergone a full-frontal lobotomy! While he obviously mourned her loss and pined for her, he suddenly became decidedly pleasant to have around. In processing this, I can only attribute his newfound affability to the fact that he no longer needed to shield her from me, or to zealously oppose any investment of her time in me, as opposed to him. How sad that this would only occur upon her demise. Strangely enough, after she passed away, he began to relish my weekly visits, much to our mutual pleasure. What a pity this was to happen so late in our lives – at 53 for me and 82 for him. Nonetheless, I am deeply grateful that we were able to enjoy one another's company, albeit only for 15 months. In early May 2017, our time together was cut short when he suddenly collapsed, lost consciousness, and died eight hours later. Having just come to terms with the loss of my mother, this came as a terrible shock to me – all the more heartbreaking since we were getting on extremely well and I had expected him to live well into his nineties, like both his parents. The day before he collapsed we had spent a happy afternoon together, reminiscing fondly about the past.

Unfortunately, mom's sister, Yvonne, married a man of similar ilk, and I've always wondered what motivated these attractive women, with their wonderful father and brothers, to share their lives with men who were controlling, damaged and abusive – an interesting thesis for someone studying psychology! I think my mom knew that she had to take responsibility for the consequences of her choice – and then perpetuating the problem by not putting her foot down years ago!

CAN DO!

Standing: Rowland Arthur Tramontino, Thelma Valentine Bailey née Tramontino, Lionel Albert Tramontino. Sitting: Yvonne Louise Wehner née Tramontino, Seconde Albert Tramontino, Lorraine Ann Chaplin née Tramontino.

I know it's not always easy, but it's imperative for women to take a stand against men who are abusive, be it physically, emotionally, or verbally. Men also need to take a stand and realise that such behaviour is unacceptable and teach their sons to respect women.

One of my mother's many wise decision was to ensure that from a young age we grew spiritually by attending 'Sunday School', then later 'Teen church' and 'Friday night Youth' meetings – all of which role modelled the important values of Christian life. Besides offering a sense of belonging, this also initiated a close personal relationship with God, who has always been my anchor in times both good and bad. I believe that my faith has made me who I am, and it has grown deeper and stronger over the years.

Growing up in a poor household

A qualified draftsman, my father was very good at designing and constructing beautiful woodwork items for his children and our home. An extreme introvert, he elected to remain sitting in a corner, drawing out his days, happily doing his job, despite the fact that his work paid poorly. He earned very little throughout his life, as he was distinctly lacking in ambition and entrepreneurial drive, and it never occurred to him to ask for a reasonable annual increase. Consequently, my grandfather contributed to the household by assisting mom every month, while my aunt was kind enough to bring us groceries once a week. From an early age I knew that hard work brought success and I thoroughly enjoyed working at Pick n Pay Hypermarket in Durban North every Friday afternoon and Saturday and during school holidays in Grade 11 and 12. We came to rely on the hand-me-downs proffered by our Tramontino cousins for school uniforms. With this ongoing support from extended family, my parents somehow found a way to make ends meet. It has always amazed me that we never seemed to feel the effects of having next to nothing. Somehow they found the means to pay for the odd, non-essential treat like class photos, sports outings, and birthday gifts. Ironically, my friends loved coming over, because there was always Coca Cola and appetising food available, especially my mom's delicious (almost famous!) Tramontino spaghetti. As children, we were oblivious to the fact that mom never bought new clothes for herself. How could I not have noticed! ■

Grandpa Seconde Albert Tramontino.

CAN DO!

Kevin and mother, Lorraine, two weeks before she passed away at 75, in 2016.

2

Upon finishing school

Off they go to become men: Kevin, Navy; Dale, Army; and Ashley, Air Force.

Joining the navy

All white, 17-year-old male matriculants received official letters from the South African Defence Force assigning them to the army, navy, or air force. I was fortunate to get the navy, which meant being drafted to Saldanha Bay in the Western Cape. However, my call-up was for July instead of January, so I applied to work at Barclays Bank in Durban and was accepted as a trainee for six months – at a salary of R348 a month. I'll never forget my excitement at being accepted, but

CAN DO! ✓

then my disappointment at having to start work in the Durban North Branch on the forthcoming Monday – just a week after completing my matric exams in December 1980. This gave me no respite whatsoever. In those days, one started at the most junior level – which usually involved franking envelopes for posting (a task now made defunct by electronic mail). Today, most youngsters would frown upon having to do such menial work. This turn of events certainly took me on a different trajectory to my dream in high school of entering the hotel business and a career in hotel management, but as it turned out I thoroughly enjoyed my banking career.

Bridging the gap in the military service

Even though I'd hoped to have the December holidays to 'chill out', I didn't hesitate to take up this opportunity: There was certainly no such thing as taking a 'gap year' that has become so popular today, or having the chutzpah to ask if one could rather start in a month's time in the interests of having a much-needed holiday! In fact, military training could be regarded today as the gap year that male school leavers were forced to take. In my view, it was functional and useful, but for the wrong reasons. It served to inculcate self-sufficiency and maturity – attributes that are largely missing in South African school leavers today, as military training is no longer compulsory.

Interestingly, Israeli youth are conscripted for up to three years of compulsory military training, during which they learn to take responsibility for themselves, their peers, and the national safety. In making the transition to adulthood, teenagers commonly regard doing military service for the State of Israel as both a privilege and a duty. Contrary to this, in South Africa the 17- to 19-year-olds today who are lucky enough to complete their schooling either go straight to university or college, or find themselves unemployed and drifting aimlessly, lacking in maturity and a sense of direction. Young men of yester-year – who did military service before embarking on further study – emerged from the experience much more mature, resilient, and ready to assume the responsibilities of everyday life.

While for some children a gap year might mean a waste of time, in general one should look to do something rewarding and meaningful during this time. Although I did not have the benefit of a gap year, after working two to three nights a week answering phones for a company to supplement my banking income, I applied for four month's leave very early in my banking career, during which I relished the experience of working on a kibbutz in Israel. As a Christian, living and working in this disciplined but supportive environment was the most enlightening experience. I learned so much about culture, cooperation, collaboration, and hard work. I strongly encourage parents to grant their children similar gap years, or some sort of volunteering experience. The Americans are good at encouraging this. As part of my daughters' gap-year experience, I paid for them to travel with me to places like Moscow, Prague, Dijon, Paris, and the Netherlands.

Going forward, I never took life's opportunities for granted, but made sure to seize them and turn them into something bigger. Even though I was officially recruited to the navy from July onwards, the bank's policy was to keep me on their books as an employee, with a token salary of R48 a month for two years. In those days, this paltry sum amounted to useful pocket money.

My time in the military proved a great learning experience. I was naïve and unprepared for the crazy, almost surreal world I was about to join. My jaw dropped at the first sound and sighting of the rough, suntanned, officers and recruits – sleeves tightly rolled up to reveal heavily tattooed, powerful biceps, spewing vile profanities sprinkled with unintelligible English or Afrikaans. It was a world in which your sanity and self-esteem depended on blind obedience, and whether the corners of your bed had been mitred to 90 degrees or whether you could endure standing guard outdoors in winter from midnight to 4 am, rifle in hand and at the ready. Between the icy weather, and hours more suited to a leopard guarding her cubs in the dead of night, I vowed never to get a job which required doing such unproductive, demoralising work – let alone throughout bitter nights, when most

CAN DO!

people are cosily asleep in warm beds! I was now more determined than ever to up-skill myself, so that I could do something meaningful with my life to excite and energise me.

Racist propaganda

In an effort to stir up racial hatred, our apartheid government came up with the derogatory term *die swart gevaar* (the black danger) – to create the impression that all white people were in dire need of protection from our hidden 'enemy', namely black-skinned people. Upon reflection, I am astounded by how ignorant and self-involved most white South Africans were to be so accepting, unquestioning, and habituated to the government's racist motives! While our two years of military training were imposed for the wrong reasons, it certainly toughened us, and fast tracked us to independence, maturity, and a more disciplined lifestyle. It was interesting to see the underlying tension between the Afrikaans- and English-speaking conscripts, which stems all the way back to the Anglo-Boer War (1899–1902). English-speaking chaps were referred to as *rooineks* (red necks) by the Afrikaners – a derogatory term that has persisted to this day. I later learned that this antagonism dates back to Britain's imprisonment of Dutch women and children in horrific concentration camps. The term *rooineks* originates from the fact that the British soldiers' necks were sunburnt from wearing pith helmets which did not protect them from the sun, along with the red collars of their military uniforms.

Apartheid and the media

The state-owned South African Broadcasting Corporation (SABC) was for many years a monopoly controlled by the white minority National Party government. One of its strategies involved controlling the media as much as was possible, with the aim of limiting our sense of the strong anti-apartheid lobby that was taking hold across the world. Long after the rest of the world had access to television, the government resisted its introduction, claiming that it would 'undermine the moral fibre of South Africa', although in reality, it feared that television would dilute state control of press and radio. It also saw the new medium as a threat to Afrikaans and the Afrikaner *volk* (people) because it would give prominence to English. I was amused to learn that Prime Minister Hendrik Verwoerd compared television with atomic bombs and poison gas, claiming that 'they are modern things, but that does not mean they are desirable, and that the government has to watch for any dangers to the people, both spiritual and physical'!

In January 1976, when TV was first launched, only a few select programmes were available from a single channel, for a few hours each day, featuring very selective news content. As a family, we had to go to our neighbours, the Basels, to watch TV, as this was a luxury commodity that only the wealthy could afford. While the censor board prevented us from seeing anti-apartheid protests and marches in the US, television's eventual arrival was mistimed, because just six months later, on June 16, graphic and disturbing images of revolt and repression in Soweto, which came to be known as the Soweto riots, were beamed into living rooms across the world. Black schoolchildren across the country angrily objected to the official decree that Afrikaans be used as a medium of tuition – resulting in thousands of young cadres being delivered into the struggle. Given the fact that the majority of black children spoke neither English nor Afrikaans as their home language, one can only imagine the debilitating effects of this appalling new piece of racist legislation. No government explanation would ever temper the visual impact of the iconic photograph that was beamed across the world, of a dying 13-year-old Hector Pieterson, draped helplessly in the arms of a distraught friend as he fled the scene of the shooting by riot police, with Hector's traumatised sister, Antoinette, running alongside.

Breaking out of the mould

Having all come from wealthy families, my cousins automatically went to university. I left the navy in July 1982 and rejoined Barclays Bank, which ultimately became First National Bank. Of one thing I was certain: I was determined to study to break out of the poverty

CAN DO!

mould. While doing my army service, I studied for my banking exams and passed them. Upon my return from military service, I applied to do a BCom degree, but my parents couldn't afford to send me to university. In 1986, the bank introduced an undergraduate sponsored study programme, so it was with much enthusiasm that I applied, only to be profoundly disappointed when I was declined. The spaces were allocated to much older, longer-serving employees. Feeling somewhat disillusioned, I decided not to apply again in 1987. Thank goodness my manager encouraged me to try again, which I did, and was delighted beyond words to finally be accepted.

> **Never underestimate the importance of words of encouragement and how empowering they can be for someone else. Take an interest in someone's well-being and future.**

Thus began five years of part-time study, during which I excelled and earned many distinctions and prizes. I soon realised how hard work pays off, for my efforts were rewarded with good increases and steady promotions. I was later granted a merit bursary from the University of South Africa to do Honours, which I opted not to pursue, as my family commitments and job took priority, having by then become too demanding. ∎

3

Joining Barclays Bank
and early married life

The bells are ringing – Kevin marries Robyn née Daneel, January 1989.

CAN DO! ✓

Kicking off in Durban

As a young recruit to the bank, I worked at various branches in KwaZulu-Natal. I was enthusiastic and energetic and moved up the ranks quite rapidly. Henry Golding, the accountant at Durban North Branch, caught me by surprise one day by instructing me to answer the switchboard for a few months. 'But this is a job for women,' I thought. The culture was hugely sexist in those days. Women could not become managers and controlling the switchboard was traditionally a position reserved strictly for women. What had I done wrong to deserve this? I was incensed and felt ready to resign.

Having always believed that I should not be too shy to speak up, I asked Mr Golding what I'd done wrong. I can vividly recall him being somewhat taken aback, and responding, 'No, on the contrary, you've done so well, we thought you're the best person to fill the gap, as it's such an important front-of-house position and we have nobody else suitable.' Many people underestimate the importance of this role, and the fact that one needs an experienced person on switchboard. Many years later as a senior manager, I would stress the fact that our switchboard operator-cum-receptionist was in fact the first point of call for customers. I encouraged my staff to only appoint experienced, more mature people who were better poised for this role. Our best switchboard operator at FNB was (and still is) a blind male called Marc. It was with a renewed vigour that I took on this role.

During my early years at Durban North Branch, I made many lifelong friends. One of them, Lesley Jorgensen spent many hours patiently teaching me to drive in her car during lunch hours and after work. She had nerves of steel. I thoroughly enjoyed the many curries made for me by the Moodleys in Verulam. By 1987, at the age of 24, I was promoted to the position of assistant accountant – a big role in those days for a youngster. I was given lodgings in a huge three-bedroom home in Eshowe, an hour and a half up the coast from Durban. Life was great, I was young and on a mission to progress in my career, since I enjoyed working in the bank. It was in Eshowe that Dave Wright, the accountant, taught me about attention to detail, and that one's admin processes are critical for success. But it was far from all work and no play. My early banking days were balanced with invigorating surfing after work with my friend Paul Mindry, not to forget suffering the occasional headache on a Saturday after a drink too many the night before!

It was there that I met and fell in love with my beautiful wife-to-be, Robyn née Daneel, who was working at the bank as a teller at the time. Before I arrived, Dave Wright had repeatedly claimed that the newly appointed assistant accountant named Kevin Chaplin would definitely be 'the one' for her. But pestering her about this served only to put Robyn off, for when I arrived and tried to chat up this beautiful girl, she responded coldly. Nevertheless, I couldn't get her off my mind, and eventually plucked up the courage to phone her for a date. To my delight, she agreed. Robyn will attest that my persistence paid off: Thankfully she fell in love with me too. We chose not to tell the staff about our relationship for at least four months, which was fun. When we walked into a Friday night social holding hands, it was well worth the wait to see the shock on their faces – especially those of Dave and good friends Wilna Venter, Colleen Chateau and Essie Rorke, who had tried so hard to match-make. We married and settled in Durban in 1989, where I worked as a corporate analyst – at which point we bought our first home. I must explain that what made this purchase possible was the solid financial grounding I'd had from my mother, who always lived within her means, budgeted carefully every month, and bought nothing on HP except essential assets like a house and car. I can still picture the little notebook in which she meticulously listed every expense, including bond repayments – tallied up against my father's monthly income.

A huge problem in South Africa is that people are overextending themselves, spending wastefully on depreciating assets and not budgeting. All too often, one hears of men who either run off or pass away, leaving their wives and family to flounder financially with dire consequences. Ideally, women should be skilled enough to become co-breadwinners, as one never knows what the future might hold.

CAN DO!

And then the babies came – Kirsty Leigh (left) and Sarah Louise Chaplin, 1995.

Invest time in your marriage

Two of the greatest moments in my life have undoubtedly been the birth of our two daughters, Sarah Louise and Kirsty Leigh – who continue to bring infinite joy and blessings. Sarah, our first child, was born while we were living in Johannesburg. I was so preoccupied with the euphoria of showing off our gorgeous baby to all our friends and relatives, that I neglected to consider Robyn's needs. As if on a presidential election campaign, I dragged both mother and daughter along to meet all my friends and family in Durban, oblivious to Robyn's brittle state of exhaustion and desperate need for sleep. In hindsight, this was a ridiculous 'road show'. I got the fright of my life when Robyn dropped the bombshell that she wanted a divorce, but it was exactly the shock I needed. Determined to save our marriage, this forced me to step off the treadmill, tune into her space and start meeting *her* needs rather than my own. Working at it was challenging and things were very tense for a while, but it was the best thing that could have happened. We started dropping Sarah off at my mom and making quality time to 'find' one another again. There is no doubt that children put immense pressure on a marriage, and it's all too easy to give up when the going gets tough. Although we've been happily married for 30 years, it still requires a constant effort to stay connected, whilst ensuring that we don't take anything for granted.

> **If you invest time in your partner and work at the relationship, your marriage can succeed. Keep working at staying connected and being supportive. It is far better to 'check in with' than 'check on' your partner!**

I always try to take a stand when I hear of people who are not 'playing the game'. Every so often, one hears of a man who has decided to abandon his wife when, for example, another woman comes into his life, or his wife has gained too much weight, or complains of being perpetually tired. In my view, this is morally wrong: For a marriage to work, one has to play fair and be empathetic – especially when young babies or children are draining the last reserves of one's energy. When a marriage is sailing through choppy waters, it often leads to anger and insecurity. This is the time when people start checking on their spouses' cellphones and personal computers, treating their partners with often undue suspicion.

> I think that the most significant work we ever do, in our whole world, in our whole life, is done within the four walls of our own home.
> STEVEN COVEY

CAN DO!

Dedicate time to your children

Many years ago, my good friend Suzanne Ackerman-Berman told me that she had insisted that all their children sit down together with them for dinner, every evening. This made a great deal of sense to me, so I started doing this with my own children when they were young. The rule was that every night, the TV would have to be switched off for a full hour, which would officially become 'family time', regardless of whether it suited them or not. I'll never forget how angry they were at the time, vehemently protesting, 'Daddy, that's so unfair, none of our friends have to do this. What are we going to talk about for a whole hour?' My sense was that I had to be thick skinned and intractable about this. There were times when even Robyn accused me of being too pedantic about sticking to the 'full hour rule'. After some weeks, I was informed: 'All our friends laugh at us, we are the only family who does this crazy stuff.' To which I replied, 'Well then you must have told them for them to know about it. It's just a pity their families don't do it!'

Happy family times.

Much like a bull elephant, I stood my ground tenaciously. Inevitably, after ten minutes or so, they would start chatting about their day, and soon, we were enjoying one another's company and sharing what the day had to offer. These days, the problem is compounded by the distractions of other appealing multimedia, such as cellphones, iPads, and hand-held gaming devices. It is amazing how much interaction we can lose, such as joking around, creative play, sharing of ideas and concerns and expressions of love. Sarah, now 28, and Kirsty, now 24, reflect on those shared, precious family moments with much fondness and appreciation. It's one of the best things I ever did to build our relationships, and a great example of Ubuntu, which is also about spending quality time connecting with your children. Statistics show that today parents spend less than 10 per cent of their

Marital bliss.

CAN DO! ✓

time communicating and engaging with their children. Remember that while it's fun to watch TV together, this is not communicating with your children – although, to some extent, it does give you common ground from which to launch a conversation, provided you set aside the time. 'Teachable moments' are unplanned, naturally emerging opportunities for learning or discussion where a parent can offer certain insights to their children.

'Money can't buy me love' – The Beatles

From the start, I ensured that I showered my kids with love. I must balance this by saying that I didn't overcompensate in the form of financially indulging them or 'buying their love' when they were growing up – to the contrary in fact. When I started working, I had to pay my parents rent for board and lodging. Now that my children are beyond their teens, and driving, I've insisted that they contribute half towards the purchase of their cars. The concept of what constitutes 'spoiling one's children' is complex and open to debate. We've taken our children on superb holidays, both local and overseas, which we feel is an important investment of time and money that will precipitate deeper connections with them. But we certainly do not give them every material item they might desire. I recollect Kirsty saying, 'Daddy, you always say "no" when we want the latest gadget, but then you take us on lots of holidays?' My reply: 'Because when I'm long gone, you will always remember the holidays but not the gadget!'

Shabbat (Sabbath) gatherings

Over the years, Robyn and I have acquired many wonderful Jewish friends, and we have often been invited to share their traditional Shabbat (Friday night) dinners. We love the concept of honouring God and uniting the family over a weekly dinner as part of a reconnection with one's faith. Interestingly, this Jewish ritual dates back to the days when the Jews were still slaves in Egypt. Emanating from this is Judaism's vision of a society offering its people dignity, equal rights, and hope.

In observing the Sabbath, one allocates a fixed date once a week for the family to sit down and say their prayers, celebrate their joys, and define themselves as part of the 'we' rather than the 'I'. It is a night when parents don't have to rush off. Instead they give their children their greatest gift – that of time, uninterrupted by work, technology or outside distractions. I think it's a wonderful way for the family – and often the extended family – to stay connected, while engaging in meaningful discourse. And what an amazing way to connect with fellow Jews, all doing the same thing at virtually the same time, across the globe!

Many people are given to wonder why Jewish people are so successful. Generation after generation prized themselves on studying the Torah (Jewish written law), so, with an inbred culture of learning, intellectual pursuits have always been part of the Jewish narrative. Across the board, Judaism stresses learning and analysis, along with robust debate. From an early age, children are taught to substantiate their thinking or argue the point as opposed to simply memorising doctrine. I've no doubt that the ritual of gathering for a Sabbath dinner

Jewish tradition at our Christian wedding.

CAN DO!

has given them ample opportunity to exchange information, practice the art of lively, robust debate, and hone their persuasive skills. If one adheres to all the 'no work' rules of Shabbat, it's also intended to function as a day of complete rest and renewal – which many of us sorely need. This concept is something most families can easily adopt, and one certainly does not have to be Jewish to do so! ∎

4

Semi-grating to Johannesburg

From Barclays to First National Bank

Due to mounting sanctions against South Africa because of its apartheid policies, Barclays Bank disinvested in South Africa and sold its shareholding in the bank in 1986. The following year, the bank was renamed 'First National Bank of Southern Africa Limited' and it thereupon became a wholly South African owned and controlled entity. Prior to this, junior managers were able to work in the UK for a year. I had always wanted to travel, but with Barclays having disinvested, the option to work overseas was no longer available. I was so disappointed, but nonetheless remained determined to somehow configure my life in such a way that I would find the means, time, and opportunity to explore the world. In Xhosa, *'ukuhamba kukubona'* means 'travel opens a window to the world'.

In 1990, I was promoted to the position of National Industrial Relations Manager – which required moving to Johannesburg. Despite having believed some years earlier that I'd never want to leave Durban, I grabbed this opportunity, which represented an interesting challenge and, of course, a significant move up the corporate ladder. This would prove to be one of my formative 'can do' decisions.

Ask for what you believe is reasonable

So in 1991, the big move away from home, friends, and family began. Since we wanted to drive up from Durban with lots of our stuff, and Robyn was seven months pregnant at the time, I needed a bigger, safer car than the one which I'd bought second hand, some years earlier.

Knowing that my new package included a large new company car, I requested that I take delivery of it a week before my arrival. I was told by the HR Department in Durban that this would not be possible, since my promotion would only become effective upon commencement of my new appointment, that is my first day of work in Johannesburg. I decided, with my grandfather's adage of 'never say die, get up and try' to make a special request to the Johannesburg office. To put it bluntly, I refused to take no for an answer. Sure enough, with little time to spare before the date of our pending 'semigration', I took delivery in Durban of what was to be my first brand new car – a magnificent blue Ford Sapphire, which looked and handled much like a solid Mercedes. The hand of fate works in inexplicable ways. We cruised safely virtually all the way to Eshowe, en route to Johannesburg, but at twilight, a drunkard stumbled onto the road right in front of me, and hit my windscreen, smashing it with a horrific thud – a collision which was unavoidable. Somehow, he bounced off the bonnet and smashed windscreen, and disappeared completely from sight. After a desperately frantic search, we were astonished to find him lying curled up on the roof of my car, groaning in mild discomfort, his life having been saved miraculously by his deep state of inebriation! With a new windscreen and badly dented bonnet, we continued on our way. Of course, the dreaded moment came when, upon arrival, I had to break the unhappy news to my new boss and the HR department. They were very understanding: these things happen. The car was duly repaired and we kept it for four more years.

Never be afraid to ask for what you think is reasonable, if you believe you can motivate it strongly. If you deal with a difficult situation calmly, most people are reasonable and life carries on.

Furthermore, when I accepted the post, everyone said, 'You can't work for a man like Louis Mol. He's so unreasonable and autocratic.' People seemed to be terrified of him, but I was not scared off by this and decided to take on the challenge. Early on he issued an instruction that

made me feel most uncomfortable. Challenging him in a diplomatic way, I asked if we could discuss the matter. Initially, his face turned blustery red, but he soon calmed down. I don't think anyone had ever challenged him before! This proved to be the start of a great, mutually beneficial working relationship. I learned so much from him, and my three years in this role proved to be a most productive, interesting learning experience.

Focus on the positives

Having preconceived ideas can prove severely limiting, particularly if one is not prepared to compromise or if one is unwilling to change one's views. Despite having been repeatedly told that I was crazy to leave Durban for Johannesburg, which apparently was 'awful', I changed my mindset to 'hey – let me just give it a shot'. Instead of focusing on the negatives such as crime, which was of course an ongoing concern, I focused on the positives and made the most of every day. As things turned out, it was one of the best things I ever did, and our young family spent ten super-happy years there. As a child, I had never been to a game farm. It was our move to Johannesburg that enabled our family to take the most meaningful holidays in game reserves. I am still astounded by the number of people who tell me how much they hate living in Johannesburg. Perhaps this stems partly from their reluctance to explore the offerings of this magnificent region. My grandfather, Seconde Albert Tramontino, was part owner of the Nest Hotel in the Drakensberg, where we spent all of our July holidays as children. I can still recall the love and warmth we shared with our extended family during those idyllic holidays.

Schedule family getaways

When I met Robyn she introduced me to game reserves in KwaZulu-Natal, where she had enjoyed many memorable holidays. So while living in Johannesburg, every second month we would take Sarah and Kirsty to one of six game reserves, which are all within one or two hour's drive from the city. For six to eight weekends a year, I'd

CAN DO!

use the timeshare I'd purchased to take the family to wonderful spots like Mabula Lodge, Mabalingwe Nature Reserve, Kwa Maritane, or Bakubung in the Pilanesberg. All of these easily accessible and affordable places are breathtakingly beautiful. We'd arrive on a Friday afternoon, stay for the weekend, and leave early on the Monday morning to return them to school on time – having woken and dressed them in their school uniforms well before the first glimmer of dawn! For me, these shared encounters with wildlife were both relaxing and invigorating, and I would return to work refreshed and ready to tackle any similar such wildlife at the office! It is amazing how much you can pack into two and a half days when you plan it and there are always thrilling, manifold ways to optimise one's time.

I am astounded by how many people don't make time to get away, particularly since it doesn't have to cost a lot. If you make the effort, you can find anything within your budget. The mere fact that you are with your family, away from the usual distractions, affords you the unique opportunity to bond, share ideas, and connect with one another on a meaningful level. At the start of each year, one should schedule this precious time away. It will do you, your marriage, and your children the world of good.

Weigh up the risks

In 1991, after our daughter Sarah was born, Robyn and I decided that she should take more than the six months maternity leave that was due to her, and she duly resigned from her job. But within two years it became evident that we couldn't afford her remaining unemployed. After much discussion and prayer, she returned to a mornings-only job that had become available at the bank. When Kirsty was born, our finances only allowed her to stay at home for 18 months, after which she returned to mornings-only work. However, she became most unhappy and was soon desperate to leave. Despite the financial pressure this placed on us, I supported her decision to resign and work from home by using her talents in craft and design. Robyn soon made a range of attractive items like bags, cushions and jewellery that sold well, and still do. I believe that it can be counterproductive to a marriage to exert undue pressure on your partner to go back to work, particularly while young children are still very needy. There is no joy in coming home to a miserable partner and children! A preferable option would be to try and cut down on costs, and find ways to possibly supplement your income, while your partner could possibly look to work from home – perhaps even start a small cottage industry. In my case, I prayed hard and worked even harder and the risk paid off. Shortly thereafter, I was given a promotion, along with a much-needed salary increase. There are times when one shouldn't be too afraid to take a risk and make a tough choice – especially if your partner's happiness is at stake.

Remember that you inevitably grow wiser because of the risks you take and your mistakes. Weigh up the value of the risk and its potential benefits, and decide whether it's worth it. Develop a strategy to move forward should it not work out in your favour, and trust your instincts.

It's also always about the power of prayer. This doesn't mean sitting back and waiting, but rather doing everything you can to seek and seize the opportunities that God puts in your way, whether it be doors opening or closing.

Look for opportunities to realise your dreams

When my daughters were young, my desire for international travel was very much on the back-burner. Despite this wanderlust being unaffordable at the time, I was constantly on the lookout for opportunities for travel. I noticed that the Wildlife Society was selling raffle tickets. The prize for selling the most tickets would be an overseas trip. A welcome challenge – which I embraced with the passion and drive of an Olympic athlete! I sold tickets to virtually anyone who passed me in the street, along with the help of friends and colleagues, without whom I couldn't have done it. Everyone who assisted me got a free ticket in the draw for every nine tickets sold, and free movie tickets for every two books of tickets sold. My heart almost did a somersault when I heard that I'd won a trip to Austria: Boy, did I relish the great feeling that the hard work had paid off! Realising that I could not rely on luck to get what I wanted, it was empowering to know that I could achieve everything in life with hard work. That sense of 'can do' spurred me on to sell the raffle tickets for another two years, and I won the top seller prize each year, affording me overseas trips until the growing responsibilities of family and career precluded me from selling. ■

5

Shifting landscapes

Our historic transition

When I joined the bank in 1980, black people were restricted to being cleaners, and Indian and coloured people were for the first time allowed to serve in the front line. For me, having been denied the opportunity of befriending black people as equals, this was a sad loss. It was only when I began to interact with black, Indian, and coloured people while working in the bank, that I came to realise the extent and nature of the warm, multicultural heritage I had missed out on. What an awesome opportunity for change!

The early 1990s heralded a period of long-overdue and immensely exciting transition in our country's political history. FW de Klerk had risen to power as state president, after having ousted PW Botha from office in 1989. It was largely due to Nelson

Mandela's disciplined, astute negotiations, coupled with FW De Klerk's courageous commitment to dismantling apartheid, that our 'rainbow nation' was able to emerge.

This was the dawn of our first multiracial democracy – exciting but also frightening times for many white people,

Kevin and former President FW De Klerk.

CAN DO!

who were widely regarded as the oppressors. People were not sure what to expect from the pending onset of black majority rule. The ban on the ANC and other organisations was lifted, various security regulations were abolished, all political prisoners were freed, and Nelson Mandela was released after being incarcerated for 27 years.

The eyes of the world were fixed upon us: 1994 will go down in history as South Africa's most momentous year. Mandela voted for the first time (along with the nation) on 27 April, and on 10 May he was inaugurated as our first democratically elected president. Along with the rest of the nation, I was immersed in the euphoria surrounding this miraculously peaceful transition.

> When FW de Klerk opened parliament on 2 February 1990, few expected anything more than familiar rhetoric. What he proclaimed astounded Parliament and rippled in breaking news around the world. On that historic day, he would declare the end of apartheid, by stating that in the face of growing violence it was in the interest of all to begin a process of political negotiation to establish 'a new and just constitutional dispensation in which every inhabitant will enjoy equal rights, treatment and opportunity'.

Hurdles are not barriers

In September, later that same year, I became FNB's human resources manager in Gauteng – a position I held for almost four years. Although they had wanted me to go back to the credit division and lending money after my industrial relations post, I requested instead a stint in human resources, believing that I had the necessary qualifications: I had studied Industrial Psychology and Labour Law in my BCom, whilst majoring in Accounts and Business Economics.

The opportunity to take the career equivalent of an Olympic high jump came in 1997, when I was promoted to human resources (HR), finance and administration director of FNB First Commerce. By anyone's standards, this was a huge promotion. The senior HR manager and the general manager in charge of making such senior appointments must have seen sufficient potential in me to warrant taking such a gamble, despite my youth. I was only 34, several managers were at least ten years older than me, and they believed they were far better poised for this much prized position.

Understandably, from day one, my unexpected appointment resulted in bitter envy and unhappiness from some peers, so this scenario presented me with seemingly insurmountable challenges. Some peers turned out to be devious, but luckily I was wise enough by then to manage this. I've never allowed hurdles looming on the track ahead to diminish my self-confidence, courage, or ambition. Hurdles are not insurmountable barriers, I prefer to see them as markers or milestones which enable one to set the bar higher, having successfully made the leap at a lesser height. The resentment I encountered was almost tangible, and some even made a concerted effort to 'stab me in the back'. Fortunately I was always one step ahead, particularly since I had the full support of my seniors and other colleagues who kept me appraised.

> If you don't succeed at your first attempt at doing something, you cannot say that you have failed until you've actually quit. If you think about it, life is really a test of overcoming one hurdle after the next. Success is determined by your level of persistence and, if necessary, making the right course correction. To survive and thrive, one needs to be resilient and bounce back when life knocks you down. No one ever became a champion ice skater without falling painfully, many times.

BEE – appointing the first black managers

Undaunted, I maintained a warm, positive attitude, and used my natural ability to connect with people and tackle the issues head on. Those were still early days in terms of promoting black people to managerial positions, but with the benefit of my HR experience, I saw their potential and went out of my way to nurture and encourage them. They soon realised that I was genuine about wanting them on board and developing them so they could advance.

CAN DO!

With the advent of Black Economic Empowerment (BEE), it was incumbent upon us to start appointing black managers for the first time. While the implementation of BEE has been a complex process, riddled with issues and challenges, the country was not only ready for this transition, it was long overdue. Given the racial tension which bubbled beneath the surface at the time (and often still does), one may well ask: How did they learn to respect and trust me? As I recall, my warm rapport with black people began while working in Johannesburg as the HR manager. I believe it was just about being genuine, learning to speak Xhosa, and connecting in the true spirit of Ubuntu.

Nelson Mandela said, 'If you talk to a man in a language he understands, that goes to his head. If you talk to him in his own language, that goes to his heart.' I would ask my staff, for example, how do you say, 'How are you?' Then I would repeat it *'Unjani?'* till it became an everyday part of my lexicon. I love phoning a black friend and saying, *'Molo sisi. Ndiyakukhumbula kakhulu.'* She wonders who this guy is, trying to get fresh with her, because it means, 'Good morning sister. I am missing you a lot.' When she finds out that it's me, she always laughs, and says that I sound exactly like a black man! As an aside, I must share my secret as to how I taught myself to speak elementary Xhosa. I set myself a target of learning just one sentence a week and then simply repeating that sentence over and over until it sticks like superglue. In hindsight, this was another important 'can do' achievement that would become a significant part of my everyday lexicon.

Whichever country you live in, you will encounter people who speak a different language to your own. If you are looking to build relationships and develop a rapport with your fellow citizens, I encourage you to go the extra mile by learning to converse with them in their home language. In so doing, you will learn to live inside their space, rather than hovering on their periphery. That said, don't try to master it in too short a time. Learning just one sentence a week will ultimately facilitate a simple conversation, which shows you care.

Despite the country having evolved into a 'rainbow nation', my father still struggled with the new democracy. To my extreme embarrassment, from a political perspective he still remained living in the past. He couldn't accept that I left the bank after 26 years to engage with the broader community, dedicating much of my time to outreach work and making a difference to people's lives. If you have a strongly founded, morally based conviction that pursuing a certain path is in your and society's best interests, it may sometimes require defying your parents, and going against their so called 'sage' advice.

However, this approach comes with an important caveat: Sometimes, your parents and your close friends, who have the advantage of being on the outside looking in, are able to see the whole picture, and give you the best advice. They know your history and they know you well. Generally, they are the people who know your strengths and weaknesses better than anyone else, and they are the people who care the most for you. My advice would be to listen carefully to what they have to say, weigh it all up in terms of your sense of reality and your personal vision, and then make a calm, measured, unemotional, and hopefully sensible decision.

Banks merging and mingling with momentum

In 1998, the First Rand Group was established by the merger of First National Bank (FNB), Rand Merchant Bank (RMB), and Momentum. FNB First Commerce EXCO (executive committee) consisted of Bradley Bothma (CEO), Ian Wands (Credit Director), John Wilson (Marketing Director), and myself. Although I was at least ten to fifteen years younger than my colleagues, this position afforded me unimagined growth and learning, particularly since they were all older, wiser, and more experienced than me. With Bradley, Ian, and John proving to be such excellent mentors and colleagues, my business acumen and experience grew tenfold in terms of learning how to make big decisions, manage a team, and grow a business. Being a national position, it afforded me excellent experience.

CAN DO!

Retrenching people isn't fun

As a result of the merger, the bank had restructured once again – after already having done so several times. In 2000, as an ambitious 37-year-old making big strides, I was implementing all these big decisions on a national level. Then suddenly another restructuring was announced. What we initially thought was a merger turned out to be a takeover. As the head of HR at FNB First Commerce, I had the unenviable task of retrenching a few thousand people which is undoubtedly one of the hardest things I've ever had to do.

I can still remember the awful experience of having to retrench one of our more senior staff members, a man in his fifties who had been at the company for the better part of his working life. On the first day of his retrenchment, he called me, saying in Afrikaans, 'I'm sitting outside my house in Cape Town, dressed for work but I have not been able to tell my wife. I don't know what to do.' Of course I empathised with him, but I advised him to break the dismal news to her sooner rather than later. At that dreadful moment I knew that I didn't want to stay in HR any longer.

For those lucky enough to escape the chop, the rule was that everyone, from the top down, had to reapply for their jobs. The hardest thing was for me to see experienced, top people like Ian, 56, Bradley, 50, and John, 49, forced into early retirement at such a young age. People were traumatised – many had not even given a thought to updating their CVs in over 30 years! From bank tellers to directors, we were given the option to reapply, either for our existing jobs, or for other positions in the bank. The company did away with 'general manager' titles and since the GM of Cape Town had just retired, I opted to apply for what was then called 'sales and service director' in that city. I reflect on my years in Johannesburg as a season in my life that I thoroughly enjoyed. I learned a lot and made the most of my time. One should try and capitalise on every season in one's life, no matter the climate or force of the wind.

Cape Town beckons the Chaplins.

Follow the moral high road

While considering the move down to Cape Town, many of my colleagues cautioned me, saying that I'd never get it right, since Cape Town was one of the poorest performing areas in the bank. This didn't faze me in the least, it only served to make me more determined than

CAN DO!

ever to succeed! I was made responsible for all the branches in the Cape Town CBD which included Sea Point.

As already mentioned, everyone was affected by the rule that we had to reapply for our jobs. Part of my strategy in this new position was to surround myself with the right, and best, people – managers that were competent to handle the various branches, relationships, service, administration, etc. I particularly wanted people with the work standards and ethics I had come to value. In addition, I sought out staff who would keep me on my toes. These included Hilary George (branch manager), who did so in such a positive and constructive way, because she respected me and I respected her. ■

6

Four years to turn the tide in Cape Town

Cape Town City wins the trophy: Wendy Lucas-Bull, CEO First Rand Retail Group, hands the trophy to Kevin. Looking on are Trevor Strydom; CEO Western Cape; Michael Jordaan; CEO FNB; Elizabeth Matlakala and Cheryl Haggett, Sales and Service Director colleagues.

Director – FNB Cape Town City

Having applied for the position of sales and service director, it was with some disappointment that I received a phone call to say that I'd been given this position in Durban as opposed to Cape Town, my first choice. While there were loads of applicants for these few top positions, and this was certainly a feather in my cap, I had the strong conviction that a return to Durban would represent a step backwards, given that I'd moved on from there ten years earlier. Life in Durban was by then way too familiar and all pathways were already over-worn with my footprints. As the saying goes, 'Been there, done that.' Despite it being

CAN DO!

an easy, prestigious option, I was unafraid to decline this seemingly good offer, and summoned the courage to request that I rather be considered for Cape Town.

When one is faced with a choice, it's often tempting to take the soft option, which usually means falling back into your comfort zone at the expense of future personal growth and development. The job of running Cape Town was beckoning, and I had a hunch that being forced out of my comfort zone would be the launching pad for a dynamic new journey. As things turned out, in May 2000, I was thrilled to be given this wonderful opportunity and delighted to embrace all the new challenges it presented. Upon attaining this new position, my responsibilities were far greater, for I was fully accountable for the bottom line in my area. It was exhilarating for me to run the business as if it were my own!

I won't forget people like Ian Wands, director of credit, who became like a father to me. When I took the job in Cape Town, the excellent advice he gave me was, 'My boy, when you get there, be sure to network effectively.' That was a skill I focused on honing from the outset. I was most saddened when Ian passed away in his early 60s.

I learnt so much from our CEO, Bradley Bothma, about standing up for what one believes is right and not becoming a fence sitter. He was a remarkable businessman and mentor who taught me to be creative, to think big, be bold, to plan, and strategise wisely.

Despite all the naysayers and prophets of doom, I managed to turn things around in Cape Town. Together with the help of my excellent branch, relationship, admin and service managers, and the support and guidance of my excellent bosses Alan Stephenson and then Trevor Strydom, Cape Town City became one of FNB's top performers within four years, to the extent that we took the business from the bottom five nationally, to number one out of 33 areas in 2004. This was measured by cost to income ratio, revenue growth, product mix, customer satisfaction, sales, and costs. At this point, credit must also go to the input of several wise mentors such as Raymond Ackerman (founder and ex-chairman of Pick n Pay), Philip Krawitz (chairman of Cape Union Mart), and Archbishop Desmond Tutu – all of whose influence I shall discuss in more detail later. I cannot stress strongly enough the importance of finding your own 'guru' or mentor.

TEN GOOD REASONS FOR MY SUCCESS IN THIS ROLE:

1. **Setting a clear vision of what we wanted to achieve as a business, and getting everyone to buy in.**

   As the saying goes, 'If you fail to plan, you plan to fail.' I made sure that our compasses were aligned at all times. We discussed this vision and how we could achieve it, on an ongoing basis.

2. **Creating an exciting and dynamic culture of excellence, appreciation and creativity.**

   I made it a constant focus and introduced various initiatives. This entailed visiting branches, checking for excellence in the appearance of the branch, which is just as important as the quality of their customer service. Some of my staff were head-hunted and offered double pay by our competitors, but they declined these offers as they loved the culture we had built within our sector. Our half-yearly award evenings also ensured public recognition of their achievements and ongoing commitment.

3. **Remembering people's names.**

   During branch visits I took a genuine interest in our staff and made a point of remembering their names. Raymond Ackerman taught me how important this is, to build relationships with your staff. For many years while doing his rounds, Raymond personally greeted every member of staff, in every store, until the business grew too big for this to be possible. Although the book is somewhat dated, in Dale Carnegie's *Secrets of Success* he emphasises: 'A person's name is to that person, the sweetest and most important sound in any language.' Over the years, people often asked me to explain my secret to remembering all their names. There's no secret – I simply take a genuine interest in people and this has always helped me to remember them well enough to put names to faces. Moreover, the staff valued my taking a personal interest in them.

CAN DO!

The reality is that most of us don't concentrate when we are being introduced to new people, but I've developed the habit of listening carefully and repeating names verbally and mentally. If you realise that you aren't concentrating while being introduced, or can't recall the name, there's no harm in saying, 'Sorry – please repeat your name', or in politely asking, 'How do you spell your name?'

Later, being responsible for hundreds of staff in my area (almost 200 in the Adderley Street branch alone), I obviously couldn't remember each person's name, so when I visited a branch I'd usually walk around with the manager, who would be called upon to occasionally assist by whispering the relevant name into my ear! Ultimately, I streamlined and down-scaled the workforce by reducing the number to less than 100 at our Adderley Street branch. At the end of every year, I bought a small gift for each member of staff, and made the effort to visit branches to present the gifts in person. It's amazing to see how well people respond to this in terms of boosted confidence, performance, and self-esteem.

4. **Holding quarterly sessions with branches.**

These sessions served as a regular reminder of our vision and goals. We sometimes had a fancy dress or a 'P' party to just get the *gees* (Afrikaans word for vibe or spirit) going. I'd learnt the idea of a 'P' party while staying on a kibbutz in Israel. People are invited to come dressed as something that starts with the letter P, which offers the widest variety of easy dress-up options. For example, one can come dressed as a pimp, policeman, prostitute, princess, post-box, pimple, pharaoh, or pregnant woman. If you are a person who doesn't like to dress up, you can get away with arriving dressed head-to-toe in pink or purple! The fancy dress becomes a 'mask' or masquerade, behind which people can let themselves go and relax – which is, after all, what one is hoping for! This was a way of creating a bit of excitement and fun around telling my staff what I wanted them to achieve.

As a team, we vigorously looked at ways to reduce costs and increase income. Every quarter, I did 'road shows' for the catchment area of our branches, during which we'd set the strategy for the quarter and year ahead.

5. Holding weekly one-on-one meetings with managers and monthly meetings together.

We discussed actual sales figures versus targets, the challenges and areas of difficulty, the areas for improvement – all the while eliciting their ideas. It kept us focused on the vision and the task at hand. My high demands proved quite taxing on our staff, and despite one manager, Michel Leroy, telling me that my stiff sales targets and meetings were stressing him out, most confessed to appreciating and respecting me big-time because of this!

6. Emphasising the importance of the customer.

I always used the example of our caring tea lady, commonly known as Aunty Koelsum, who, upon passing an unmanned desk, would answer the phone, greet the customer and take a message if she heard someone's phone ringing more than three times. She would even scold staff if she saw them not answering their phone within three rings. That exemplified a level of passion and commitment sorely lacking in many people today. Possessed of an unwavering sense of care for our customers, this much-loved lady went on to teach herself to operate the switchboard. She became something of an icon at FNB. When the switchboard operator went on lunch, Aunty Koelsum would stand in for her and do the job with the efficiency of a queen bee!

7. Following up with customers.

Staff were taught that there is nothing worse than agreeing to go back to a customer by a certain date, and then failing to do as promised. If they hadn't resolved the matter by that date, they were to be sure to phone the customer back to say they were still busy working on it and to ask for x amount of time to settle the matter. Nothing infuriates a customer more than an unmet commitment. In my view, it's a cardinal sin – for it's not only a sign of inefficiency and unreliability, but a lack of interest in meeting the needs of the customer.

CAN DO!

Top Achievers at a glittering awards evening.

8. Hosting half-yearly award evenings for excellence.

This did not have to be a very costly event. On occasion the prizes were simply movie or theatre tickets, but what counted was the acknowledgment that their work was being appreciated. This was also a great team-building exercise. Bucking tradition, the inclusion of spouses at the first such event in Cape Town was really well received.

9. Surrounding yourself with positive people who support and encourage you, who also challenge you to be innovative and proactive.

I've always avoided employing people who say, 'Yes sir – how high sir?' I chose instead to head-hunt people who were smarter than me, since one can learn nothing from an echo! I believe that in any healthy organisation, it's essential to allow people the space to thrash things out. You can learn much more from the people who cross-question your judgments, as this forces you to motivate your decisions with sound reasoning. You become a better leader with a team that stretches you. A strong leader should never be afraid to appoint people who are more skilled than he or she is, nor should such people be regarded as a threat. Drawing on and nurturing their attributes will inevitably ensure your own success.

FNB Cape Town City – top performing area. Standing: Kevin, Michel Leroy, Rhonda Smith, Sihaam Miller, Dave Eastment, Vivian Khumalo. Front: Ruby Bake, Medie Bardien, Hilary George.

10. Standing by your values and principles.

While in the role of sales and service director at FNB Cape Town, I had learnt that one of our top branch managers when I was in Johannesburg, Naomi Kahn, had been unfairly accused of all sorts of things and emotionally intimidated by a very senior FNB manager. I told my boss, Trevor Strydom, that I wanted to call Wendy Lucas Bull, then CEO of the retail bank, to tell her what was going on. Trevor strongly advised against this, saying that I would probably be fired if I did so. However, seeing something which I felt was morally unjust, I knew I had to take a stand and act on it. Despite Trevor imploring me not to do so, I phoned Wendy. She appreciated my confiding in her because my doing so enabled her to investigate. One should not be afraid to do the right thing in life: Stand by your values and principles, and make that critical call.

CAN DO!

Consulting Raymond Ackerman

Some of the best learnings I was able to implement came from Raymond Ackerman. During the many inspiring hours I spent with him, I soaked up every word of his invaluable lessons like a sponge and couldn't wait to implement his ideas. One of the most influential was his 'four legs of the table' concept, on which he based his book and which he used to build Pick n Pay. I connected most profoundly with his views on people, who inevitably play a defining role in the success of any business.

In summary, four metaphorical pillars or legs ensure the stability and success of any good business. This overarching philosophy underpinned everything I implemented – so much so that Raymond often joked that he should receive royalties! While the tabletop represents the customer, the four legs of the table comprise:

First leg: Strong administrative and financial controls. These are critical to success.

Second leg: Merchandise, advertising, and product. Establish what the customer wants, as opposed to what we think the customer wants. How is your merchandise displayed and marketed?

Third leg: Corporate social responsibility. Your customers will continue to support you when they know that you care. What you give, you get back.

Fourth leg: Your staff. Treat them as your most important asset. Raymond taught me the art of making one's staff feel special. From December 2000 I decided to buy a little gift for each staff member annually, as mentioned earlier. I enlisted the help of my wife Robyn, and daughters Sarah and Kirsty, who came shopping with me for hundreds of gifts. These were individually wrapped and personally labelled by them! What a joy it was to spend two full days going around to all the branches and handing each person a gift.

In sum: If one leg is wobbly or missing, your table will collapse and so will your business. By adhering to all four 'legs' of this principle, your business will succeed – much like it did for mine.

'No' is the start of nothing

When I took over FNB in Cape Town I noticed that several of the branches were housed in rather grand, historic buildings that were in fact architectural monuments or heritage sites. It did not take long for me to establish that many people didn't know exactly where our Adderley Street or Long Street branches were located. I realised that to survive in this competitive new age, we needed appropriate FNB signage on these beautiful buildings, but was told that this was strictly forbidden. Bitterly disappointed, I approached the South African Heritage Resources Agency (SAHRA) to obtain this permission. When this was again declined, I threatened to close down or move the branches unless signage was permitted. Occasionally, one has to take risks. I knew that I had to be persistent, and I wouldn't take no for an answer. If I didn't get prominent signage on those buildings, I could never make the business profitable. Gone were the days in banking where one could rely on the belief that everyone knows where the local bank is situated. Competition was fierce and one had to find ways to distinguish oneself in the marketplace. In this case, my fight was somewhat risky, because it could have attracted negative publicity (as well as positive), and had the potential to turn into an ugly or controversial locking of horns with the relevant local authorities. I also had to ensure that my staff didn't know I was doing this, because the uncertainty surrounding the stability of their jobs could have proven unsettling. I'm pleased to say that we won and obtained the necessary approval: Today there is clear, prominent FNB signage on the face of these magnificent buildings. A visit to one of these branches offers one an aesthetically charming experience of our impressive architectural heritage.

Overnight township sojourn

In early 2000, the company launched a pilot programme aimed at taking all the sales and service directors from around the country into the black township of Soweto, where we would be expected to spend the night. One must bear in mind that this was just five years into our new democracy, at a time when white people never ventured into the townships and they were still regarded as foreign territory, dangerous, and crime infested.

The overnight sojourn was organised by Mike Boon – an external consultant. He informed us that we were to be the guinea pigs: the first ones from the bank to go into Soweto. We were told to wear no jewellery, to meet at a taxi rank in Jeppe Street, and just bring R20, along with the necessary clothes for an overnight stay. We were divided into pairs and instructed to take taxis from a rank in the middle of Johannesburg to Baragwanath Hospital, where we would congregate. In our hyper-vigilant state of trepidation, my colleague Jonathan Dunwoody and I noticed that we were the only two white people on the taxi. To put this in context: We were all victims of cultural and racial stereotyping, which led us to have preconceived ideas about what was or wasn't safe – given the prevailing degree of interracial violence and media hype surrounding it. Our next task at the taxi rank in Soweto was to befriend someone and ask to be taken to his or her home. Many of our colleagues were stricken with a blinding fear of the unknown and had to work at overcoming longstanding, stereotypical beliefs and expectations.

At the taxi rank, Kevin and Jonathan Dunwoody, Sales and Service Director, Durban.

Making the impossible possible

Little did we anticipate the warm hospitality proffered by a woman who took us under her wing and welcomed us into her humble home, offering us a cup of tea and cake. Later that afternoon we made our way back to the taxi rank, where we shared our respective stories and sentiments. We were then taken by taxi on a drive through the streets of Soweto. At dusk we were dropped in pairs and told to walk down the road to a given house number, where we would sleep the night. Although in reality we were not in any danger, we all thought that we might be. (Unbeknown to us, incognito security guards had been positioned strategically at our various destinations.) It felt strangely surreal to knock on the door of a shack belonging to a complete stranger in Soweto and to say, 'Hello! We believe you're expecting us.' It was just a private, dimly lit and simply furnished family dwelling in which we were given dinner and offered blankets and a place to sleep on the floor, with access to a barely functioning outside tap and toilet. (Most township homes do not even have the luxury of running water and toilets.) The next morning, my partner and I walked back to the station and returned by train to the Rissik Street station in Johannesburg, where we shared our experiences over coffee and vetkoek – a traditional South African delicacy consisting of deep-fried dough.

Some FNB colleagues told of having at the outset been traumatised or fearful at the prospect of going into the township, but they went on to find this to be an invaluable learning, bridge-building, and inter-cultural encounter that brought about a myriad of fresh perspectives – not to mention a major paradigm shift. From my personal perspective, the experience was unforgettable – one that would form the catalyst for me to help my own staff to change their focus completely and to connect with a wider range of people of colour, particularly the broader township community.

Implementing township visits at FNB Cape Town

While working in Cape Town, this insight led me to ask whether any of our white and coloured staff had ever been into the black townships. Absolutely shocked to learn that *not one* of them had done so, I decided

CAN DO!

to expose them to this experience, in the hope that this broader perspective would infiltrate the business. I thought, 'Right, so let's take them in!' Yumnah Ehrenreich, admin manager at our Adderley Street branch, called to say, 'Kevin, I'm not going in there! Those guys will steal my car!' To which I replied, 'Yumnah, how can you be so racist?' But she remained adamant. Her response to my suggestion that she join me in my car: 'No, that's worse – you drive a Mercedes!' Given that I had about 100 managers comprising branch, relationship, admin, and service managers, I ended up hiring a vehicle and taking them in groups of 20 into the township, making five trips. I faced an unexpected obstacle from Shamiela Basardien, service manager at our Heerengracht branch. She called me indignantly, 'Kevin, I hear that you're taking us into the township, and we're going to a restaurant. You of all people should know that I'm Halaal. How can you disrespect my religion like this?' I responded, 'Shamiela, do you really think there are no Halaal restaurants in the township?' My persistence paid off: I cajoled the 'Yumnahs' and the 'Shamielas' into making this expedition – despite their imagined fears and concerns. I subsequently witnessed many heart-warming, lightbulb moments as they hugged and thanked the 'mamas' who worked in the restaurant. They then thanked me in turn for facilitating this wonderful experience. The following week, I was happy to hear that Shamiela, always infinitely focused and target driven, felt comfortable to go into Gugulethu with her staff, where they opened many new accounts. Thereafter, our managers started to regularly take their staff into the townships. The paradigm shift emanating from this experience changed my business on many levels. For example, until then our tellers had barely greeted corporate black messengers and basically treated them with disdain. All of a sudden, there was a discernible warmth underlying all such transactions across the colour spectrum – from messengers, customers, and corporate clients. This represented a turning point for the business. Our customers somehow sensed that a shift had taken place, in alignment with our new democracy. Today, I am blessed to be friends with some of my ex-staff.

Managing the damage

Within six months of my arrival in Cape Town, FNB launched a rather controversial new banking product for high net-worth individuals. This campaign proved a total disaster, which resulted in many frustrated and angry customers. I was faced with the unenviable task of managing a deluge of displeasure and needed to somehow turn things around so as to win back loyalty. It's important to take full responsibility for one's mistakes, so we needed to apologise. We did this by inviting all our 2000 high net-worth customers to a series of splendid evenings, entertaining roughly 200 per function. These were held over about 10 evenings within a two- to three-week period. During the planning phase, my sales and service director colleagues from other areas thought I was crazy. They suggested the evenings would be bound to fail, and I would be 'like a lamb to the slaughter'. Instead, by openly acknowledging that we were at fault, the events proved a huge success, to the extent that several customers wrote to thank us afterwards – and other sales and service directors followed suit.

> Never be shy to apologise if you've messed up. It is far better to face it head on, manage the damage, and show genuine contrition.

Constructive criticism

While no one likes criticism, I have always believed this to be essential for personal growth, since one can learn a lot from negative feedback, especially if it is given constructively. As part of the performance review process, most successful companies today ensure that all members of staff obtain performance feedback from both their managers and subordinates. If your staff or colleagues have a negative perception of you, you would be well advised to take cognisance of their opinions and make a concerted effort to work out how best to address this. In one of my performance appraisals as HR manager in Gauteng, my boss, Basil Proctor, said that he respected my ability to take criticism, and that I always picked myself up and bounced back in a positive way – all the better for it!

CAN DO!

Introspection is invaluable to a harmonious working environment.
If there is a negative perception about you, address it, either by
discussion or changing the way you function.

Grace before meals

Bradley Bothma, my boss in Johannesburg, also taught me the importance of giving expression to humility and appreciation by saying a short non-denominational grace before meals at appropriate staff functions. This practice is one of the most common and universal forms of spoken-prayer, the one sacrament many of us hold onto after others have faded from use. Now is the time to be bold! Although I'd attended hundreds of corporate events previously, hearing him say grace made such an impact on me that I immediately knew it was something I would implement in my own business and personal life. So, from the outset in my new role, we always said grace at functions, even when I hosted monthly customer lunches with my relationship managers. I won't forget a lunch we had with my peers, one of whom was Muslim. I checked with him beforehand if we could say 'grace' and he happily agreed. Afterwards, George New was so angry that he remarked in front of everyone, 'Kevin, with Essack being a Muslim that was in poor taste.' Essack Eusuf-Moosa quickly sprang to my defence, saying, 'No George, I actually enjoyed it – and Kevin said, God!' I must add that in cross-cultural contexts, it's important to respect and embrace the differences between people's religions when praying.

As sales and service director, the first event I ever implemented and hosted in Cape Town was an awards evening held at the Cape Sun for the top 100 performers of my area. I felt that it was time to start being bold and saying grace would also be a powerful and inclusive way to cross-culturally unite our Muslim, Christian, and Jewish attendees. Afterwards, the number of people who came up and thanked me was amazing. Somehow, it helped to give the business a soul. All these years later, it still continues to be a regular practice at our Ubuntu Breakfasts, which I will discuss later. ■

7

Inspiring mentors

A proud moment when FNB and Pick n Pay collaborated to present a vehicle to the Lions Feeding Project, 2002 – Raymond Ackerman, Suzanne Ackerman-Berman and Kevin Chaplin.

Raymond Ackerman

A defining moment of my career occurred in 2000 when Raymond Ackerman's daughter Suzanne, who had previously introduced me to her father, called me and said he would like to invite me to accompany them on a trip to Gugulethu. Despite being busy, there was no way I would not free up my diary to spend time with this much revered businessman. Sometimes we make a seemingly small decision that, in hindsight, becomes a defining moment. This one was to be one

CAN DO! ✓

of the best I ever made! Had I not done so, Raymond would never have agreed to mentor me. The purpose of our trip to Gugulethu was to visit the Zama dance school, a project close to his heart that he founded (and still funds), where students from disadvantaged backgrounds learn to express their emotions through dance and music.

Raymond's humility in terms of shunning the limelight blew me away. Insisting that no praise or fuss be made of him, this notable philanthropist remained on the periphery after the dance show. When asked if he would like to say a few words, he encouraged his wife Wendy to rather step forward. It soon became clear that they enjoy a most remarkable relationship. On the way back, I asked Raymond if he would be prepared to mentor me, to which he humbly replied, 'Me? Are you sure?'

Thus began an awesome journey of learning, in which inspiring ideas were shared and discussed at regular meetings held over the next few years. This included getting to know Wendy who works tirelessly on their philanthropic efforts, including Amy Foundation. Wendy regularly visists Amy Foundation after school centres to read to children. One of the lessons Raymond taught me is to take a certain percentage

Raymond Ackerman won the Outstanding Young South African award in 1965, along with Gary Player, and by 1966, at the age of 35, he was the managing director of 85 Checkers stores, which he started. After a dispute with the management, he left. In the same year and in response, using the investments of 40 friends and a bank loan, Raymond bought three stores in Cape Town trading under the name Pick n Pay. Under his leadership, Pick n Pay eventually grew into one of Africa's largest supermarket chains. There are 265 Supermarkets, 20 Hypers and 298 Franchise stores as well as Clothing, Liquor and Boxer stores in several African countries. The Pick n Pay Group employs around 80 000 people.

Raymond is well known for his philanthropic activities, and he remained chairman until he stepped down in 2010. He is now honorary life president and still stays in close touch with the business.

of what your business earns and give it to charity – over and above one's personal donation or tithe, as prescribed in the Bible.

From the time he bought his first three stores, Raymond didn't wait to make big profits before giving back to the community. From month one he made a difference. Every business, regardless of size, should allocate a portion for social responsibility. This consciousness often filters down to the staff and has a ripple effect on other businesses and competitors.

Raymond helped me to understand not only the importance of being socially responsible in business, but also the need to do it wisely – by ensuring that people are aware that you're doing your bit. Although one's primary motivation should not be to obtain public recognition, corporate social responsibility (CSR) is just that – a responsibility. Therefore, donations should not be anonymous or given under the radar. Ideally, one must aim for a fair return in terms of marketing and branding for your business.

In the early 2000s, a large bank was visibly shouting its good deeds from rooftops, while another was also doing similar work, but marketing it rather poorly. With this insight, I got involved in the Table of Peace and Unity, which I shall discuss in Chapter 8. Raymond taught me about the metaphorical concept of building a house: 'The more you give, the more you will get back.' Eventually, you will get so much back that you will need to build more rooms and expand your house. He autographed my copy of his book, *Hearing Grasshoppers Jump*, with the following inscription: 'Dear Kevin. With best wishes, and remember the "house".' I would like to believe that I have never forgotten it. For information as to how this was implemented, please refer to Chapter 8.

> *Kevin's enthusiasm and passion are what make him successful, along with the fact that he has very set, clear goals – always a key ingredient for success.*
> RAYMOND ACKERMAN

CAN DO!

> *Kevin's passion is infectious. He is a man whose mission is to leave this world a much better place than he found it.*
> PHILIP KRAWITZ

Philip Krawitz

I also wish to express my gratitude to Philip Krawitz, Chairman of Cape Union Mart, another influential mentor who was kind enough to give me many hours of his valuable time. Today his company is the country's largest family-owned, unlisted clothing retailer. We first met when he called me to request a meeting after hearing that the GM of FNB Cape Town had retired. This was in the early days of the RMB takeover, and since the new management had decided against the formality of wearing ties, I went to our meeting wearing a jacket without a tie. How we laughed as he happily removed his own, explaining that he always kept a tie on hand just for the bank. It was this warm interchange

Philip Krawitz with Western Cape Police Commissioner Mzwandile Petros and Kevin (Chairman of Business Against Crime Western Cape), 2003.

Cape Union Mart was founded in 1933 by Philip's grandfather and namesake, Philip Krawitz. The founding family are still actively involved, and run the business together with a proficient team of professionals. From their very first store on the corner of Corporation and Mostert Street in Cape Town, the group now consists of 108 Cape Union Mart, 74 Old Khaki, 35 Poetry, 32 Tread + Miller and 37 Keedo stores. Many employees have been with the company for more than two or three decades and the company prides itself on attracting and retaining some of the best talent in the retail sector. Philip said, 'Contrary to what has happened in the manufacturing sector, and particularly in the clothing industry, the Group has never had a strike and never retrenched a single worker. This is a remarkable achievement, given that we employ more than 3000 people!' Cape Union Mart takes great pride in its Corporate Social Investment (CSI) Programme, in which they spread their support over a myriad of good causes such as poverty relief, education, healthcare, economic upliftment, assisting the intellectually or physically challenged, the homeless, the aged, vulnerable children, environment, arts and culture and fighting racism.

that paved the way for us to click immediately. To my amusement, Philip once said, 'I learnt early on that banks will only lend you money if you don't need it.'

When I asked Philip to mentor me, he willingly agreed. During this time, he shared his core business ideologies and strategies, along with important philosophies on how he managed his stores and evaluated their performance. Of significance were the tools he used to measure his product lines and each store's performance. He explained that even if all his stores made a profit, the worst performing one would be subject to closure, with a new store opening in its place. He lives by the philosophy of giving back to the community. 'As a family, profit is not our only objective. We're one of the biggest contributors of profit to CSI programmes. I probably have more fun giving away money than making it and we want to create jobs,' said Philip. Once again, much of what I learned in my time with Philip was put into practice at FNB.

I first met Kevin, my dearest friend and colleague, when he held a secure, top position in a well-known bank. He was warm, humble, and affirming from this first meeting, and remains so till today. I salute Kevin for giving up a secure, comfortable position and following his dream and deep conviction to serve and enhance so many lives. We have been able to maintain a long-distance, long-standing friendship because of our shared passion and deep commitment to the amazing community to which we have both dedicated our lives. With many blessings, I thank him.

HELEN LIEBERMAN

Helen Lieberman

The road to success lies through connecting with others. In the course of building strong and successful relationships each one leads to another then another. As alluded to earlier, my connection with Philip Krawitz was to link me to a whole new network of remarkable people, who would each play a significant role in my life and in various outreach projects. One of the exceptional women he introduced me to was the legendary Helen Lieberman, who founded Ikamva Labantu, a South African grassroots organisation founded during the apartheid years. Helen is the founder and honorary president of Ikamva Labantu, which means 'the future of our nation'. As a young speech therapist working in a hospital at the age of 21, she could not stand by and ignore the suffering of patients who were discharged without adequate care, so she turned her attention to the disenfranchised, impoverished South African townships. Today Ikamva Labantu is one of the largest non-profit organisations (NPOs) in South Africa working to develop over 1 000 projects to sustainability. What began as a small, localized initiative has grown over the years into a vast organisation with connections throughout the world. Helen's work in this field has been exemplary and recognised internationally.

Leading by example, she is a model of excellence of what is possible if you simply get into your car and go into the townships to do what you've set out to achieve!

Some years ago, while still working at FNB, Philip invited me to join the board of Ikamva Labantu, and I became actively involved until I took over the running of the Amy Foundation, at which point I felt it appropriate to tender my resignation. We still remain good friends and I am an ardent supporter of Helen and Ikamva Labantu.

Aviva Pelham

Another exceptional contact made through Philip Krawitz was his special friend Aviva Pelham. In a remarkably successful career spanning more than 40 years, Aviva has delighted and enchanted audiences as an opera singer and actress, both locally and internationally. She gives generously of her time in training promising young performers – from schoolchildren to adults – and is an accomplished director. She recently wrote, produced and starred in a mesmerising one-woman show called *Santa's Story*, which recollects the tale of her mother's escape from Nazi Germany as a young Jewish girl, and how she made her way to Southern Rhodesia (Zimbabwe). There Santa married a virtual stranger, who was to become Aviva's father. I jumped at the opportunity to help market and sell tickets for this enchanting performance and was thrilled to learn that this production has played to packed houses both locally and internationally.

It did not take Aviva and me long to find an exceptional synergy in our work. This evolved into a close friendship that saw her travelling tirelessly and fearlessly into the townships to work with Amy Foundation children, at a time when most white people were too afraid to venture into the area. For many years, she has choreographed hundreds of township children from the Amy centres to perform at our gala dinners and other functions. Possessed of an astute ability to scout for talent, she has shared her knowledge generously by moulding many youngsters into superb vocalists and

CAN DO! ✓

performers. One cannot underestimate the depth of her commitment, and the level of dedication this requires.

> *Kevin, you have vision, courage, perseverance, imagination, integrity, hope, faith and infectious positivity. Never listen to the naysayers and keep believing in your wonderful self. With much admiration! It's always a joy to work with Kevin. He is a warm, loyal, dedicated gentleman who has achieved a great deal, attracting local and international attention to the Amy Foundation. He's always shown me so much respect and gratitude. He's always enthusiastic and ridiculously positive – and a most inspiring person to know! Underlying everything about him is this strong flow of energy – nothing he says or does is mediocre – it's all about passion and never giving up. Perseverance is one of the keys to success and he has it in huge doses. He keeps focused and never loses sight of his goal.*
>
> AVIVA PELHAM

Archbishop Desmond Tutu

'The Arch' was another great luminary to make a significant impact on my life. When I met him at the first Table of Peace and Unity, we immediately clicked, and this was followed up with a one-on-one meeting that formed the basis of a friendship to last a lifetime. I would visit him regularly thereafter to learn from his wisdom. It was the Arch who first coined the popular phrase 'rainbow nation' to describe the people of South Africa in celebrating our country's rich linguistic, cultural, and religious diversity.

I was pleased to be able to persuade him to move all his personal banking business, as well as that of the Desmond Tutu Foundation, to FNB. He was kind enough to invite me to attend many special events with him, and despite my busy schedule, I did my best to attend, particularly since there was much to be learnt from him.

As Archbishop Tutu is the patron of the Tygerberg Children's Hospital, one such occasion was a visit to the neo-natal Kangaroo Unit that was established to cater for babies who are born several weeks or even months prematurely. I was blown away by the fact that Professor Kirsten and his team have boosted the survival rate for babies weighing less than a kilogram at birth, from 35 per cent only a couple of decades ago to nearly 80 per cent today. With a severe shortage of beds in the neonatal wards, mothers who came to hospital with their premature newborns were often sent home alone. But this created another problem. Apart from being unable to bond with their babies, the latter were not being breast-fed. Being so tiny, the babies were at high risk of infection. Due to over-crowding and formula-milk feeding instead of breast milk, too many babies became

One of many happy moments with Archbishop Desmond Tutu, August 2012.

CAN DO! ✓

seriously ill or were dying, so the Kangaroo Unit was established to keep the mothers there, with their preemies being strapped to their chests, kangaroo style.

> *Thanks for being the amazing man you are. God blessed us with you. Keep doing what you are doing!*
> ARCHBISHOP DESMOND TUTU

Internationally esteemed patron

Some of the highlights of my life have materialised through my longstanding connection with the Arch. In October 2006 I was invited to a prestigious black-tie gala dinner to celebrate the Archbishop's birthday. Political leaders, international figureheads, local business people, and celebrities converged on the Sandton Convention Centre in Johannesburg to pay tribute to his commitment to linguistic, cultural, and religious diversity – as well as his personification of Ubuntu. The birthday party also commemorated the unveiling of an exhibition dedicated to his life and works in the library of the University of South Africa.

Two years later, Robyn and I went to his fiftieth wedding-anniversary celebration in Soweto, Johannesburg, at which he exchanged rings with his beloved Leah Tutu and the couple renewed their marriage vows. This was nothing short of delightful! What touched me the most at the reception was the colourful rainbow of attendees sharing this celebration, since I'd never attended an event with such a rich diversity of people – and what fun we all had together!

The Arch's energy is so inspiring that we decided to ask my Mom if she would be prepared to look after our daughters for another night. When she happily agreed to this I immediately changed our flights and without hesitation drove from Sandton to Hartebeespoort Dam. Phoning for accommodation on the way, I was surprised to learn that there was nothing available. Starting to sweat I prayed hard. On entering the outskirts I impulsively took the first turnoff and to our immense relief, we stumbled upon a guesthouse which had a room available. 'Thank you, Lord!' The owners, Hessel and Etresia van Der Walt, were amazingly warm and hospitable, even giving us the honeymoon suite with rose petals sprinkled on the bed, along with some after dinner singing by Hessel. This kick-started a lifelong friendship with our two Afrikaans friends, who to this day call us their *Engelse vriende* (English friends). Etresia told us years later that when I rang the bell, she thought Robyn was my *skelm* (mistress)! Perhaps that explains those rose petals ....

In 2006, the Arch was kind enough to take on the role of Patron of the SA Ubuntu Foundation, and Patron of the Amy Biehl Foundation South Africa the following year. In 2013, when he won the Templeton Award for humanitarian services, he could choose three non-profit beneficiaries who would be party to this prize. We were overjoyed when he kindly chose Amy Biehl Foundation as one of them, since this honour represented a massive capital injection of R100 000. As patron, whenever possible, he attended our gala dinners. Over the years he has literally given of his time as a prize, where we've auctioned off a 'Tea with Tutu'. One year, at a well-attended auction, the bidding for this prize under auctioneer Joey Burke was so fiercely contested between three people that it seemed a pity for only one person to get it: All three were prepared to pay between R33 000 and R35 000 for the pleasure of his company. After the auction, I asked the Arch if he would give us two more, to which he happily agreed. Since the bidding was so close, I followed up on this by asking the second and third highest contenders if they would each be prepared to pay R33 000 – and they generously agreed. So collectively, we raised a much needed R100 000 from that one auction alone!

From the Arch, who is renowned for his infectious chuckle and delicious sense of humour, I learned about the importance of humour, standing up for moral rectitude, and never being a fence-sitter – often at the risk of being outspoken and causing controversy. I've been so enriched by his faith and wisdom. Every gathering,

CAN DO!

regardless of who was in attendance, opened with a prayer. It's not a question of 'can we', but simply 'let's pray together'.

Madiba Magic

Forever emblazoned in my memory will be the time I first met the much-revered Nelson Mandela. The occasion was Archbishop Desmond Tutu and Mama Leah's fiftieth wedding anniversary. After Robyn and I went up to take communion in the church, we returned to our seats and were astonished to come face to face with a beaming Madiba and his charming wife, Graça Machel, who both warmly shook our hands. I was so taken by the softness of his large hands and his magical aura, but moreover by his humble, almost bashful response to the compliments and praise I bestowed upon him. Afterwards, Robyn and I couldn't leave the church fast enough to call our daughters to tell them who we had just met, and how blessed we felt to have had this amazing experience.

A second encounter with Madiba occurred when we were seated right behind the world-famous icon at Hlumelo Biko's wedding in King William's Town, Eastern Cape. This afforded me an opportunity to simply gaze at him, mesmerised by the presence of this exceptional human being who, for me, is Ubuntu personified. At the memorial service held for Mandela after he passed away in December 2013, Barack Obama gave a powerful tribute, saying, 'Mandela understood the ties that bind the human spirit. There's a word in South Africa – Ubuntu – that describes his greatest gift: his recognition that we are all bound together in ways that can be invisible to the eye; that there is a oneness to humanity; that we achieve ourselves by sharing ourselves with others, and caring for those around us.' Little did I dream that the word 'Ubuntu' and all it symbolised, would propel me toward an entirely new and exciting trajectory in terms of my future career, but I shall elaborate on this in Chapter 10.

This rare, privileged opportunity to watch Mandela's facial expressions just centimetres away flooded my mind with memories

A rare privilege: Kevin and Robyn Chaplin with Nelson Mandela, 2007.

of his struggle and the price he paid to achieve justice for his people and peace for our nation. Again, I ensured that I did not miss out on the opportunity to shake those soft and forgiving, careworn hands – a tangible link to his greatness, albeit only for a few unforgettable moments. Isn't it remarkable how the simple act of touch, of holding someone's hand can connect two people in a meaningful way? It's no

CAN DO!

wonder that the imprints of Mandela's hands have become a highly sought-after artefact to memorabilia collectors around the world!

At Mamphela Ramphele's sixtieth birthday party, Robyn and I were blessed a third time, when we were able to hold his hands and actively engage with him as photos were taken. What a privilege! Awed by the presence of the greatest statesman of the twentieth century, it was as if nothing else mattered. I can't recall exactly what we spoke about, but he laughed at something I said. It was always a joy to be in the presence of our country's humble mentor, who taught me that true greatness starts and lies within. Madiba's ability to connect with people and make them feel so important is the essence of true leadership. ■

8

Corporate Social Investment/Responsibility (CSI/CSR)

Yvonne Chaka Chaka leads the way.

What you give, you get back

I've always believed that we face a perilous future unless civil society and business play a more proactive role in giving disadvantaged

CAN DO! ✓

communities better opportunities for upliftment, particularly in the light of our destructive social environment. I cannot stress enough the importance of a company and its employees being involved in some form of outreach work, commonly referred to as CSI or CSR (corporate social investment/responsibility). The benefits include 'first mover advantage', demonstrating inspiring management, enhancing corporate reputation and stimulating new marketing opportunities, attracting investment, and motivating employees. Research shows that employees working for a business passionately committed to CSI projects show greater commitment to the company, lower absenteeism, lower staff turnover, and higher productivity. Furthermore, aligning your business with inspirational values changes the culture in the company to one that looks beyond the 'me' – so that staff will display greater willingness to recommend and support the company.

CSR is not just about supporting an event. For half a century, existential psychologists have been examining what gives people meaning in their lives – and 'doing something for others' ranks highly in the list of findings. People who feel they are making a difference, leaving a legacy, or helping others are more likely to find meaning, fulfilment, and spiritual enrichment. Conversely, those who believe their lives are meaningless are more likely to commit suicide. As I reflect upon all those CSI events I supported, the outcome reinforces exactly what research has shown. It changed the way my team thought and behaved.

Organisations that take volunteering and 'doing good' seriously, answer an inherent human need to find meaning. Employees who can appreciate the positive effect of their work are intrinsically driven to do more. This is not only the right thing to do, it makes good business sense.

> Those who are making a difference to their communities and their environment will be the new leaders of the twenty-first century.

The teachings of Raymond Ackerman and Philip Krawitz altered my whole outlook on running a business. One of the first changes I implemented with my branch and relationship managers, arose from the decision to reconfigure the customer entertainment budget to buy tables at charitable gala dinners to entertain our customers. As expected, this emphasis on charitable events was an excellent form of PR, and they particularly enjoyed mingling at those high profile, black tie affairs. When we bought these tables, I insisted on inviting black, coloured, white, Indian, Christian, Jewish and Muslim, Afrikaans, and English-speaking customers. Time after time, we were the only organisation with black people at our table. Often, I'd go up to the organisers – for example the Paediatric HIV Foundation – and ask why there were no black attendees. To my astonishment, all too often, the reply was, 'Well, we don't really know where to find them!' This gives one a sense of the extent to which things were still out of kilter.

Night of 100 stars

Helen Berger took over the running of the glitzy Night of 100 Stars when Adele Searll passed away in 1998. These memorable evenings offered a splendid dinner and featured sophisticated performances by top singers and dancers. Helen approached me at one of the first customer functions I hosted in Cape Town, asking whether I'd heard of their amazing campaign, and seeking advice as to who she should speak to, now that the General Manager of Cape Town had retired. Naturally, I agreed to talk to her. I was so impressed by the magnificent fundraisers they'd organised, that I became one of their biggest supporters – such that I ultimately bought hundreds of tickets for our clients over the years. I was in the fortunate position of being able to leverage my position at the bank, drawing on our large database of high net-worth individuals. This proved a win-win for all, since the clients regarded it not only a great night out, but a brilliant networking opportunity. My relationship managers and I were able to treat the clients to something special, whilst contributing to a needy cause.

CAN DO!

Many top executives don't realise how much good they can do by leveraging their positions of influence within their organisations to make a difference. You simply need to look for the opportunity to make your role more meaningful. Besides enriching the lives of your staff and your clients, you are well poised to help the needy by spending your CSI and entertainment budget on supporting NPO work – for example by buying tables at gala charitable dinners (among many other such opportunities).

I urge you to give serious thought as to how you can turn your role into being much more than 'just a job'. If you are one of those who would love to make a difference, the easiest way to start is to effectively utilise your position of influence, by swinging into action and injecting it with some of your own drive, passion and energy!

> 'It didn't take much for me to persuade Kevin to come on board as a major sponsor of this annual, super-chic event. From the get-go he was incredibly helpful and supportive to us and he made the job of selling off a thousand seats that much less burdensome. In those days, R150 to R200 a seat was a considerable sum! He also seemed to have the knack of sourcing artists who agreed to perform for no payment. Over and above this, FNB would sponsor a full page in our programme, which assisted in covering costs. The fact is that when Kevin is driven to achieve something, he's unstoppable. When I think about it now, over the four years in which he was involved, we probably raised a small fortune together!'
>
> HELEN BERGER

Table of Peace and Unity

Within a month of my arrival in Cape Town, I was invited as a VIP to represent FNB at the first ever Table of Peace and Unity, where an elite group of 350 guests sat down to a three-course luncheon and top-notch entertainment, on the spectacular slopes of Table Mountain. I

The Good Food and Wine Show: cooking with Italian Chef, Valentina Harris; Isabel Hancock, GM of Swiss Air; Kevin and UK Chef, Richard Corrigan.

liked the inclusive concept of a rabbi, imam, and priest – along with representatives from a vast spectrum of our local community – sitting down to break bread together at a multicultural event, respectful of all races and religious affiliations. This annual fund-raising initiative was the brainchild of Christine Cashmore, a well-known businesswoman, foodie and philanthropist who started the Good Food and Wine Show nationally. It was destined to become a winner as a way of contributing to a united and peaceful South Africa.

Over the years, this remarkable project raised millions of rand for children's charities. The magnitude of the event grew such that it was hosted in three cities. In 2013, I helped her to broaden the scope of the concept internationally to Holland and Austria. Christine and I became good friends, and she went on to assist me in sourcing support for the Amy Foundation Youth Skills Training Centre – but more about this later.

When I was invited to attend again the second year, I was troubled by the fact that while others were paying a large sum to be there, I was among the invited VIPs who did not pay for their tickets – seated in the middle with the mayoress. Third time around, I felt that I couldn't accept a free seat again and sensed that I needed to come up with a fresh take on this concept, so I approached Christine to ask how I could help. She responded that I could donate towards covering costs, but I knew that most of it was already well sponsored. I decided to create our very own FNB Table of Peace and Unity, which would work in tandem with theirs, but exclusively for lonely and forlorn pensioners. Initially, Christine didn't quite understand why I wanted to do this, until I explained how the elderly in South Africa are all too often abused and neglected. Despite Christine believing that we wouldn't be allowed to hold it in a bank, and that it was illegal to open a bank on a Sunday, I was determined to stage this in our magnificent Adderley Street Branch.

With my mantra that 'there is no such thing as can't', I ensured that the gracious domed interior of the Adderley Street Branch was to become the venue. I'd always felt that the dignified great bronze doors, which open onto travertine and marbled floors and walls, would make a stunning location for a function. Not many people are aware that it was the last Herbert Baker designed structure to be built in South Africa.

Next, I had to convince my team, who obviously were not event planners and already under immense pressure to reach their

Table of Peace and Unity in FNB Adderley Street Branch banking hall, hosted by branch manager, Dave Eastment.

Making the impossible possible

targets, to arrange our own version of a Table of Peace and Unity – on a Sunday, their day off! Talk about chutzpah! I'll never forget them bemoaning the fact that they were already having to work so hard, for long hours, and to make things worse, now on a Sunday. I asked them to please bear with me and give it a go, believing that they would see things differently afterwards. My branch manager, Dave Eastment, agreed to handle it, but wanted me to be there as host. As I've always believed that one needs to network strategically, I explained that I still needed to be on the mountain, because it was important for me to network and he could quite ably host the event at Adderley Street. The challenge I put to the team was to find 150 of the loneliest pensioners in Cape Town – ideally anyone who had not received a visitor for a year. They contacted several old age homes, and to my amazement (and sorrow), found hundreds! Word spread quickly that another Table of Peace and Unity was being held, for lonely pensioners. I sat across the table with the mayor, Nomaindia Mfeketo, and Patricia de Lille, who headed the Independent Democrats at the time. As the event drew to a close, I asked them to accompany me down to our own Table of Peace and Unity event at FNB, Adderley Street. Patricia was ultimately the only VIP to keep her word by visiting the pensioners, who couldn't thank her enough.

While the event was wrapping up, one woman approached the podium in tears, thanking FNB for changing her life and giving her the courage to live for another year. That night, I received the most heart-warming messages of appreciation and thanks from my staff across the spectrum, including those who were initially so reluctant to be involved. They finally understood why this was a perfect opportunity to show our people that FNB is a business that cares for our community. Given the excellent coverage on both radio and TV, I was thrilled with the outcome. As a team, we went on to run the Table of Peace and Unity successfully for several years thereafter. I've always believed that strong leadership is about assembling the right, committed professionals who work well with you to achieve a common goal.

From a corporate PR perspective, the benefit to the bank was

CAN DO!

immeasurable. Several old age homes moved their business our way, and some of the pensioners' children began to open accounts.

> **Whilst we must never forget to focus on the bottom line, we don't need to do everything purely for profit, because if you do the right thing, the profit factor will often look after itself.**

The following year, the staff involved called Ilchen Retief, my personal assistant, to say they would be doing this again. Sadly, when I left FNB in 2006, my successor decided to can the Table of Peace and Unity, as he didn't see the value in it.

Yvonne Chaka Chaka

I met the legendary African singer Yvonne Chaka Chaka at the first Table of Peace and Unity in 2000. Yvonne has made an indelible mark, both locally and internationally, as a world class entertainer, songwriter, humanitarian and entrepreneur. Little did I know that this would be the start of a life-long friendship, much to our mutual benefit.

Shortly after my move to Cape Town, Yvonne was selected as *The Face of FNB*. This marketing and brand ambassadorial role took her across the length and breadth of the country in the form of road-shows, mostly to the disadvantaged communities in the townships. Targeting 'the unbankables', such as stokvels (private contributors to informal money saving schemes), hawkers, and street traders, we would encourage them to invest their money with the bank, explaining

Dubbed the "Princess of Africa", Yvonne has been at the forefront of popular music in South Africa and the African continent for over 30 years. The Princess of Africa foundation is an NPO that furthers several humanitarian causes, such as the fight against malaria, wider health and education issues, with a particular focus on vulnerable women and girls. To advocate for change, Yvonne combines her access to high-level decision makers with her ability to voice issues faced by communities across Africa.

the advantages of banking, saving, using an ATM card, and the importance of keeping their pin code safe.

> *As busy as Kevin was, I was amazed that he had no qualms about often accompanying us and was hugely impressed with the way he instantly gelled with ordinary, simple folk who came from both rural and urban backgrounds. It didn't take long for us to develop a warm connection, which began to feel like we were close family – such that I call him 'Buti' (spelled boetie in Afrikaans, meaning brother). To this day, I phone him every time I come to Cape Town. He inevitably makes the time to fetch me from the airport, and I spend time with him and his family.*
>
> *Right from the start, and long before his commitment to the Amy Biehl Foundation, Kevin wanted to be comfortable in connecting with historically disadvantaged people, so he made the effort to learn their language – which in Cape Town meant learning to speak Xhosa. As a banker in a senior position, I'm sure that this was not expected of him and I was struck by this most respectful gesture. I believe that he genuinely doesn't see colour, and he never patronises black people. He will work with anyone whom he regards as competent and who, like him, has the best interests of the country at heart. I think his work at Amy Foundation is a natural progression from that, for it really fulfils him, as he has so much love for people. One soon learns that Kevin doesn't do things in half measures, and since he has taken over the Amy Foundation, he has successfully rebranded and restructured it to elevate it to a much higher level.*
>
> YVONNE CHAKA CHAKA

Yvonne helped me to raise money at an FNB event in 2002 that my team arranged, in which 200 of my high net-worth clients contributed to funding three non-profit organisations – Ikamva Labantu, Reach for a Dream, and the Amy Biehl Foundation. Since 2001, she and I

CAN DO! ✓

Yvonne Chaka Chaka, 'I didn't know white men could dance.'

have collaborated on hosting numerous other events. She tirelessly travels the world as a UNICEF ambassador, doing important work – much of which is unpaid. What really impresses me is the way she has raised her four sons, who have all turned out to be the most remarkable young men. One of the things missing in this country is the ability to teach young boys to be men who will treat women well. ■

9

To leave or not to leave

Early in 2004, I took the family on our first overseas holiday, which entailed four weeks in Europe. Shortly before leaving, we heard an amazing woman of faith named Annalaura Colavita giving her testimony in church. When I heard she was a missionary from Italy, I was determined to meet her, but little did I know that her family lived near the timeshare resort we were going to in Italy. Thus began a close friendship with Annalaura, who tirelessly works for God and has become like family. Despite her own family being wholly unsupportive of her missionary work, she started a charity shop, Ntsikelelo Africa, selling second-hand goods, which she still runs today, with 30 per cent of the profits supporting missionary work, 35 per cent going to Amy Foundation, and 35 per cent to quadriplegics.

Before my departure on our family holiday to Europe, since all the branches were now running on well-oiled wheels, with good branch, relationship, and admin managers in control, I gave Ilchen Retief, my PA, strict instructions to call me only if someone had died, or if I was being retrenched! (The latter had become increasingly easy to joke about, as retrenchments had become ever more frequent and no one was immune to this possibility.) She did contact me, but thankfully not for either. Half way through the trip, I received an SMS instructing me to phone my boss urgently. To my astonishment, it was to tell me that he wanted to promote me to provincial manager of the Western Cape!

Prior to this, two of my branch managers, Rhonda Smith and Ruby Bake, had given me the prayer of Jabez, which has since remained part of my daily prayer, 'Lord, bless me indeed and enlarge my territory. Keep your hand upon me and keep me from evil.' This prayer has since increased to include many other people that I pray for daily. When I got the message about the promotion, I remember thinking, 'I didn't want the prayer to work so quickly!' I had been enjoying my role as sales and service director immensely and would have been content to stay in it for a few more years. Besides not feeling ready for this new challenge, I was racked with guilt about the prospect of leaving my phenomenal team, which I'd so painstakingly structured and strengthened over the years. However, knowing this was an amazing opportunity, I decided to embrace it and give it my all. I was appointed provincial manager for Western Cape in 2004 and remained working happily in this role for two years.

Taking stock of where you're headed

Every now and again, it's prudent to take stock of where one is, where one seems to be headed, and most importantly, where one wishes to be. In 2005, at the age of 42, I passionately fulfilled the responsibilities required of this new position (while most of my colleagues were already well into their 50s). It was customary for most employees at the bank to retire in their mid fifties, but being so young, I felt that I could not stay doing that same job for the next fifteen or so years. With nowhere else to go in Cape Town, my next logical step up the corporate ladder would have meant returning to the materialistic, whirlwind Johannesburg lifestyle. Of one thing I was certain: I had no desire to live there again! Durban on the other hand, was too small, while Cape Town was without doubt, my spiritual home. My daughters Sarah and Kirsty were enjoying 'the mother city' and as a family we loved the people and the lifestyle it offered. The privilege of working with remarkable people like Raymond and Wendy Ackerman, Suzanne Ackerman-Berman, Philip Krawitz, Archbishop Tutu, Helen Lieberman, Lauren and Arthur Gillis, Aviva Pelham, Helen Berger and many others – all in Cape Town – still beckoned with a compelling lustre.

With my having ruled out a return to Johannesburg, the writing was on the wall: it was time to move on. Since FNB was so good to me, I did not want to work at another bank. Most importantly, I wanted to be involved in something that could really make a difference and I strongly sensed that Cape Town was where I could make it happen. I prayed hard, and asked God what his purpose was for me.

Besides prayer, I also believe that when you want to do something new, it's unwise to keep it to yourself, because then it will never happen. Have faith but take action in whatever you believe. In the Old Testament, Jeremiah 29:11 says, 'For I know the plans I have for you, declares the Lord, plans to prosper you and not to harm you, plans to give you hope and a future.' With this in mind, I slowly started sharing my thoughts about leaving (wayward thoughts indeed)! Naturally, I would have to be very careful about who I chose to discuss this with, because I was still in a position of leadership, and couldn't let my staff know what I had in mind – least of all my employers, as I still wanted my bonus and increase!

Robyn and I discussed the fact that I wanted to leave within the next three years and she was wonderfully supportive, which meant the world to me. If I'd had a wife who spent loads of money on flashy clothes and cars, I would never have been able to afford to take this gamble. When I told my daughters, Kirsty, who was then nine, became terribly distressed. I allayed her fears of being poverty stricken, by saying, 'God has blessed me for 25 years. Why would he stop blessing me? He's going to bless me even more.' And boy oh boy, he sure has! I could never have dreamt the amazing journey that lay ahead.

Reverse racism

By late 2005, I mentioned to Lynne Brown, then the MEC for Finance under Ebrahim Rasool, that I was keen to leave FNB. She proposed that I apply for what sounded like the job of my dreams: heading up Cape Nature, which administers all the nature reserves in the Western Cape such as Cape Point, Table Mountain, Cedarberg, and De Hoop. They needed someone to turn things around financially. 'Aha – so that is God's plan for me,' I thought. 'Now I know.' I applied for the position, using Lynne as my reference, along with Cameron Dugmore, then Minister of Education, as well as Ebrahim Rasool, all of whom knew me reasonably well. (Ebrahim Rasool served as SA Ambassador to the United States for five years, between 2010 and 2015.)

With all these high profile, influential contacts, it seemed that I had it in the bag, particularly as Lynne wanted me, and it was ultimately her decision. Next, I got a phone call from Tasneem Essop, the newly created MEC for Tourism and Environment, who said, 'I know that Lynne has promised you this job, but I can't give it to you because you're a white male. If I make this appointment, I'll be lambasted by the media, so quite simply, I can't do this.' Despite my protestations, it was a no go. I was distraught, because apart from travel, my other passion had become the bush, wildlife, and nature conservation. In terms of attitude, I had to pick myself up and stay positive in the knowledge that this was clearly not part of God's plan for me.

Within a week, I learnt that the CEO of Rand Merchant Bank, Cape Town, had resigned and they were looking to replace him. RMB was part of the First Rand Group, as is FNB, but at least it was a different bank, which would read well on my CV. I believed that I was the perfect candidate for this position, given that my strengths lay in leading a team and building a business – and so this must be God's plan for me, I thought. When I called their head office in Johannesburg with regard to applying for it, I was told that the board had recently taken a decision that no white male would be eligible for the position, which was subject to BEE (Black Economic Empowerment) compliance laws. So certain was I regarding my suitability for this position, and because it sounded intrinsically racist, this misshapen rejection came as a shock. To test her, I responded, 'But how do you know that I'm white? I'm actually coloured!' Sounding somewhat distressed, she immediately apologised, but I thought it best to put her out of her misery by explaining that I was in fact white. Nonetheless, I suggested that she be careful not to judge people's race by their voices or make such racist assumptions in the future.

When I expressed my displeasure at this blatantly racist decision, a senior executive suggested that I take the matter up with Paul Harris, the CEO of the First Rand Group. With the changing political milieu, my low melanin count was clearly not doing me any favours. Although I struggled with this form of reverse racism, I appreciated the need for implementing affirmative action policies. After mulling over the matter for two or three days, I changed my mind, and agreed that they in fact were doing the right thing. At the time, all the senior positions at FNB and First Rand were occupied by white males and change was long overdue. How would we ever see transformation if we kept replacing the senior posts with white males? Time for me to take a step back. 'OK, so if that is not a part of God's plan for me, then what is? Where to from here? If it is to be – it's up to me to start something myself!'

Balancing the scales

There is no doubt that the 'born frees' of today are facing many challenges. I often hear of white school-leavers feeling most aggrieved that despite their excellent credentials and qualifications, they are being discriminated against in terms of admission to university and later, positions in the South African job market. They believe that the prevailing BEE system is unfair, since they personally had nothing to do with endorsing apartheid, which prevailed well before their time. I explain to them that you cannot simply eradicate centuries of discrimination, which dates right back to the time when the Khoi and San people were victims of segregation and domination by white supremacists. Still today, the vast majority of white students come from privileged backgrounds, and therefore have a distinct advantage over black counterparts who have been raised in shacks, with minimal parental support, infrastructure, and resources. It is not uncommon for these children to come from single parent homes lacking basic amenities such as electricity, flushing toilets, running water and certainly no work desk or lamp. Since we are one of the most unequal societies in the world, the government has had to come up with some way of balancing the scales – giving rise to BEE. That said, I strongly believe that young white males and females should not feel threatened, because business managers, be they black, coloured, Indian, or white, will ultimately want to hire the best person for the job. If you don't walk around with a chip on your shoulder, and you put your heart into excelling at what you do, you will eventually overcome the colour-bar obstacle. In the application process, you might be declined several times, but if you really persevere, there will eventually come a time when you do get accepted. When opportunity knocks, be sure to distinguish yourself by your 'can-do' attitude, as opposed to a self-limiting 'cannot' approach. If you don't have an innate sense of confidence and optimism, you're far less likely to succeed.

UCT talk on entrepreneurship

At about the same time, in 2005, I was asked to do a talk on entrepreneurship for a group of post-graduate students at UCT. I was introduced to the students as the provincial manager who had been at FNB for 25 years. 'Oh dear,' I wondered, 'Why would they want to listen to me talk on entrepreneurship, if I've only worked for a corporate all my life?' Somehow, I knew that I needed to highlight the entrepreneurial

Good memories at Bankcity in Johannesburg.

aspects of my career at FNB. Although I was no business mogul or high-profile industrialist, I explained how and why I'd never spent more than three to four years in the same role and shared my ideas of how one can be entrepreneurial within a corporate environment.

For me, this was a 'light-bulb' moment: I would need to move on from FNB and not apply for another job or put my CV out. The time had come for me to effectively 'walk the talk' by starting something afresh. When I reflect upon this period of uncertainty, it is amazing how timing and synchronicity worked to enable me to change direction, in a way that demanded delving into my reservoir of courage to find my true sense of purpose. So, for the next twelve months, I assiduously worked on structuring a business plan to spearhead my own organisation – while still giving my all to the bank.

Boss behaving badly

After I made the decision to leave, my new boss did something that really annoyed me. Without discussing it with me beforehand, he arranged for one of my employees to be transferred to one of the government departments that FNB had started. Despite the fact that he was my boss, I was livid that he did not have the courtesy or respect to check if I was fine with this. Somehow, this was another sign telling me that it was time for me to make an exit, but I would not slip away

CAN DO!

quietly in the dusk. I've always believed that if one is really bothered by something, it's important to take a stand. When I accosted him about this telephonically, he said, 'Kevin, I'm driving, you're on the speakerphone, and I can't talk now.' I lashed back, 'I don't care, I can't work for someone I cannot respect.'

A little later, I found out that his immediate superior, Zweli Manyati, was in the car with him. For me, the fact that Zweli had overheard this conversation was the best thing that could have happened. It didn't take long for news of this unpleasant interchange to reach Paul Harris, then CEO of First Rand. (Paul Harris, together with GT Ferreira and Laurie Dippenaar, started Rand Merchant Bank in 1977.) The next thing, Paul summoned the bank's in-house executive industrial psychologist, Francois Hugo, affectionately nicknamed the *kopdokter* (head-doctor)! He flew down to Cape Town to mediate on this matter, attempting to resolve this impasse, but the fact is that I could no longer work for my boss, and it was time for me to move on. It also enabled me to share my views on how the regions should be structured and more efficiently run.

In the meantime, I was looking to expedite my exit in such a way that I would not lose out on shares or an annual bonus. The fact that this gave me the opportunity to fly to Johannesburg to discuss things with Paul Harris added to the logical flow of events. When I first told him my intentions, he initially attempted to dissuade me, saying that I was being short-sighted, but he changed his mind when I outlined the details of my new business plan. FNB had sent me on the Executive Management Programme at UCT Graduate School of Business the previous year and I was able to use the final required project to build the framework for the next step of my journey. My presentation to the lecturer and the fact that he gave it top marks was another sign I was heading in the right direction. As if I was rowing a boat down a gushing river splitting into several tributaries, I sensed that the current itself was surging towards a particular spot where I could confidently make a safe exit. This gave me the courage and impetus to make that big step, with an overriding sense that God was in control.

Having informed Raymond Ackerman of my plans, a month before I was due to leave, he called me to express his concern about the wisdom of my decision. He felt that I was still young, and questioned whether my personal financial position was strong enough to undertake this kind of risk to my young family during those bridging months. I replied that he had left Checkers Shoprite when he was only 35, much younger than I was, and he sure had made a success of himself!

Emanating from his concern about whether I was able to survive financially upon leaving the bank, he supplied me with a large stock of his book *Four Legs of the Table* at no cost and suggested that I on-sell them and keep the proceeds. Thereafter, he supplied them at R40 each, which I then on-sold for R 100 to make R60 per book. I will always be indebted to him for his immense kindness, concern and generosity.

At the time of my going to see Paul Harris, Francois Pienaar (of Springbok rugby fame) was the sports PR person for FNB and his contract had come to an end. Paul mentioned that they wanted to promote Francois Pienaar, who was also an astute businessman with strong leadership skills. For quite some time, I'd been proposing that they look at restructuring the bank because we were all reporting to different lines and the problem was that nobody took responsibility – Retail, Home loans, Corporate, Wesbank, FNB card were all reporting to different structures and we needed one overriding structure to consolidate and address all customer issues together. I'd given my boss my proposal, which involved streamlining the infrastructure to create an organisation that would have been leaner, meaner, and more efficient. He, however, had never approved it or taken it further, because it meant that he essentially would have been out of a job! With our reporting lines inherently flawed, Francois Pienaar was appointed the overall FNB regional executive for Western Cape. This proved to be an excellent move for the bank. I still remember him calling me to say how much he looked forward to working with me and calling me to a meeting with him to outline and exchange our ideas. While it was a great meeting, I had the uncomfortable task of having to break

CAN DO! ✓

Sarah and Kirsty Chaplin under the Eiffel Tower in Paris ask the question To Leave or not to leave?

the news that I would be departing in the next three months – I had already been to see Paul Harris and this agreement had been reached. I explained why, and he understood and supported me. I worked really well with Francois during my remaining three months, and eventually left in August 2006, more determined than ever to reach for my dreams. ▪

10

The calling of Ubuntu – 'that which unites'

The Spirit of Ubuntu – Bandi Biko, Kevin, Thoko Ntshinga and Sandeep Kumar.

One of the most profound things I learnt from Archbishop Tutu is the importance of Ubuntu. This concept was to become a seminal theme that would underpin the soul work of my life and ultimately determine my destiny. But before I go there, let's look at what Ubuntu really means. According to an old Xhosa maxim, 'umntu ngumntu ngabanye abantu' – a person is a person through other persons. I am because we are. In other words, we are human because we belong to the human community, which will function optimally if we respect and treat others accordingly. It is only by acting with empathy and humanity toward one's fellow man that a person can be at one with the spirit of the people. This is the shared humanity known as Ubuntu. Furthermore, we are who we are, mainly because of all those who have had an influence on our lives, whether it be God, our family, friends, neighbours, or educators. This belief deters us from becoming arrogant.

CAN DO!

It speaks about our interconnectedness, for no one is self-sufficient. You can't be human all by yourself, and when you practice Ubuntu, you are known for your generosity of spirit. I am because we are. It is our responsibility to take care of one another. All of us at our best are happiest when we see other people happy and fulfilled. We pray that our world can become one where we can recognise that we are members of one family – the human family, God's family – working for a compassionate, caring, and sharing community. That is why God said about Adam that it was not good for him to be alone, for we are made for complementarity, for sharing.

ARCHBISHOP DESMOND TUTU

Ubuntu recognises, in the most profound way, that we are interdependent, and that any action that I perpetrate against you has consequences for me and for my life. In other words, what I do to you lives on in me! This is in alignment with the Western expression of the concept of Ubuntu: 'Do unto others as you would have them do unto you, and do not do unto others as you would not have them do unto you.'

An African expression of 'Ubuntu' says: Your pain is my pain, my wealth is your wealth, your salvation is my salvation. It is about the individual being so rooted in the community that one's personal identity is defined by what one gives to the community. An example of a greeting in the Shona language: 'Good morning, did you sleep well?' The reply: 'I slept well if you slept well.' 'How has your day been?' 'My day has been good if your day has been good.' In other words, we are so connected that if you did not sleep well or are not having a good day, how could I? The greeting would apply to everyone in one's midst – whether it be a stranger or family member. We were lucky to have had Mahatma Gandhi, another great icon who espoused Ubuntu, living in South Africa for over 20 years – albeit through turbulent times. He was an honest seeker of truth, a fearless defender of the weak, and an uncompromising practitioner of non-violence.

Ubuntu inspires us to open ourselves to others, to learn from one another, whilst recognising the diversity of cultures, traditions, languages, values, and customs of all humanity. An Ubuntu perception of the other is never fixed: It enhances the self-realisation of others whilst allowing them to be and to become without reducing the other to any specific characteristic or sterotype.

We live amidst such a rich mix of people. As I had grown up during apartheid South Africa, it was only when I matriculated in the 1980s that I got to socialise with people of another colour, and I soon realised that by and large, there is a sense of camaraderie and warmth amongst South Africans of all races. It is our diversity that makes South Africa so unique and so respected around the world. When I meet people visiting from overseas, they frequently comment on the great energy and friendly smiles of our people and marvel at the country's natural beauty.

I believe that Ubuntu has played an important role in uniting us. For most black South Africans, Ubuntu is not a detached social theory – it is a central facet of their lives – and for many it's their primary means of subsistence. It's important to add that Ubuntu is not a belief system that is limited to black South Africans. According to a survey of high net-worth individuals from countries around the world, South Africans were the second most generous nation after Americans. They also gave more freely of their time to charitable work than people from all but three other countries. The survey ascribed their generosity to the spirit of Ubuntu on the one hand and to the vast inequalities that continue to plague our society on the other.

In 2011, FW de Klerk invited me to talk about Ubuntu at a conference in Cape Town to celebrate the occasion of the twenty-first anniversary of the historic speech in which he announced the release of Nelson Mandela. I used this as an opportunity to share my belief that one of the strongest forces uniting South Africans is the practice of Ubuntu, for it values the good of community above self-interest, by helping people in the spirit of service – irrespective of culture, religion, race and language. In so doing, you are trustworthy and look to share

CAN DO!

natural resources fairly, which does not mean that you have to be weak or feeble in business. On the contrary, to succeed one needs to be tough, decisive, supportive, and bold – all the while considering the success of the group above that of the individual.

Starting the SA Ubuntu Foundation

Many people have asked me what triggered my decision to start the South African Ubuntu Foundation (SAUF). If ever I needed an affirmation that it was the right decision to leave the bank, it was the unpleasant argument I had

> I always knew that deep down in every human heart, there is mercy and generosity. No one is born hating another person because of the colour of his skin, or his background, or his religion. People must learn to hate, and if they can learn to hate, they can be taught to love, for love comes more naturally to the human heart than its opposite.
>
> NELSON MANDELA

with my boss – a small but integral part of a series of defining moments that occurred at the time. After the entrepreneurship lecture I'd given at UCT, what I knew for sure was that it was time for me to 'walk the entrepreneurial talk'. And so began my journey of self-discovery. The change I'd seen by taking my staff to the townships, along with an event I arranged in Khayelitsha (which I'll elaborate on later) ignited a spark of recognition that I sorely wanted to be a catalyst for change. During my last nine months whilst still at the bank, I drew up a four-point business plan comprising four distinct areas in which I wanted to focus.

Since I had a great affinity for making black, coloured, Jewish, and Muslim friends, and connecting with them as colleagues and clients, my initial focus would be on breaking down some of the barriers between people of different race, language, culture, and religion. Perhaps my natural ability to connect across the cultural spectrum was reinforced by the mind-blowing experience I'd had way back in 2000, visiting the townships in Johannesburg.

Still today, I am often the only Christian at many a Jewish or Muslim function. Recently, I was the only non-Muslim guest at Auntie Koelsum Baradien's seventieth birthday, which was attended by about 150 Muslims. At my friend Ethlyn Sussman's Shabbat one evening, much to my amusement, I overheard her son saying that he would bet her R100 that I was Jewish. Although she knew I wasn't Jewish, she went along with the bet and made him pay! My connection with Ethlyn began in 2000, when I was alerted to the fact that she was looking to move her banking away from FNB. Averting this led to a long friendship, which included attending her daughter Justine's wedding, becoming friends with her brother-in-law Ellis Henen, and assisting her son Brett through some very trying times. Which all goes to show that when potential ex-clients become close friends, it's likely to become hugely rewarding!

It is always the highlight of my week to celebrate Shabbat with dear Jewish friends, like Aviva and Paul Sulcas, Helen and Michael Lieberman, Zvi and Nilly Baruch (who are now like family, and whose daughter Michal's wedding we had the privilege of attending). Jewish weddings are always so spirited and vibrant. All of these people have warmly opened their arms and homes to me and my family. I strongly believe that if there was less prejudice in the world, it would be a far more peaceful one. If we wish to live in harmony and peace, we must respect one another's religions and views.

The idea for the SA Ubuntu Foundation was precipitated by something disturbing that had taken place in 2005, while still working at FNB. I decided to assist the Amy Biehl Foundation in raising much-needed funds. I had invited all my high net-worth clients to a function at a driving range located in the township of Khayelitsha, which had been created by Peter Biehl (the late Amy Biehl's father). I invited people of mixed race and culture to enjoy one another's company – kicking off the evening by hitting some balls in the range, followed by a dinner dance in the township. To say that I was shocked by the 'decline' responses is an understatement, particularly since I was accustomed to people responding enthusiastically to my enticing invites from FNB, offering

CAN DO!

all manner of entertainment at hotels. For the first time ever, without exception, all our white and coloured customers declined, proffering elaborate excuses as to why they couldn't make it. Conversely, we received 100 affirmative RSVPs – but all from black people! How ironic! Clearly, this was 'affirmative action' (or rather inclusivity) going horribly wrong.

Calling on good friends for help

To make matters worse, no white or coloured government ministers were able to attend either, and both ministers Lynne Brown and Cameron Dugmore were unavailable. The black ministers, however, all agreed to come. When I phoned Cape Town's premier, Ebrahim Rasool, to tell him that no whites or coloureds were coming, and from an interracial perspective, we were looking at hosting a 'damp squib'– he too agreed to join us, along with his wife and son. As things transpired, I was the only white and he and his wife were the only coloured people there! Despite all this, we went on to enjoy an awesome evening, dining and partying together well into the night – enhanced by the presence of the delightful Bandi Biko (Steve Biko's sister).

As I reflected on the many extraordinary moments of that unique evening, a defining moment came as I drove out of Khayelitsha close to midnight. It struck me that the warmth and camaraderie, where I was the only white person amidst black people, should not be a one-off, nor remain an exclusive experience to me alone. I had to start something that would bring people of all colours together in the embracing spirit of Ubuntu. Little did I know then that Bandi, who has such a zest for life, would become a great friend with whom I would share many a laugh in the years to come. In 2016, at my daughter Sarah's wedding, she had enormous fun dancing with another dear friend, Pam Golding – the inspiring doyenne of the South African property industry who founded Pam Golding Properties. Both Nobandile (as I like to call Bandi) and Pam have a joie de vivre that is contagiously uplifting. Equally, Pam and I have enjoyed many laughs over a glass of good whisky at her lovely home, but I was most saddened when this much admired and highly respected property game changer died in April 2018, at the age of 90.

To kick-start the SA Ubuntu Foundation venture, I would draw on the huge database of clients with whom I had built a relationship at FNB. My first and most important port of call was Archbishop Desmond Tutu, who had spoken passionately about South Africans having become an 'Ubuntu nation' or 'rainbow nation'. I knew I needed some important names behind me for people to take this seriously. Given our warm and caring relationship, the time was right to call on my trusted mentor. I went to see him, accosting him with the words, 'Arch – you're a fraud.' 'What do you mean?' he replied. 'You're telling the world we're a rainbow nation, but in reality, we are not. Look at what happened with the golf driving range function and at most events and functions in Cape Town. The attendees are either all white, all coloured, or all black. We are all leading very separate lives and never effectively integrating and interacting with one another. The Jews are mainly living in Sea Point or Fresnaye, the blacks are living in townships like Gugulethu, Khayelitsha, Langa, Phillipi, the coloureds mainly in areas like Athlone, Grassy Park, and Manenberg, and the northern suburbs like Bellville, Plattekloof, and Durbanville are home to mainly whites (until recently, mostly Afrikaans-speaking whites, such that the northern suburbs were often referred to as being behind the boerewors curtain). It's not necessarily racism but a function of people remaining in their traditional comfort zones. In terms of the business sector, South Africa is far from an authentic rainbow nation.' I told him that I'd decided to start an 'Ubuntu Foundation' to address this in some way, which meant leaving the bank. Since his name had become virtually synonymous with the term, I needed him to be my patron. Needless to say, he willingly agreed.

Over several glasses of good red wine, I also brainstormed on many occasions with Mamphela Ramphele, who agreed to back me as well. Next, I enlisted the support of a close friend and strongly principled woman, Hilda Nikiwe Ndude, who at one time was very senior in the ANC and appeared in that iconic photograph between Nelson and his then wife, Winnie Mandela, on the day of his release. Hilda was so upset at the way Thabo Mbeki had been treated that she was instrumental in starting COPE as a breakaway political party from

CAN DO!

the ANC. When I first met Hilda, she was the chairperson of the V&A Waterfront, to whom I was presenting on behalf of FNB in the hope of winning their banking business. So impressed was I with the wisdom and insight of this powerful woman, that I wanted to meet with her separately afterwards. Somehow, I couldn't come right until my good friend Yvonne Chaka Chaka's fortieth birthday party, at which Robyn and I were seated next to Hilda. I also engaged during the same period with other dear friends like Thoko Ntshinga and Thembi Mtshali. From a networking perspective, when you meet people who impress you instantly, it's important to nurture these special connections by following through. This was the case with both Thoko and Thembi – both actresses, remarkable women, and now great friends.

This was one of the toughest times of my life, because I couldn't tell my staff at FNB. Although I was their leader, my mind was in two places, and juggling both well – building another business plan but still 100 per cent committed to my job. It was stressful and draining. For the first time in life, I had to do this on my own, without staff to back me up.

I must acknowledge the role of Dr Henry Payne from New York who first came to South Africa 20 years ago to run successful diversity workshops and has returned annually ever since, and who was one of the first people to support me in starting the SA Ubuntu Foundation, along with the Ambassador of Belgium, Jan Mutton. The Ubuntu breakfasts that Jan sponsored personally at the ambassador's residence were very special and set us on the path to future success. Both became good friends and are now also avid supporters of the Amy Foundation.

Core to building the SA Ubuntu Foundation, and any organisation for that matter, is a strong board. I was blessed from the beginning to have board members Taswell Papier, senior director at law firm ENSafrica and now a judge on the bench; Professor Fatima Abrahams, Department of Industrial Psychology, University of Western Cape (UWC) and board member of various corporates; Nilly Baruch, Union of Jewish Women; Vernon Kirsten, Global Reservations Marketing; followed later with Vuyo Koyana, Pan African Market, consultant and facilitator; and Nokuzola Cossie, trust and estates lawyer. ■

11

My four-point SA Ubuntu business plan

Let me tell you about an exciting concept called 'Ubuntu'!

CAN DO!

1. SPEAKING AT CORPORATE CONFERENCES, WORKSHOPS AND FUNCTIONS

Having been in much demand as a public speaker at conferences and university events while working at FNB, it struck me that I'd been doing all these talks and had never taken a fee. When asked what my fee was, all I'd ever requested was for FNB's banners to be displayed and our logo to be in the programme. My biggest challenge upon leaving the bank with a young family to support was to somehow ensure that I could earn an income from day one. I could speak on a variety of topics, such as the economy, the art of running a successful business, and positive thinking. One of the topics I'm often asked to speak about is how I managed to turn FNB Cape Town around in four years. Essentially, I foresaw this venture as becoming one of my sources of income, and it dovetailed well with the ideology behind the SA Ubuntu Foundation. However, it certainly would not offer sufficient income for me to make a living and put my children through school, at only 42. I would need to think of some more adjuncts to this business.

When I think about the content of my most popular presentations over the years, the focus has been on 'being the very best that you can be' and 'achieving success and balance in your business and personal life'. The subject matter is generally based on my personal journey, backed up with interesting and relevant anecdotes. I also discuss what made me successful when I came to Cape Town, and I talk on the importance of having a positive attitude and strong leadership. In alignment with the content of this book, the themes of 'Making the Impossible Possible', and my 'CAN DO' approach, have been added to my list of available topic options for speaking engagements.

2. UBUNTU BUSINESS BREAKFASTS

At the time of compiling my four-point business plan, the issue of our country's racial divide still hung heavily on my heart. Having participated in numerous social and fund-raising events

One of the many Ubuntu Breakfasts – Ilchen Retief, Vernon Kirsten, Barbara Gamzu, Elisabeth Brandt, Kevin Chaplin, Taswell Papier, Sindiwe Magona, Ahmed Kathrada, Thembi Mtshali-Jones, Silviu Rogobete.

over the years, it shocked me that few black people ever attended them. To my knowledge, there was no successful business forum in which people of all races could socialise in a relaxed, convivial environment, which lent itself to sharing common ground. This was the type of Ubuntu that was so sorely needed in our country. Having always had a wonderful rapport with black people, I thought back to my Johannesburg years, and recalled the fact that many of our black managers had said that I was the first white director they fully respected, as they could see that I genuinely believed in them and wanted to promote them for the right reasons. I've also always been widely accepted by Jews, Hindus, and Muslims, many of whom still remain close friends of mine.

I awoke one morning with a life-changing epiphany. Given my vast network of contacts across the board, I could become a catalyst for change. By harnessing this in a meaningful way, I could bring people across the colour spectrum together to share one another's company in an informal environment. I hit upon the idea of holding an *Ubuntu business networking breakfast* once a month, to break down the barriers between black, white, coloured, Indian, Christian, Jewish, Muslim and Hindu people.

CAN DO!

Our first Ubuntu breakfast was held in 2007 at Greenways Manor in Bishopscourt with Hlumelo Biko, son of Steve Biko, as the speaker. The owners of the hotel, Thomas and Susanne Faussner-Ringer, were most supportive, and owing to their friendship we were able to start the Ubuntu events. We have come a long way since then, and today these monthly Ubuntu business networking breakfasts cater for 120 business executives of diverse backgrounds in terms of colour, culture, and religion. They are well attended by government officials, CEOs, MDs, small- and medium-size business owners, heads of department, and representatives of a wide range of local and international entities. Ubuntu Business Networking enables attendees to hear and discuss presentations by influential business, political, and cultural figures in a setting that encourages people of all races and cultures to network, become well acquainted, and truly embrace each other. I always know we're on track and feel a sense of gratification when I see the rich mix of attendees every month. This unique initiative brings South Africans, international residents, and visitors together around the table to develop lasting friendships, business connections, and partnerships. It also provides them with emerging business insights, offers cutting-edge leadership perspectives, stimulates collaborative opportunities, and models inspiring ways for trusting, cross-racial partnerships to emerge within South Africa's economic sector. Attendees are inspired to use their inherent abilities to the fullest, while contributing to, and benefiting fairly from, South Africa's growing prosperity.

The Ubuntu breakfasts draw inspiration from a host of positive people and enable Kevin to remain in the public eye, while giving exposure to Amy Foundation. Besides being a great ambassador for his cause, he's a great public speaker as well. He really believes in this country, and these breakfasts generate so much positivity.
YVONNE CHAKA CHAKA

A FEW RESPONSES FROM BREAKFAST ATTENDEES:

I thought your Ubuntu Foundation initiative was wonderful and long overdue. It was great to interact with people from varied and very interesting backgrounds. The new contacts I made will surely enhance our work.

LIHLE SIDAKI

Aubrey Matshiqi was one of the best speakers I have ever heard. I took so much away from what he had to say about current day South Africa – and what we all need to do in order to make sure that this country remains the gem that it is. After attending many of these breakfasts over the past ten years, I am certainly motivated to continue the work I do.

BRAD BING

Ingrid Stoepker, Yolanda Yawa, Elizabeth Matlakala, Kevin Chaplin, Annalaura Colavita, Siya Mapoko.

CAN DO! ✓

Thanks to your breakfast, Kevin, I met Rekha Jaga, and we are now working together in my business. A big thank you!
PHUMI NHLAPO

You often do not realise the impact of giving strangers the opportunity to interact and network as you do at your breakfasts. At one of those breakfasts I met Clive Harvey Fox, the Indigo Man, who was publishing books about inspirational people. I put him in touch with a woman whose book I was editing. Morag Mackay was involved in a motorbike accident the week before her matric dance. She spent eight months in Conradie Hospital, lost an arm, and had to learn how to breathe, talk, and walk again – a beautiful and remarkably positive woman. He was amazing with her and thanks to him her book has come out. In it she thanks him for his support. Sometimes someone comes into your life who sees your success before you do, who believes you are a kindred spirit in the most special sense. For me Clive was that person. He inspired, he mentored. Meeting him and working with him was part of a bigger plan. He was inspirational and motivational, unbelievably good at encouraging people to find the hidden gifts in adversity. He believes that difficulty makes you grow, that without purpose, life is meaningless. What we see as darkness and challenge is a sacred doorway to the light. So had it not been for your breakfast, these connections would not have been possible and her book would not have seen the light of day.
GWYNNE ROBINS

Kevin, it's thanks to your breakfast that I met Eben Human of Assignment 3 and we are now in business together. Imagine a black woman and a white Afrikaner man!
NOKUTHULA MGWEBILE

Gary Kirsten

The words of some guest speakers continue to inspire, and they somehow remain relevant throughout their careers. Over the twelve years that we've run Ubuntu breakfasts (12 a year), I've only invited three or four speakers twice. Gary Kirsten is one of them. This former Springbok cricketer notched up 101 test matches and 185 one-day internationals. Having coached and mentored some of the greatest players in cricket history, including India's national team, Gary understands the dynamics of optimum performance.

At the last breakfast Gary spoke at he gave us insight into how he transformed Team India into a unit that would win the World Cup. The insights Gary gained as coach transcend cricket. His skill at creating a winning culture is inspirational. Responding to popular demand after his first address in 2009, I invited him to speak again in 2016. His sentiments on teamwork and leadership resonated strongly with me, since they have always been at the core of my own management style. For the benefit of my readers I summarise Gary's advice here:

PRIORITIES: To get the best out of your team, try to ensure that they become richer, not just financially, but in terms of their experience. (I always saw this as my role at FNB: Getting the best out of my staff – and growing them in all respects – would be more likely to benefit our clients.)

CULTURE: For the best results, create a culture of integrity driven by a solid value system. (You should only work for an organisation in which you are in alignment with the values of the leader. If this is not the case, you are not being true to yourself and you shouldn't work there.)

RESULTS: If you do everything right, and sound values are in place, the results will take care of themselves

What is your leadership mantra?

A. Don't come into a new leadership position with your own preconceived ideas. Take the time to understand where your team

CAN DO!

are coming from, and what makes them tick. Gary would not have won over his players and I would not have won over my staff at the bank if we had enforced our own preconceived ideas about how to do things. Listen well and be open to discussion and change.

B. When you're working with brilliant people who are all operating as individuals and not as a team, you're never going to win. The best way to get people to want to be part of a cooperative team, is to get them to understand what they can do for their teammates and what their teammates can do for them. They need to believe that there is more value in playing as a team – and being accountable to the team – than achieving their personal goals.

C. The power of any intervention is directly related to the interior conditions of the person. What are the person's ulterior motives? Are they genuine? Do they come with a genuine desire to improve themselves and their performance, or to address the issue in question?

D. Legitimate intentions: If people can see that your intentions are in their best interests, you will be able to lead them. Very importantly – commit and be authentic. Work out what they need to see in you as a leader, and lead by example.

Testing and toasting the new Ubuntu logo

I often marvel at the number of invaluable connections made at our Ubuntu breakfasts. When David Grier spoke in March 2016, one of our attendees was marketing lady Julie Gresse from a dynamic advertising agency called MadWorld. After the talk, Julie spoke to Solomon Potgieter, CEO, who offered to help us reinvent the Ubuntu brand. The original logo had become outdated, having been designed by my wife Robyn over ten years earlier, so it was indeed time for a new look. Madworld's top designers created something special for us and presented our team with five options. We narrowed it down to two choices and got attendees to vote for their preferred logo at the next breakfast in May 2016. Thus was born our fantastic new logo. Thanks must go to Kristoph Kunze for his continued work with our website and Oliver Genthe for the breakfast invitations. Once again, the networking web was hard at work!

The power of synchronicity

After many of my talks at conferences and events (held both locally and overseas) people have approached me to ask where they can read more about what I had said. Over the years, I've refined and crystallised my thinking, and for quite some time I've toyed with the idea of sharing my philosophy and experience in a motivational book. Given my busy travel schedule and extensive work and family commitments, this notion had remained on the back burner but always lurked at the back of my mind.

While working at FNB many years ago I met Toby Shenker, the ghostwriter and editor of this book, in the course of supporting the Union of Jewish Women – an impressive outreach organisation, for whom she wrote and fundraised at the time. In 2013 she happened to attend an Ubuntu breakfast. When Toby introduced herself as a memoir writer, a light flicked on immediately, given that this notion was still very much in my mind. After the function we arranged to meet and discuss this notion, and so the seed began to germinate. We have since worked together to create this book (albeit sporadically, given our other commitments), and I'm delighted that my objective has been reached. This is one example of the important connections that occur at our Ubuntu breakfasts, month after month.

One might be tempted to dismiss my reconnection with Toby as a random coincidence, but I believe there is more to this than a chance meeting. Deepak Chopra said, 'One must try to develop an awareness of coincidences while they are happening. It is easy to see them in hindsight, but if you catch coincidences at the moment they occur, you are better positioned to take advantage of the opportunities they may be presenting.'

We cannot ignore the way synchronicity affects our lives. If we consciously 'tune in' to these seemingly coincidental events, amazing things start to happen, empowering us in ways we could

CAN DO!

never imagine. Conversely, if we ignore such 'messages', the results can be anything from disappointing to disastrous. God brings certain people into our lives for a reason, and it is up to us to embrace these moments and seize these opportunities as building blocks, from which exciting new things can fall into place.

Letting people down – not in the spirit of Ubuntu

I've always believed strongly that if you commit to something, you should not let people down, regardless of any change in your mood or circumstance – barring grave illness or disaster! While hosting events and Ubuntu breakfasts in Cape Town, I was horrified to see how many people who had accepted our invitations actually failed to pitch up. We eventually learnt to cater for 10 to 15 per cent less than our positive RSVPs. It's shocking when people do this, and they need to show respect for others by honouring their word. If you have to cancel, then try do so at least two days beforehand.

I recall being invited by the US Consul General to an event in 2001, which Robyn and I happily accepted as we were both free. Owing to unexpected delays in the building process of our new home, it turned out that we had to move in on the very same day of the 5 pm cocktail party. By 4 pm, the furniture had just been offloaded. To Robyn's immense distress, I insisted that we go, simply as a matter of principle. Keeping my word is something I hold dear. To make matters worse, we had no electricity supply, so we had to rush to the house of our friend's Bryan and Maria Bernfield to shower. Needless to say, Robyn was furious that I made her go to the cocktail party, and it took her months to forgive me! People need to take a serious look at themselves when they merrily change their minds at the last minute to conveniently go on with their preferred agenda for the day. Surely people realise the loss and inconvenience this represents to function hosts, who have in all likelihood incurred enormous catering costs, and devoted much attention to appropriate seating arrangements, etc.

Making the impossible possible

3. ACADEMY OF ENTREPRENEURSHIP

In my banking days, one of the things that really troubled me was the fact that black people were all too frequently being ripped off by instalment agreements. Making a simple purchase like a R3 000 fridge, for example, would often result in undue penury. To afford the items, they would enter into agreements consisting of reams of fine print, which involved paying them off over several years. The items would end up costing double by the time they were paid off, and if they missed two or three payments, interest upon interest charges built up until they could no longer afford the repayments and the items would be repossessed. Clearly, there was (and still is) a gap in the transaction process: understanding of the financial implications was lacking. I recognised the need for financial literacy and education about its empowerment potential. It also bothered me that many young entrepreneurs could not obtain the finance necessary to start their own businesses – and that new business ventures tended increasingly to fail during their first three years. An academy of entrepreneurship was sorely needed.

Regardless of the potential, banks were always declining applications, and I was seeing hundreds of complaints every month. So how could I help? I wanted well-qualified mentors and coaches to provide the knowledge and information needed to set up viable business plans. I set about building a model: how to train youngsters from across the spectrum to become entrepreneurs; help them access finance and set up their businesses; and then mentor and coach them to success.

To see if I was on the right path, I presented this model to the SA Institute for Entrepreneurship run by Margie Worthington-Smith. My concept was in perfect alignment with the institute's vision, and Margie thought I was onto a winning formula. Now I knew that I had enough to start my own organisation. From a personal perspective, I thought that starting this academy was part of God's plan for me, as the SA Institute of Entrepreneurship had given me the affirmation to pursue it. However, shortly after leaving FNB and starting SA Ubuntu Foundation, I was invited to head up the Amy Biehl Foundation. I took a conscious decision to put my plan to run this academy on hold: I had to be realistic. Taking control of the Amy Biehl Foundation meant I could not do everything I had planned. I had to prioritise. But I am getting ahead of my story ....

4. UBUNTU FESTIVAL

The idea of holding a festival came to me when Ilchen asked if she could take Monday off to go to the Klein Karoo Nasionale Kunstefees (KKNK). This is a visual and performing arts festival held annually in Oudtshoorn, attended mainly by Afrikaans-speaking people. Knowing that white Afrikaans people are drawn en masse to the KKNK – and that mainly black people are drawn to the Cape Town International Jazz festival – I had a brainwave. Why not create a festival that brings people of *all* cultures together through food and music? So that's how I came up with the last part of my business plan. But more about the exciting Ubuntu Festivals later. Music has a proven power to cross barriers; create communities and unite nations; form bonds between different races, cultures, and religions; and to affect the heart and the mind, from the richest man to the poorest child.

August 2006 saw me embark on this journey. With all four components in place, I was finally in a position to launch what I would call the 'South African Ubuntu Foundation'.

The SA Ubuntu Foundation – Vision and Mission

And so it was born. Our vision embodies a world in which all people are inspired to use their inherent abilities to contribute to, and benefit fairly from, South Africa's growing economic marketplace and prosperity, its democratic values and processes, and its commitment to empowerment. We aim to realise this vision by promoting and fostering a truly prosperous and harmonious rainbow nation. To achieve this, we run initiatives and activities that break down the barriers between people of different colour, culture, religion, and language in the hope that they will truly embrace one another. ■

12

Musings of a keynote speaker

In action – doing what I love best.

CAN DO! ✓

A Eureka Moment

In 2003 the then Rector of Cape Peninsula University of Technology (CPUT), Professor Marcus Balintulo invited me to be the keynote speaker at the first World Wide Web conference in SA, which was hosting 500 international delegates. I was delighted and flattered to accept this honour, but the reality is that I knew virtually nothing about the World Wide Web, and I'm certainly not an 'IT' guy. When I raised my concerns about this, Marcus assured me that I could choose any topic I liked, and he gave me three months to think about my topic, which was ample time. With a month to go, and the programme needing to be finalised, they began to hound me for my topic. For the first time in my life, I had a mental blank, a white-out of sorts. Trevor Strydom, my boss at the time, suggested that I back out. I even asked our PR and communication department in Johannesburg to come up with a title and content. They couldn't think of anything either, and suggested I withdraw. The night before I was due to submit my chosen topic, I went to bed in a state of panic: 'Maybe I should tell them I've had to leave the country suddenly, or perhaps taken ill? But the Bible says that you mustn't lie!' I prayed to God to help me: I was at a complete loss, given my aversion to letting people down. Somehow, I eventually fell asleep.

My eureka moment occurred at 4 am. I woke up with a jolt and jotted down some ideas for a talk. I didn't know that a package had arrived in the post that day. It contained a public speaking guide to which I'd subscribed some months before. It offered ideas, topics, and tools for public speaking, as well as the full script of other people's speeches. The deal is that you are allowed to use the contents of an existing talk if you're a subscriber. Unbeknown to me, Robyn had put it next to my bed. Having turned on the bedside light, I was nothing short of astounded to find it lying there, miraculously awaiting me! I opened the book and there was a talk, right on the mark, given by a professor in Canada on the World Wide Web and technology. I was able to draw on it and adapt it to my own ideas and experience. Talk about the power of prayer! This example of its power should help convert those who don't believe that prayer works. Regardless of your religion, prayer positions you better to take advantage of opportunities that present themselves. We become empowered in ways we never imagined possible. I can assure you that no one was more stunned than I to receive a standing ovation for that presentation that almost didn't take place!

After leaving FNB in 2006, part one of my four-part plan – speaking at corporate conferences and functions – gave me cause to concretise my thoughts on how and why I had succeeded at FNB, and to share some of the lessons I had learnt in the everyday world of business. In the course of espousing some of my key life philosophies, I also wanted to share much of what I had learnt from my big-hearted, outstanding mentors, whose teachings I've alluded to earlier. What a unique opportunity to 'pay-it-forward'!

In 2007, I was invited to speak at the graduation of 500 CPUT students but was told that the university did not pay its speakers and had never done so. I explained that I was no longer in banking and I earned a living through public speaking. University officials countered that I should regard their invitation as an immense honour. Nonetheless, I stood my ground, and they paid me, although the payment was only 50 per cent of my normal fee. I believe that people sometimes don't truly value what you do for them unless there is some form of payment involved, and as such, you can often be unfairly exploited. You need to believe in yourself and demand what is fair and reasonable. No one else will do so, for in most instances, you are your only opponent! I was subsequently told by Professor Andre Du Toit at CPUT that I was the first guest speaker to have held the students' full attention throughout.

HERE ARE SOME OF THE KEY MOTIVATIONAL THOUGHTS AND IDEAS I'VE SHARED OVER THE YEARS:
Interior landscaping

Control your thoughts and you will control your life. Take charge of yourself first thing in the morning. When you wake up, do you say, 'Good morning Lord. What a beautiful day!' Or do you wake up and say, 'Oh Good Lord! It's another morning.' While they might sound similar, they reflect mindsets that are worlds apart. Do you come across as lacklustre, and having the world on your shoulders, or someone putting a shoulder to the world to make good things happen? Imagine how different your day would be if you could wake up every morning and ask, 'What excites me about today? How can I add a sense of exhilaration to my day? What changes do I need to make, to convert boredom into enthusiasm? To whose life can I make a difference today?' In the words of the famous South African extreme adventurer David Grier, 'Get up every morning, get into your boat with the correct attitude and paddle, paddle, paddle. The solutions are there and only you can find them. Everyone's personal Everest is different. I had to find my personal catalyst to conquer this. Rather regret having done something than regret not having done it. Learn to live like a renegade.'

It all has to start with what I call 'interior landscaping' – and by this I mean taking a good look at ourselves, our relationships, and our purpose in this world. People who think, 'I've done it all, I've been around, I've arrived,' will be unlikely to improve themselves or seek fresh opportunities. We should always be open to introspection, to establish how we can evolve to live more mindfully. Am I as good as I think I am? For me, the first lesson pertains to one's attitude. Attitudes are contagious. Is yours worth catching? If people walk into the room, do they duck to avoid you, or do they come into your space to be with you and hear what you have to offer? Are you an energy sapper or an energy giver?

I like what Robin Banks talks about in his Mind Power course – the ABC of Victims and Victors. Are you a Victim or a Victor? It's never too late to change from being a victim to becoming a victor. Start today! And if you know someone who espouses the victim behaviour, help that person become a victor.

Victims: **A**ccuse, **B**lame, **C**omplain.

Victors: **A**ttitude – is positive, especially during the tough and difficult times. **B**elieve – in the cause and speak with belief and conviction despite all the challenges. **C**hoices – know that life is about choices. Things are not always going to work, things are going to go wrong but make the choice to find the solution and be part of the solution.

Surround yourself with positive people

My advice is: don't walk away from negative people – *run* away from them! Tell them that you don't relate to negativity. Give them the opportunity to change and if they don't, make a conscious effort to get them out of your circle of influence. Just as positive people can lay solid

> If you change the way you look at things, the things you look at change.
> DR WAYNE DYER

foundations to enable you to reach for the stars, so negative people lay the unstable foundations for a rocky road to nowhere. Surround yourself with positive people and you will go far. This does not mean that one must be oblivious to criticism, in fact, one should

usually welcome it – especially if it's constructive. One of the biggest compliments I got in a performance review was that I'm able to take criticism on the chin and address it proactively. Most people become negative and are often surly or difficult to work with after they've been criticised. Over the years, I've written up performance appraisals on many people who might have had the necessary technical acumen, but I rated them down for having an overriding negative attitude. Usually, this comes to them as a shock – a rude awakening, but they will most surely benefit in the long run if they seek to address it.

The magic of enthusiasm

With unlimited enthusiasm you can succeed at almost anything you hope to achieve. Your passionate enthusiasm will ensure that you work hard and prepare relentlessly to accomplish your goals. I love

> Remember that 20 per cent of the people are against everything all the time.
> ROBERT KENNEDY

CAN DO!

the quote, 'Reach for the stars. If you miss, at least you will hit the moon!' After a talk I gave recently, Lauren Gillis (Founder of Relate Trust) stood up and said the following: 'Kevin personifies passion and enthusiasm. (Greek word: entheos ism – entheos meaning 'inspired by God'.) It is said that when one is enthusiastic, then one activates the God within.' How could anything be more amazing than loving what you do and knowing that it matters?

I met Kevin many years ago, when he worked for FNB, and what struck me was his enthusiasm for social responsibility. He was like a sponge and in the course of our many talks about my beliefs and his, I was particularly impressed with his ideas and values.

His enthusiasm and passion is what makes him successful and the fact that he has very set, clear goals – always a key ingredient for success. Not only were Wendy and I really impressed with the work of the Amy Biehl Foundation and the very deep and sad story of Amy Biehl, but also the concept of perpetuating her memory and work.

It is thanks to Kevin's dedication, enthusiasm, and energy that this worthwhile project is so well established today. We have several items linked to Pick n Pay that emanated from our discussions, and while we have not raised much money for our company, we have taken great pleasure in helping him to achieve his important goals.

RAYMOND ACKERMAN

As a quick update, I would like to add that Raymond introduced me to Richard Brasher when the latter took over as CEO of Pick n Pay in 2013. When Richard got to know me, he promised us continued support, explaining that in addition to the Ackermans, Pick n Pay would also be donors. Richard has also contributed in his personal capacity, by donating the substantial speaker's fee he earned from a talk he delivered for Investec – literally paying it forward!

Optimism vs Pessimism

I'm saddened by the number of people who are pessimistic. A sense of optimism is the most important trait to acquire. In a study done in the Mayo Clinic in Rochester, by looking at patients 30 years later, it was found that people classified as optimists had a 19 per cent higher chance of still being alive than the pessimists. Those who saw things as getting worse as they aged died seven-and-a-half years earlier than those who had a positive view of ageing. In a University of Kansas research, student levels of hope formed a greater predictor of their ability to make it through university successfully than their high school results. When realistic optimists face challenges or problems, they won't automatically give up, or imagine the problem to be insurmountable, instead they will think laterally, and come up with plan A, plan B, or plan C.

To work with Kevin is a roller coaster ride of organised chaos! To put this into perspective, Kevin and I share the same view of not accepting an 'I can't' attitude, given that our starting point involves agreeing that whatever the scenario, we will make it work! As you can imagine, this can lead to chasing visions and having to tailor our dreams to suit the reality. Even so, it is worth travelling the road of 'I can' to see how far you can go before stepping down to reality. We always end up better off than we would have, had we started thinking, 'I can't'! There are the people who believe their glasses are half empty as opposed to those who believe that theirs are half full. Kevin believes his is full to the brim daily. This is evident in everything he does, which makes him an amazingly positive person to work alongside.
ALISON McCUTCHEON OF RAINBOW EXPERIENTIAL MARKETING

I often relate the story about the two shoe salesmen, which goes as follows: They go to an island to sell shoes. Upon arrival, they notice that no one is wearing shoes. The one phones his office to say, 'Cancel

CAN DO!

the order, nobody here wears shoes.' The other one calls his office to say, 'Double the order, nobody here wears shoes!' That illustrates the power of being optimistic.

Afiefa Behardien, my chief operations officer (COO), often sighs when I come up with ideas that seem overly ambitious, 'Oh Kevin, the eternal optimist!' But at the end of the day, she has to admit, 'Hey, you were right! We did it.' Having a 'can do' approach means that I tend to set high goals and achieve them. Likewise, if I wasn't optimistic, I probably wouldn't have taken on the task in the first place!

Live with love and kindness

There are so many ways we can live empathetically – whether it be emotionally, spiritually, or financially. All that is required is the mindset to do so. Kindness is a great power and an instrument of your true nature, so use it

> I've learned that people will forget what you said, people will forget what you did, but people will never forget how you made them feel.
>
> MAYA ANGELOU

often. When in doubt, as the saying goes, 'Kill 'em with kindness!' The essence of all the scriptures and religions can be summarised in just four words: 'Love All, Serve All.' Judaism, Islam, Christianity, Buddhism, and Hinduism all teach the same truth. Just as many schools worldwide teach identical subjects in different languages, ultimately, the essential message is the same. Take a genuine interest in others and be known for the strength of your character.

Laughter is the best medicine

Humour is infectious. The sound of boisterous laughter is far more contagious than any cough, sniffle, or sneeze. Find things to laugh about and share them with your colleagues and friends. When laughter is shared, it unites people and builds friendships, while increasing connectivity and intimacy. There is infinite wisdom in the old adage, 'Laugh and the world laughs with you; weep, and you weep alone.'

Laughter is a powerful antidote to stress, pain, and conflict. Nothing works faster or more dependably to bring your mind and body back into balance than a deep, hearty laugh. It triggers the release of endorphins – the body's natural feel-good chemicals, which promote an overall sense of well-being and can even temporarily relieve pain. Humour lightens your burdens, inspires hope, and keeps you grounded, focused, and alert.

Laughter boosts the immune system. Living with levity can strengthen your immune system, boost your energy, and protect you from the damaging effects of stress. Apparently, a good giggle decreases stress hormones while increasing infection-fighting antibodies, thus improving your resistance to disease and heart failure.

Laughter relaxes the body. A full-bellied, hearty laugh relieves physical tension and stress, leaving your muscles relaxed for up to 45 minutes. The phenomenon of inducing physical changes in the body has been well researched and proven – such that people who watch funny sitcoms, for example, have been found to enjoy a higher level of well-being. With so much power to heal and renew, the ability to laugh easily and frequently is a tremendous resource for surmounting problems, enhancing your relationships, and supporting both physical and emotional health. Best of all, this priceless medicine is fun, free, and easy to use!

Smile at as many people as you can. I've always advised my staff to smile at people as they pass them in the street. A simple form of acknowledgment – like a warm, cheerful smile – can make someone's day. It doesn't get cheaper or easier than that! Some might think you are crazy when you smile at them, but smile anyway and spare a thought for the people you have uplifted in some way by smiling at them. There's a story about a man who committed suicide by jumping off a bridge. When his family found

> Your sense of humour is one of the most powerful tools you have to make certain that your daily mood and emotional state support good health.
>
> PAUL E McGHEE

CAN DO!

his diary the next day, he had written: If someone smiles at me on the way to the bridge I won't jump. So always smile at people, for you never know whose life you might save.

Start a gratitude journal

As discussed earlier, I grew up with insufficient means, but my mother taught me to never focus on what we didn't have. One of the easiest ways to infuse your days with positivity, is to start a gratitude journal. This will encourage you to write down and list, on a daily or weekly basis, all the things that you're grateful for. Essentially, it shifts the focus away from what you haven't got to what you have. We all have our problems, and a long list of needs. But instead of wallowing in regret, disillusionment, or envy about all the things that you feel should be yours, yet have somehow eluded you, it's infinitely more helpful and uplifting to try and focus on everything you can be grateful for – be it a roof over your head, a job, good health, children, access to education, food, or the beach. You will feel more appreciative, blessed, and positive as you take on the challenges of each new day. Trust me, it works!

Ideally, you should make it a practice to be grateful every day for *everything* – the good, the bad, the pleasure, and the pain. You will notice quickly that it's impossible to have a bad thought or feeling when you are in the state of being thankful. There is no such thing as an 'ordinary moment', so accept and surrender to every moment and every sensation (good or bad) and try to find the beauty in each experience, person, or place. If you look for it hard enough, you will find it. The simple act of considering the good things in your life will distance you from negative thoughts that are a barrier to laughter and joy. It helps to sit somewhere 'sacred' to meditate and relax – whether it involves going into the bush or just the garden to enjoy nature, or simply by listening to music.

Don't count on a prospective inheritance

Over the last few years, one of the more bizarre and extremely distressing issues I've had to grapple with is the small, or rather not so small matter, of being disinherited by relatively close family (excluding my parents). Believe it or not, this has happened not once but twice – involving seemingly wonderful people with whom I had always enjoyed especially warm, supportive, and enduring relationships!

Unfortunately, old people, having become vulnerable, are easily deceived and often open to abuse – particularly when dementia creeps in. Without wishing to go into the circumstances of each particular instance, in each case, the person's will was changed at the eleventh hour, after having been unduly influenced (and deceived) by another close relative, who had a strong vested interest in ensuring that the bulk or all of the inheritance in question swung another way. In the case of an uncle to whom I was particularly close, he had even sent me a copy of his will a few years earlier, to indicate how much he loved me and the extent to which he was happy to include me.

Besides the disappointment of losing out on much-needed money at the time, what shocked me was how malicious and greedy people can become when money is involved. When I learned of their evil manipulations, I knew these relationships would never be the same.

> *If you woke up this morning with more health than illness, you are more blessed than the million who won't survive the week. If you have food in your refrigerator, clothes on your back, a roof over your head, and a place to sleep, you are richer than 75 per cent of this world. If you have never experienced the danger of battle, the loneliness of imprisonment, the agony of torture, or the pains of starvation, you are ahead of 20 million people around the world. If you can hold up your head with a smiling face and are truly thankful, you are blessed, because the majority can, but most do not. If you can hold someone's hand, hug or even touch that person on the shoulder, you are blessed, because you can offer God's healing touch. If you can read this message, you are more blessed than over two billion people who cannot read anything at all.*
>
> AUTHOR UNKNOWN

CAN DO!

I had to eventually bury my anger and bitterness, pick myself up, and get on with my life. I had always known that I would have to work hard for my money, so I took the view that it was not meant to be, and God was in control. When something nasty has been done to you, the very act of forgiveness will enable you to move on with some degree of fortitude.

Eliminate self-limiting beliefs

Many people sabotage themselves in the way they think, act, and respond to things. Limiting our beliefs in what we can or can't do is like drawing a circle around ourselves in the sand. This becomes an artificial construct that exists only in our own thinking. Invariably the construct is not based on reality or anything that's been tried and tested. Stop making excuses for your mistakes, and don't spend your life apologising or explaining yourself – just try to get on with the job and do it well and to the best of your ability! Equally important is to learn to forgive yourself. Sadly, many parents put their impressionable children at a serious disadvantage by reinforcing their negative opinions, which soon become deeply ingrained perceptions of self. Perhaps you were told that you were too clumsy to play sport, too fat to ever lose weight, or too stupid to be good at maths. It will be helpful to establish the origin of these self-limiting beliefs and process the likelihood of these being accurate or simply self-limiting perceptions. Just because it might be difficult to lose weight, or a big challenge to achieve some performance goal, does not make it impossible. Here follows a wonderful tale about elephants that illustrates the point.

As my friend was passing the elephants, he suddenly stopped, confused by the fact that these huge creatures were tied to a stake by only a small rope around their front legs. No chains, no cages. It was obvious that the elephants could at any time break free, but for some reason they did not do so. My friend saw a trainer nearby and asked why these beautiful, magnificent animals just stood there and made no attempt to get away.

> '*Well. When they are very young and much smaller we used the same size rope to tie them. At that age it was enough to hold them. As they grew up, they were thus conditioned to believe that they couldn't break away, so they never tried to break free.*'
> *My friend was amazed. Just because they believed they couldn't escape, they remained stuck, right where they were.*
>
> AUTHOR UNKNOWN

Perhaps you are someone who feels like your life is constrained by metaphorical chains? Much like these elephants, many of us are hindered by old, restrictive beliefs that cannot possibly serve us. How many of us have avoided trying something new because of an ill-founded, false notion which says 'I can't'? How many people go through life hanging onto a belief that they cannot do something simply because they failed at it once before? There is often a strong social component to our behaviour, and the prospect of being ridiculed, criticised, or rejected is enough to powerfully inhibit us. From an early age, I made a conscious decision *not* to accept the false boundaries and limitations created by my difficult father and our impoverished circumstances. I made a choice to respond to life's challenges with 'CAN DO', as opposed to 'I can't', and I've no doubt that this attitude is what altered the trajectory of my future.

> Whatever you can conceive and believe, you can achieve. Your attempt may fail, but never fail to make an attempt.

WATCH

If you forget everything else, the WATCH acronym is an invaluable tool for life. It's fairly easy to remember, since each letter stands for something worth remembering. The easy way to keep the following in mind is by looking at your WATCH, which stands for: Words, Attitude, Thoughts, Company, and Heart. You won't forget it!

W – Watch the Words that come out of your mouth. Each word you

CAN DO!

say can build a person up or break that person down. The nature of your sentiments says something about the way you think and who you are. Consider how differently you would respond to someone who comes up to you saying, 'Gosh Kevin, you're looking great!' as opposed to, 'Gosh Kevin, you've put on weight!' I know which one I would respond to best. If you can say a positive thing to a staff member, you build that person up, as opposed to a negative, which does the opposite. Also, if you are a person who shouts or swears when under stress, once these harsh or insulting words are out of your mouth, you cannot take them back and you will quickly lose the respect of your staff and colleagues – and once lost, it's almost impossible to earn it back. Have grace under pressure. The bottom line: Learn to control yourself. THINK before you speak.

T – Is it True?

H – Is it Helpful?

I – Is it Inspiring?

N – Is it Necessary?

K – Is it Kind?

And most importantly will your spoken word be pleasing to God. Before I speak at a conference, workshop or any event I ask God to please bless the words that come out of my mouth and may they be pleasing to him and give him the glory.

A – Watch your Attitude. With the right attitude, you can reach a higher altitude. And with a positive attitude, not only will you attract the right people, you can achieve almost anything to which you set and apply your mind. The good news is that bad news can often be turned into good news when you change your attitude. When you walk into a room, do people avoid you or do they naturally gravitate towards you?

Your attitude will also contribute to how effectively you communicate. Effective communication involves: 7 per cent Words; 38 per cent Tone of Voice; 55 per cent Body Language.

Attitudes are contagious. Is yours worth catching? *When you are faced with a problem, adopt the attitude that you can and will solve it.* It is your attitude at the beginning of a task that will often determine your success or failure, and it's your attitude towards life that will determine life's attitude towards you. Develop the attitude that there are more reasons why you should succeed than reasons why you should fail. Give yourself freedom to try out new things, and don't be so set in your ways that you can't grow. Too many people put their lives on hold because they are too scared of what other people might say or think if they should fail. Such concerns will not only hinder your progress, they will also prevent you from taking a chance. Good friends however, will help you to laugh at your mistakes!

How will you use today's failure to ensure tomorrow's success? The best lessons are usually learned from failure. As Virgin Group founder Richard Branson said, 'The brave may not live forever, but the cautious never live at all.' Take time to reflect on the mistakes you have made. Evaluate how you could have improved on the situation and write down the lessons you have learnt.

T – Watch your Thoughts. From a young age, we are taught that making a mistake is bad. Painful memories of past failures trigger negative emotions like fear and anxiety, which prevent us from achieving our potential. We become what we think about. Control your thoughts and you will control your life. Have thoughts that lead to action. If I hadn't taken action in alignment with my thoughts, I'd still be at FNB, or I'd still be sitting in Durban. Focus on positive, proactive thoughts as opposed to negative ones, since proactive thoughts lead to action that can result in change for the better. So many people don't follow through on their thoughts or ideas, and sure enough someone else then does it before you. I so often hear people say, 'But I had that idea!' Well, too late – as the saying goes, 'You snooze, you lose!'

C – Watch the Company you keep. Make a conscious decision to surround yourself with the right company – supportive people who'll build you up, which of course includes choosing the right spouse! Much of what I've been able to achieve is attributable to my wife Robyn, who has been immensely supportive of my every move. Sometimes you

CAN DO!

are going to have to ignore people who find countless reasons to say, 'Don't do it.' That said, be sure to differentiate between the naysayers and those who offer sage advice. Ultimately, you should explore your options, think laterally and arrive at your own solid reasons to justify why you should do it!

I remember reading that Barack Obama welcomed Hilary Clinton into his team after a long and bitter battle for the presidency. Questioned by the media as to why he had made the seemingly inexplicable decision to create a 'frenemy' out of his toughest adversary, Obama reportedly said that if you surround yourself with clever people who challenge your thinking constructively, it might well be that they will be better than you at certain things. Having them in your team, however, will boost your performance and ultimately achieve a mutually beneficial outcome. I believe that it's healthy to work with highly intelligent people whose points of view differ from mine, for they might well present a better, fresh, and inspired alternative to what I had originally seen as the only way to go. This dynamic will force both parties to constructively thrash out their thinking as they crystallise their ideas. Remember – you learn nothing from an echo, but you certainly stand to benefit from a vigorous debate!

H – Watch your Heart. Have a giving heart. Cultivate a generous heart and generosity of spirit. Of course, in business my priority and responsibility was to make a profit. As a result of doing and focusing on the right things – in my case, putting customers and staff first – the profits were sure to follow. Emanating from the Table of Peace and Unity, for example, new customers started banking with us. These were ways for people to see what we were about, and say, 'I like what you're doing here. I want to bank with you.' One should cultivate a heart that cares, for it's not just about giving money. It's also about giving of yourself: by mentoring someone you can both make a difference. When you go to bed at night, you might wish to make a point of asking, 'To whom did I make a difference today?' People often complain that their bosses never teach them how to do X or Y. You need to share your knowledge and pay it forward. When you're at a traffic light, buy 'The Big Issue' magazine, or buy a 'Funny Money' flyer – these are produced to enable unemployed people to earn some income.

THE FOUR QUADRANTS TO A MORE BALANCED AND SUCCESSFUL LIFE

Using a flipchart, I like to draw a quadrant representing the four key parts of life which are essential to happiness and well-being: The spiritual, physical, intellectual/IQ, and emotional/EQ. One has to have all four of them in sync. Since all four require conscious attention, if one is missing or lacking there will be a heavy price to pay, just like the four legs of the table in business.

Physical: You don't have to run marathons or become a prize-winning body builder. Maintaining a healthy diet and a basic level of fitness will see you through the day. Whether it's going for a walk, a cycle or even yoga, you need to get the blood flowing to both the body and brain to keep your muscles toned and to feel invigorated. I like to run five mornings a week for at least 40 minutes, and there's no doubt that being physically fit helps me to cope better during the day. When you exercise, your body releases chemicals called endorphins, which interact with the receptors in your brain. Among other things, endorphins reduce your perception of pain – in a similar way to morphine! Psychologically, the feeling that follows a run or workout is often described as 'euphoric'. Commonly referred to as a 'runner's high', it usually leads to a more positive, energised outlook on life and improved self-esteem. Make sure you are not one of those people whose only exercise is jumping to conclusions, running down their friends, side-stepping responsibility, and pushing their luck!

Eating the right foods and a healthy balanced diet is also essential. As we know, there are innumerable tips on healthy eating, but one that resonates with me is the importance of eating foods with tryptophan like avocado, turkey, chicken, greens – which all carry serotonin, the

CAN DO!

'happy chemical' to the brain. As a food lover, I try to balance this by reducing my intake of bread, rice, potato or pizza. One of the best things I did six years ago was to start taking a health product called Juice Plus, which I will discuss later.

Spiritual: Although this is difficult to define, it's the way you feel on a deeper level. For you, it may be less about religion and more about personal development, being connected to others and seeking inspiration from something greater than yourself. Whether you find inner peace through religion, spending time with nature, meditation, or reading spiritual literature, nurturing your spiritual side will enable you to get in touch with your true self and live contentedly in the present as you move forward with a sense of joy. I believe that we're all on the same journey; we're just taking different roads to get there. Quieten your mind when it wants to take you astray, as this will open your heart, but remember to love yourself completely at the same time and give that mind a break as it's only doing its job.

Here are some quick tips to start you off on your unique path:

1) *Know there is no 'normal' when it comes to spirituality, religion or beliefs. Your beliefs are unique to you.*
2) *Be grateful for the differences that surround you. These differences allow you to mould your own journey into exactly what you want, rather than following the crowd.*
3) *Keep seeking for your greatest you. With each day that passes, you have the opportunity to wake up and do better than you did yesterday. This enables you to feel better each day, too!*
4) *Love your entire journey, not just the feel-good moments. More times than not, it's the painful events in our lives that help mould us into the beautiful spiritual beings we are.*

MIND BODY GREEN by KATIE O'BRIEN

> The happiest people in the world are not those who have perfect lives but those who have learned to enjoy things that are less perfect.
>
> DR VIJAI SHARMA,
> CLINICAL PSYCHOLOGIST AND
> BEHAVIOUR SPECIALIST

Intellectual: Many people are so busy running the treadmill of life, they forget the simple things like stopping to take stock. It helps to read books, do courses, and keep your brain stimulated with, for example, crossword puzzles or sudoku. Make sure to be computer literate, read widely, and keep up to date with current thinking, financial and social trends as well as world affairs. Education builds us. It's never too late to get a degree or diploma, or to do a short course, even part-time if necessary!

Emotional: EQ is now even more important than IQ. The word 'emotion' in Latin means to move out from or stir up. So, if you have no emotional intelligence, how can you expect to move forward? In the old days, seeing a therapist was taboo. Today the world is so much more complicated, so everyone should see one! It need not be an expensive, highly paid professional. On the contrary, it can just be someone you trust, a good listener who can enable you to unburden and process your thoughts, feelings and actions. It must of course be someone in whom you can confide and most importantly, whose opinions you value. There is much wisdom in the saying, 'A burden shared is a burden halved.' By tapping into and examining your issues, you are more likely to be able to take charge of yourself and your future, and to become emotionally well rounded.

My father had a high IQ but a low EQ, which is one of the reasons he was so miserable and anti-social. I can't help wondering how different his life would have been had his mother taken him to a psychologist. Now is the time to let go of your past, to take control of your emotions and your feelings, and above all to believe in yourself. Live every moment and laugh every day – especially at yourself!

CAN DO!

Fit into a changed society

One of the speakers at our monthly Ubuntu Business Breakfasts was the highly esteemed Professor Jonathan Jansen, Vice Chancellor and Rector, University of the Free State, who wrote an article headed 'How to be white in the new South Africa' (*The Times*, 17 September 2015). Contained therein are a few salient points, which I feel could benefit young South Africans and people all over the world, in terms of how they relate to others. Here are some excerpts which may be of relevance.

First: Get a grip on yourself. You are not better than the other person because of your skin. Skin colour is an accident; by the roll of the dice, you could have come out differently. Acknowledge that you are a child of privilege. If you start off with the idea that everything you have is a consequence of the hard work of your parents, you are probably from another planet. Yes, they probably worked hard, but centuries of separation and privilege – white affirmative action, in essence – gave your family an emphatic advantage at the expense of black people. That is why you do not live in a shack or never attended a crappy school. Acknowledging this simple fact sets you free, big time. Envying it will make it difficult to ease into this new country, since you would never understand how we came to be so unequal.

Always be on the lookout to learn from your friendships. Make sure your friend teaches you an African language or Indian culture, or Afrikaans history or mathematics. Look to learn, but also to share something worthwhile that your friend does not have access to. Learn something new about others but do not reduce black culture to Mafikizolo and gumboot dancing. Black culture, like all cultures, is richly diverse and constantly changing. Learn to appreciate the traditions and expectations of your different friends and their families. Call the parents of your Afrikaans friends Oom en Tannie (Aunty and Uncle) if that is what they expect, and listen to older black people with deep respect and do not, I repeat, do not call them by their first names or assume familiarity. ■

13

Amy Biehl Foundation on the horizon

Amy Biehl. Photo: Orange County Register.

CAN DO! ✓

As I reflect upon my working life, the image of two distinct halves comes to mind. Although the latter half of my career was built upon the skills and lessons learnt in the former – and both proved equally demanding – each has a very different story to tell. The pivotal point was reached when I moved on from banking in 2006, at a time when the country seemed to be struggling to find its feet in a post-apartheid era. So much still needed to be done by the government to improve the plight of those who had suffered the ravages of apartheid. By and large, it was left to civil society and the corporate sector to step in, to help bridge the gap. Along with this came a set of new challenges. The second chapter of my life involved immersing myself largely in uncharted waters with as much drive and passion as the former, however, my involvement in running and growing the SA Ubuntu Foundation and Amy Biehl Foundation (later to become Amy Foundation) came from a much deeper, more spiritual place. Before I explore this in more detail, let me first give you the background to the Amy Biehl story, its immeasurable relevance to the anti-apartheid struggle, and how it shifted perceptions – both locally and internationally.

Who was Amy Biehl?

Amy was an attractive, dynamic Stanford graduate student who came to South Africa from the US at the age of 25, as a Fulbright scholar, to complete a one-year student exchange programme at the University of the Western Cape (UWC) Community Law Centre. The university had been established in 1960 for coloured people as part of the government's policy of racially segregating higher education. In 1993, during Amy's stay in Cape Town, she focused on the position of women in a constitutional democracy, and the efforts made to include substantive, rather than only formal equality, in the Bill of Rights. She also helped with voter registration for the upcoming SA election – the nation's first multiracial election, scheduled for April 1994.

Whilst involving herself in anti-apartheid organisations on the UWC campus, she worked tirelessly with ANC members like Cyril Ramaphosa, Dullah Omar (anti-apartheid activist, lawyer, and Cabinet minister) and Bridget Mabandla (formerly the minister of public enterprises and minister of justice and constitutional development). Amy believed that Africa was the continent of the future. She was committed to making a difference. Although she was a top student, she played as hard as she studied, for she loved the beach, dancing, going to clubs, and running marathons. It did not take long for her to make friends all over Cape Town, including the black townships.

About three months into her stay, frustrated that the activists could not help her academically, she sought assistance from a lecturer, Rhoda Kadalie, the well-known academic and much respected anti-apartheid activist. Rhoda explained, 'By then, I had treated her as just another American groupie on the campus. After agreeing to help her, I proceeded to correct her paper and advised her whom to consult, whom to interview, and which materials to use. Amy stood there with her blue eyes as big as saucers, because I was the first person who actually took her work seriously. She soon trusted me, and I became her mentor, supervisor, and later a mother figure, who would guide her as to the vagaries of cultural life in South Africa. Towards the end of her stay, she was given many farewell parties; one by the future minister of justice, who really loved her and praised her effusively at a party he hosted – to the point of embarrassing Amy, who could not deal with too much praise. With South Africa being on the cusp of transition, this was an extremely tense and troubled time. Throughout her stay, I had advised her repeatedly not to go into the townships, given the violent protests and uprisings. Amy promised that she would not go.' (Rhoda has now retired as Executive Director of the Impumelelo Social Innovations Centre and remains a supporter and ambassador of the Amy Foundation.)

Tragedy struck on 25 August 1993, days before she was due to return home to the US to complete her Doctorate in African Affairs. Two of Amy's black colleagues found themselves stranded at UWC. They phoned her, saying they were desperate for a lift home to the black township of Gugulethu, Cape Town. Without hesitation, she agreed to help. Unbeknown to her, there was a political rally underway

CAN DO!

in the area. When police arrived to break up the rally with sjamboks (long, stiff whips) the mood took a turn for the worse: a mob of angry youths coalesced in violent protest. Unwittingly, Amy had somehow found herself in the midst of this enraged mob, fired up after attending a Pan Africanist Students Organisation meeting.

Under apartheid, until Mandela's release in 1990, all attempts at negotiation with the government had proven fruitless. Peaceful protests met with brutal response from the government. Over time, black activists came to believe that the best way to free themselves was through an armed struggle. The liberation movement's revolutionary theme was 'Year of the Great Storm' – the objective being to make South Africa totally ungovernable through violence.

On that fateful day, with racial tension at an all time high, Amy happened to be driving behind a Coca-Cola truck that was being stoned. The PAC's tactics involved making it difficult for truck drivers on national roads to deliver everyday items such as bread, cold drinks, and milk. PAC strategy involved stoning cars, trucks, delivery vehicles, and even ambulances. In so doing, they would force drivers to bring trucks to a standstill. If the drivers were cooperative, they were forced out of their vehicles, which would then be torched or overturned.

Reacting on impulse to the sight of a blonde, white woman who represented their oppressors, they surrounded her car and started shouting, 'Here's a settler, here's a settler!' – the term used to refer to white people. Suddenly, the focus changed from the Coca Cola truck to Amy's small car. Unfortunately, Amy became the scapegoat of their suffering and anger. In that singular moment, the beautiful, blue-eyed student came to represent collective white South Africa. She was forced out of her car, stabbed, and hit on the head with a brick. During the attack, her black friends pleaded that she was a 'comrade' and friend to black South Africans, but her assailants were merciless, steadfast in the belief that they were fighting for a noble cause. All attempts to resuscitate Amy failed, and she died on the scene – simply because she was white. Ironically, Amy was killed by the very people she was trying to help. This was a horrific case of being in the wrong place at the wrong time. The unprovoked, senseless murder created an international outrage, throwing a negative pall over our newly emerging democracy.

At a fundraiser we held for the Amy Foundation, Rhoda's daughter Julia Pollak recounted her personal recollection of Amy:

'My mother and Amy struck up a friendship that grew over several months, such that Amy became a frequent guest at our home and at the Gender Equity Unit my mother had founded on campus.

I was six years old at the time and fell in love with Amy – the way little girls idolise beautiful, vivacious young women, especially those who are kind to them. I remember playing with her long blonde hair, and asking her silly childish questions, like whether she liked having blue eyes.

I knew that my mother really admired Amy's attachment to South Africa, her love for the country, her dedication to studying Xhosa, and her commitment to discovering what was really going on. My mother would joke that Amy had more black friends than she did, that Amy knew more about Cape Town's black nightclubs and bars, and that Amy spent more time in the townships than she did. I also remember my mother lecturing Amy to stop being so kind to everybody, to stop giving colleagues lifts home into the townships, and most importantly, to be careful.

The news of Amy's death had a huge impact on me. It was the first time someone close to me had died, and it was the first time I'd seen my mother slump onto the floor and sob. I remember the complete shock of seeing the horrific details emerge on the evening news, the images of Amy's orange Mazda. But I'd like to focus on two positive things that came about through her death.

The first: Precisely because it was so shocking and tragic – Amy was the white person least deserving of retribution for apartheid – her death held up a mirror to angry young activists, and showed all South Africans the absurd, perverse consequences of collective guilt. Many activists erased the ubiquitous struggle slogan, "one settler, one bullet", from their lexicons following her

CAN DO!

death. We may never know how important that was, but I think it was a critical event that changed the course of history. The violence could easily have swelled into a full-on civil war, many more might have been killed and the prospects of a peaceful resolution might have been irreparably harmed.

Journalist Marianne Thamm, who had been my mother's tenant living in the guesthouse attached to our home, wrote that Amy's killing "shocked us out of our hot rage" such that it caused everyone to "pause and take stock".'

The reader should know that this was not an isolated incident and certainly not the only unprovoked one to take place in 1993. Various political and religious leaders pleaded with the nation for much-needed calm and reason. Amy was murdered only one month after the horrific St James massacre. In what was also claimed and later found to be a politically motivated massacre, four cadres of the Azanian People's Liberation Army (APLA), armed with hand grenades and assault rifles, barged into the St James Church in Kenilworth, murdered 11, and wounded 58 of the church's congregants while they were deep in prayer. Throughout that year, the country teetered on a precipice: Chris Hani, the beloved leader of the ANC's military wing uMkhonto we Sizwe and the SA Community Party, had been assassinated in his driveway by a white, right-wing Polish immigrant named Janusz Walus. (At the time of writing, he still remains behind bars after the Supreme Court of Appeal in Bloemfontein set aside a High Court judgement ordering his release on parole.) Outraged citizens across the country took to the streets, marching in protest, threatening to take revenge. Nelson Mandela – who had been released from prison but was not yet our president – intervened to call for calm in a live broadcast televised by the South African Broadcasting Corporation. This act of measured statesmanship enabled us to miraculously escape a potential bloodbath.

Amy's four young male assailants – Vusumzi Ntamo, Mongesi Manquina, Ntobeko Peni and Mzikhona Easy Nofemela – were all arrested, tried for murder and sentenced to 20 years imprisonment.

Although I had read about this tragic turn of events at the time, little did I imagine that Ntobeko Peni and Easy Nofemela were destined to play such a significant role in my life, thirteen years later, in the most unimagined of ways. But let me not get ahead of my story ....

Truth and Reconciliation Commission

In 1995, the Truth and Reconciliation Commission (TRC) was set up by the Government of National Unity with the aim of redressing the wounds of the past by processing human rights abuses and atrocities committed between 1960 and 1994 under the apartheid regime. Presided over by Archbishop Desmond Tutu, this court-like body was established to review requests for amnesty by those guilty of committing politically motivated crimes. It was a forum in which both victims and perpetrators could come forward and have their voices heard in such a way as to enable South Africans to come to terms with the traumas of their past.

Nobel Peace Prize winner and TRC leader Archbishop Desmond Tutu explained: 'Instead of seeking revenge, people who had been ill-treated and subjugated were ready to speak about reconciliation and forgiveness. Of course, they were given a wonderful example by the magnanimity of Nelson Mandela, who came out of prison, not spitting blood and fire, but saying we need to understand the other person and we need to forgive. Many people anticipated violence and a breakdown of society after decades of apartheid, but our country was saved from devastation by this willingness to understand and to forgive. Instead, the country transitioned relatively peacefully to a multiracial democracy, in part because of the truth and reconciliation process.'

In theory, the commission was empowered to grant amnesty to those charged with committing atrocities under apartheid, provided that two conditions were met: The crimes were politically motivated and the whole truth was told by the person seeking amnesty. No one was exempt from being charged. Ordinary citizens and members of the police could be charged. Notably, members of the African National Congress, the ruling party at the time of the trial, could also be charged.

Amy's four convicted murderers applied for amnesty, testifying that at the time of her killing they were part of a mob that had no mercy for white people, whom they regarded as oppressors. Amy's parents, Linda and Peter Biehl, were invited by Archbishop Tutu to attend and participate in the amnesty hearings. Determined to honour Amy's love for South Africa, the Biehls chose to attend the hearings. When the Biehls met Amy's killers, they came to the conclusion that the four boys had been robbed of their youth and opportunity by the ravages of apartheid.

After the hearing, Peter addressed the commission: 'We have the highest respect for the process of your Truth and Reconciliation Commission. Therefore, believing as Amy did in the absolute importance of the democratic election occurring, we unabashedly support the process, which we recognise to be unprecedented in contemporary human history. At the same time we say to you: It's your process, not ours. We cannot, therefore, oppose amnesty if it is granted on these merits. In the truest sense, it is for the community of South Africa to forgive its own and this has its basis in traditions of Ubuntu and other principles of human dignity. Amnesty is clearly not for Linda and Peter Biehl to grant.'

Amy's killers were granted amnesty and released in 1998 after spending five years in prison.

Narratives of reparation

Although snippets of Ntobeko's and Easy's story have been covered, recounted, and largely distorted by innumerable journalists working for various media over the years, the correct facts have never been accurately shared. Having spent countless hours working and travelling the world together, Ntobeko, Easy, Linda, and I have had many interesting discussions covering their past, some of which I will share.

Ntobeko told me that when he was called to testify at the TRC hearing, he felt betrayed by the PAC, because on the night in question, they were executing instructions from their superiors. They were not acting in a personal capacity. Then aged 20, Ntobeko was a leader of

> We all carry within us our
> place of exile, our crimes,
> our ravages.
> Our task is not to unleash
> them on the world.
> It is to transform them in
> ourselves and others.
>
> ALBERT CAMUS

the students' movement (up to high school level), but he was not a leader of the senior movement. He had taken an oath of allegiance to the PAC that promised service, suffering, and sacrifice of his life for the benefit of a noble cause: liberation for the racially oppressed.

Ntobeko first saw Amy's parents on TV while still in prison, and later heard their testimony during the TRC process. He was deeply moved, especially when they held up large pictures of Amy, taken at key moments in her life, such as at her graduation and more recently with the president of Namibia. At the time of the TRC hearing, Ntobeko was confused by the Biehls' words of conciliation, which subsequently played over and over like a stuck record in his head. Now that he had a sense of who Amy was, and the fact that she was one of their own, he reconsidered what he had done, and he wondered how this terrible thing could possibly have happened. Amy had basically given her life to this country. Ntobeko was lucky not to be sharing a cell with any of his co-accused, for this gave him the time for much needed introspection. He came to value the emotional pain and physical discomfort that he suffered in jail, for it offered him the opportunity to reflect upon what he had done, and upon himself as an individual – without interference. He fully understood that for him to be stuck in prison was nothing compared to the Biehls' suffering and pain – a wound that would sit forever in their hearts.

Ntobeko met with Amy's parents a number of times after he was released in 1998. On the day of his release, the country was stunned to hear the Biehls say, 'We hope society will give them the necessary support to enable them to survive in the new South Africa.' They genuinely believed it and meant it. I imagine that this statement helped to ground the Biehls and to re-direct their energies towards something more constructive.

CAN DO!

Ntobeko, who is today the father of three lovely daughters, said that he doubts whether he would have been able to show such forgiveness had he been in a similar situation. Indeed, many people have wondered what it takes for a parent to offer seemingly unconditional forgiveness. In my own view, the fact that the Biehls could find a way to make sense of the senseless by seeing past their own loss – and zooming into the bigger picture – is nothing short of remarkable.

One must remember that the skills the convicted four had acquired as underground freedom fighters were no longer required in the new South Africa. These men were indeed at the crossroads of their lives: the choices they were to make would determine their respective destinies. Most of them couldn't see themselves going back to school. Their former comrades knew that they could recruit gangsters from those ex-prisoners who were unskilled, directionless, and disillusioned. Some saw this as a tempting shortcut to personal enrichment: It was not easy to turn down such an offer. It did not take long for those who were skilled in using ammunition to get involved in cash-in-transit heists. Many of them landed back in jail within a year or two of having been released. But Ntobeko knew that this was not who or what he wanted to become. He was able to make the important distinction between politically motivated and personally motivated criminal activities. With the wisdom of hindsight, he once commented that everyone who commits murder should be made to look family members in the eye, to get a sense of their loss. I know that he deeply regrets this tragic loss of life.

Amy's legacy of inspiration and opportunity

I truly believe that Amy's story will go down in the history books as a legacy of reconciliation and inspiration. In 1997, in the interests of continuing their daughter's important work, Linda and Peter established the Amy Biehl Foundation with the aim of 'weaving a barrier against violence' (their slogan at the time), and in 1998 they started programmes aimed at developing and empowering youth in the impoverished townships of Cape Town. In so doing, the foundation was laid for an NPO (non-profit organisation) that would contribute to community building and give children hope for a brighter future. This would be achieved by providing students with educational and cultural activities as healthy alternatives to idleness and negative influences such as gang-related violence and drug abuse.

Peter Biehl shook the hands of the four young men upon their release. Truly humbled by this act of forgiveness and reconciliation, Ntobeko and Easy wanted to process what had happened with Amy's parents, so they decided to reach out to Peter and Linda and made the commitment to honour Amy and show their remorse, by dedicating their time to teaching the youth of South Africa. With this, the Biehls invited Easy and Ntobeko to join the Amy Biehl Foundation from its inception, in the hopes that the young men could use their leadership skills to do much needed repair work.

The news that the Biehls had appointed their daughter's killers to work at the Amy Biehl Foundation shocked the world and made headlines around the globe. Bombarded by the press for months thereafter, the Biehls also had to contend with a deluge of hate mail. The TRC's merciful findings did little to assuage the level of anger and hatred many people still bore.

Between 1998 and 2002, Peter and Linda Biehl worked tirelessly in Cape Town, running a variety of social programmes and business projects in and around Cape Town through funds donated in the US. The foundation funded job training and after-school programmes, which provided food, tutors, arts instruction and recreation – all to prevent youth violence.

Archbishop Desmond Tutu commented, 'What was so remarkable was not only that they forgave the killers of their daughter, but that they went so far as to rehabilitate them.' Linda explained at the time, 'I'm not sure if I can describe my relationships with Easy and Ntobeko. They make sense to me and it is what it is. You have to see someone as a human being. It's about respect for

CAN DO!

humanity and finding strength to open up to that realisation.' In the communities where the foundation carried out its work, Peter and Linda Biehl were known as *tamkhulu* and *makhulu*: grandfather and grandmother.

In the US, the Biehls' remarkable gesture of forgiveness and reconciliation was met with widespread disapproval – a bitter cocktail, tinctured with racial hatred and abhorrence. When I joined the Amy Biehl Foundation 13 years after Amy's death, I was astounded by the onslaught of racist hate mail that incessantly flooded my mailbox – such that I occasionally went cold when confronted with some of the graphically violent threats, which suggested that I deserved the same fate as Amy.

Over time, many would respond to the Biehls' decision in a different way. In an article dealing with the enduring power of restorative justice, and how South Africans need to find a new narrative for a more peaceful co-existence, Marianne Thamm wrote, 'Amy Biehl, her parents, and the men who killed her have helped, in a way, to create openings for new rhythms, languages, and modes of being human. And for this we thank them. In a country torn apart at the time by racial tension and violence, the Biehls taught us how to step out of the eye of the tempest and seek a common humanity.' (*The Daily Maverick*, October 2015.)

Today, more than 25 years after her tragic, senseless murder, the Amy Biehl story still remains one of the most powerful metaphors of Ubuntu and all that it can potentially achieve. I believe that the vision emanating from her story exemplifies the respect and reconciliation expounded in the concept of Ubuntu. In terms of its ideals, the Amy Biehl vision stands comfortably alongside the work of Nelson Mandela, Archbishop Tutu, Martin Luther King, and Mahatma Gandhi – who have all come to personify Ubuntu. Along with the thousands of people whose sacrifices have contributed to our hard-earned democracy, Amy will be remembered – via the Amy Biehl Foundation, now called the Amy Foundation – for the spirit of empowerment through forgiveness.

How I became involved in the Amy Biehl Foundation (now Amy Foundation)

In March 2002, long before I'd decided to take a new direction in my career, I received a call from the US ambassador to South Africa, Stephen Nolan: He wanted to introduce me to someone. Could I come across on the spur of the moment – that same day – as the person would be returning to the US the following day? The person turned out to be Peter Biehl. Much as I'd accepted the last-minute invitation to meet Raymond Ackerman, I again agreed to go out of my way. This time I didn't know anything about the person in question. Sometimes you need to follow your gut in the belief that things often happen for a

reason. This was to be yet another key moment and turning point in my life!

Among those we remember today is young Amy Biehl. She made our aspirations her own and lost her life in the turmoil of our transition as the new South Africa struggled to be born in the dying moments of apartheid. Through her, our peoples have also shared the pain of confronting a terrible past, as we take the path towards the reconciliation and healing of our nation.

(Extract from Nelson Mandela's acceptance speech upon receiving the Congressional Gold Medal on 23 September 1998.)

NELSON MANDELA

I was struck by the warmth and wisdom of this incredibly committed human being, and I strongly identified with the remarkable work Peter had been doing with the Amy Biehl Foundation. This turned out to be one of the wisest decisions I ever made, for shortly thereafter, Peter took ill and never returned to South Africa. It was a huge shock to learn a month later that the hand of fate had dealt the Biehl family yet another heavy blow: Peter died of colon cancer on 31 March 2002. I cannot help thinking that if I had declined Stephen's request, I would never have met Peter or become involved with the Amy Biehl Foundation in

CAN DO!

any way. I've always believed there's a reason for everything, although often one only learns the reason many years later. This remarkable turn of events is a perfect example.

Unfortunately, Peter had never taken out medical insurance, and the crippling medical bills wiped out his life savings. Linda was left virtually penniless and financially dependent on their three other children in the US. After Peter died, I received a call from his friend, Diarmuid Baigrie, asking if I could meet Linda with regard to helping the foundation. Still employed at FNB, I stepped in to assist by holding some successful fundraisers to which our clients were invited – one of them being the fundraiser for the golf driving range Peter had created in the township.

After Peter's death, Linda appointed Solomon Makosana, a former headmaster from Gugulethu, as CEO of the Amy Biehl Foundation in Cape Town. Solomon was a very special man, a top educator, and a highly respected cricket administrator, particularly in Langa township. Linda later asked me to become a board member to assist the foundation and I was duly appointed in 2005. Solomon was widely respected as a champion of the previously disadvantaged, and his administrative abilities as programme director opened many doors for the youth of disadvantaged communities. He ran several outstanding programmes, 99 per cent of which were funded by USAID (United States Agency for International Development). However, when the USAID grant came to an end in 2005, both he and the foundation floundered, mainly because the funds had dried up and Solomon had no experience in fundraising or running a business. (As an aside, the reader might find it interesting to note that Thabo Mbeki was president of South Africa at the time and that Nelson Mandela announced that he would be stepping down from public life on 1 June 2005.) ∎

14

Leaping to the rescue

I eventually left FNB in 2006 and started the South African Ubuntu Foundation. Since I had been well paid, and given shares in the bank, it was a big financial step I was ready to take. From a timing perspective, the synchronicity was eerie, for Solomon Makosana (then 58) passed away on 3 August 2006, after a months-long illness. At that stage the supply of donor funding from the US had already dried up. When Linda came out to attend Solomon's funeral, she approached me, understandably very distressed, saying, 'Kevin, we go back a long way. You've now left FNB to start doing your own thing. If you don't take over the foundation, I'll need to close it down. If you can't, no pressure, I'll understand.'

I could no longer ignore all the signs pointing me in this direction. Thanks to the influence of my original mentors, Raymond Ackerman and Philip Krawitz, I had become community minded. The nature of the project resonated deeply with me. Having visited the programmes and been awestruck by the amazing work being done by the foundation, I agreed without hesitation. Given the widespread impact it was making, there was no way I could allow a foundation of such national significance to close down. Much like a rare plant on the verge of extinction, it needed to be nurtured, watered, and grown. I agreed to take the helm, with the proviso that I would still keep the SA Ubuntu Foundation going.

> There can be no keener revelation of a society's soul than the way in which it treats its children.
> NELSON MANDELA

CAN DO!

Something had worried me about running just the SA Ubuntu Foundation: I would not be drawing on my core strength of making a difference by leading people. Starting the SA Ubuntu Foundation meant that I was working on my own. I sensed that by taking up Linda's offer, I could lead a team of about ten (then) and build it into a more substantial entity.

I was horrified to learn that the Amy Biehl Foundation was hopelessly insolvent, but I was never one to shy away from a challenge. Intuitively, I knew it was part of God's plan for me to embrace yet another "can do" opportunity to turn things around and make a significant impact.

The early days

And so began the next part of my new journey. When I took over the reins in October 2006, I had no idea what a steep, uphill ride lay ahead! From a personal perspective, I had locked all my own money into long-term investments. I did this to force myself into earning from day one. For the first nine to twelve months, I used my home loan to run the Amy Biehl Foundation, but for obvious reasons that wasn't sustainable.

Initially, I had no wish to earn an income from the Amy Biehl Foundation, so I did not draw a salary. I agreed to Linda's proposal on condition that I could do it in tandem with running the SA Ubuntu Foundation, which I foresaw would work well synergistically to raise support for the Amy Biehl Foundation, and as my source of income. As time went by, I was able to generate the funds to make the Amy Biehl Foundation sustainable, but it began to consume most of my time. With a young family to support, I could no longer afford to work the necessary hours without some form of remuneration. I can still hear our board member, Cyril Prisman, saying at board meetings that it was criminal not paying Kevin much more – we need to double his salary. I would always tell Cyril that was not necessary as it was my choice but 'thank you I do appreciate your looking out for me'. A wonderful man Cyril, who sadly passed away in 2015.

One of the biggest challenges in running an NPO is to be fully accountable to one's donors and to run it like a business on sound financial principles. One of the questions I'm frequently asked by students wishing to ultimately run an NPO, is whether they should start out by working in an NPO after graduating. My answer is simple: If you don't first get a solid business background, you're setting yourself and your organisation up for failure. Statistically, if you look at South Africa, approximately 70 per cent of NPOs close their doors after about three years, whilst new ones come and go all the time.

I knew that to build and grow the Amy Biehl Foundation, I would have to downsize and prioritise my original four-point plan of the SA Ubuntu Foundation: In the short term I would focus just on my talks and holding Ubuntu breakfasts. The rest would have to wait. It transpired that my Amy Biehl Foundation work would enable me to lead by example in the practice of Ubuntu. This new configuration would help me realise my vision of growing the foundation from grassroots level and insolvency into a unique world-class organisation, making the arrangement a perfect fit for both Linda and myself.

Ultimately, given the time I needed to invest in running and growing the Amy Biehl Foundation, I decided to indefinitely shelve part three of my plan: the concept of an entrepreneurship academy. Since then, many other structures enabling budding entrepreneurs have fortunately emerged. As it turns out I was able to realise this part of the business plan by introducing a Youth Skills Development and Training Progamme for 18- to 35-year-olds in the Amy Foundation – but more about this later.

The foundation had just moved to new offices in Plein Street, where I found myself located in an unpainted shell of a building without so much as the luxury of blinds or even toilet seats! It would be one of my first tasks to attend to this. To my dismay, half of the staff strolled in late for the first meeting. I came down hard on them immediately, saying, 'Coming late for meetings is a sign of lack of respect for your co-workers, who have made the effort to be here on time, and a lack of regard for your job. From now on, we're going to run a professional organisation. There is no such thing as "African time"!' On the subject of punctuality, I believe that consistently being on time is the product of proper planning and personal discipline, as well as showing a healthy respect for other people's time. Since I'm often over-committed in terms of managing my own time, given my busy schedule, this is one area in which I have to constantly be more vigilant and disciplined. Interestingly, enforcing this as part of our team's culture resulted in an institutional sense of punctuality, and the staff at the Amy Biehl Foundation became renowned throughout the townships for being good about time keeping. If you saw people running for the taxi, or rushing to get to the office, you could hazard a guess that they worked for Amy Biehl Foundation!

My first priority was to get the foundation's finances in order, so I started by looking to reduce the basic administrative and operational costs. When Solomon Makosana fell ill, the foundation's offices were moved to the Plein Street premises, which at the time were owned by the Georgiou Trust. The first thing I did was explain to the landlord that the foundation was insolvent. Cap in hand, I approached the Georgiou Trust, explaining the situation. 'Please don't charge me rent in future. I'll only succeed in building this organisation by keeping our administration costs to the barest minimum and there's no way I can ask donors for rent money!' Quoting Raymond Ackerman's *the more you give, the more you get back*' philosophy, I offered to give them a tax certificate in exchange for free rent. It took me three months of dogged perseverance before they eventually agreed to this, which was of course, a *huge* ask. (When it comes to running an NGO, one has to be thick skinned, especially at the first sign of rejection.)

When the building was later sold to Woolworths, I sensed this was going to be a tough one. Everyone believed that we stood no chance of staying on, rent free. In December 2006, along came Andrew Jennings, the newly appointed group MD of Woolworths, who had been president of Saks Fifth Avenue in New York. Coincidentally, Amy

Biehl's sister, Kim, had worked at Saks Fifth Avenue as a manager of one of the branches. When Kim heard that Andrew was coming to live in Cape Town, she suggested that he phone me, explaining that I run the organisation bearing her sister's name. Andrew duly did so, and warmly introduced himself. After I organised tickets for him to visit Robben Island, we struck up a special friendship which has remained steadfast over the years.

To my immense relief, Andrew allowed us to stay on, rent free, and we remain immensely grateful for his ongoing, generous support. We occupied the premises for almost nine years, until 2014, when Woolworths unfortunately had to terminate the agreement as the company needed the space for its own use. Over the years, Andrew has given us unfailing support and has distinguished himself as an exceptional ambassador for the foundation, having secured outstanding donations from many of his affluent contacts.

Kevin is resourceful, tenacious, driven and at the same time one of the most engaging and endearing people I have had the pleasure of knowing and calling a friend. Without Kevin at the helm, the Amy Biehl Foundation would have floundered many years ago.
ANDREW JENNINGS

Determined to cut costs, I tried to negotiate a free contract with Kyocera, who rented a photocopier to the foundation, but the MD was adamant that he had salaries to pay and couldn't help me. Tenaciously, I continued, asking him if he'd heard Winston Churchill's quote: '*You make a living by what you earn, but a life by what you give.*' The phone went silent. After what seemed an interminable pause, he agreed to grant us a free contract. I did the same thing with the auditors, who quipped, 'How can we do this? Imagine if all our NPOs asked for pro bono?' I reassured them, 'I won't tell them if you don't!' From then on, that's how we worked: donation first and if not

CAN DO!

possible, request a good discount. In all, this ongoing campaign to reduce costs saved us about R500 000 a year.

> **Keep costs down and don't be afraid to ask for help when you need it.**

This saving was further boosted when Reeds Motor Group's Executive Chairman, Ian Bell and his team agreed to donate a vehicle. Over time, this increased to no less than four brand new vehicles! Wonderfully generous visionaries!

Back in 2007 I needed to courier some Amy Foundation calendars overseas by Christmas. We were not succeeding and so with the attitude of 'not giving up' I managed to get hold of the General Manager of DHL, Steve Burd, who was amazing. He made it all happen and since then DHL have been great partners and supporters, giving us free courier services anywhere in the world whenever we need it. DHL will now also be sponsoring an online shop for Amy Foundation.

From a hole in one to a bare shell

After reducing costs, my next big challenge was to find enough money to maintain the beautiful golf driving range that Peter Biehl had lovingly built for over R2 million in Khayelitsha – one of Cape Town's informal settlements.

In 1983, under the principle of its Group Areas Act and institutionalised racial segregation, South Africa's apartheid government decided that all 'legal' residents of the Cape Peninsula living in squatter camps or existing townships would be relocated to a 3 220-hectare site located on the Cape Flats between the N2 and False Bay. It was called Khayelitsha, 'New Home'. Although officials claimed it would be purpose-built, this was not to be the case. Over the years, thousands of shacks would be informally constructed of timber and sheet metal by homeless people, and their living conditions remain today as pitiful as ever. With Cape Town's

Khayelitsha, the largest and fastest growing township in South Africa.

Typical street scene in Khayelitsha.

inclement weather, they are subjected to fires, lashing storms and constant flooding. These tin shacks are sweltering hot in summer and icy cold in winter. Being so tightly compacted, they are under constant threat of rapidly spreading fire.

CAN DO! ✓

Today, Khayelitsha is the largest and fastest growing township in South Africa. In the last ten years the population has risen from 400 000 to 2.4 million, 50 per cent of whom are under 19 years of age. The unemployment rate is 73 per cent, with 70 per cent living in shacks, and 89 per cent of its homes are considered moderately to severely food insecure. The high population density, lack of jobs, and extreme poverty, coupled with poor community infrastructure, lead to immense crime rates, gangs, violence, drugs, and other societal ills.

When I took over, the foundation was paying R10 000 per month for a generator at the Khayelitsha golf driving range as there was no electricity, and we were also forking out between R10 000 and R12 000 per month for the services of a security company. I was not prepared to put my own money into funding this financial vacuum cleaner, preferring to pay staff salaries, and I tried in vain to get people to sponsor the costs. Nobody wanted to sponsor a driving range. In a matter of weeks the clubhouse fell prey to criminals and vandals who methodically chomped their way through the building – initially stealing the light fittings, then the toilets, then the windows, and finally even the window frames! Within a few months, Peter's magnificent clubhouse had been stripped to a bare shell.

> **Sometimes we have to make tough decisions and be willing to accept the outcome.**

Hard as it was, I was forced to abandon this venture in the interests of keeping the main project of the foundation financially afloat. Despite it having become a white elephant over time, it was devastating to lose the facility that had once been Peter Biehl's pride and joy. Making this decision was not easy, and it was not for lack of trying to find sponsorship. ■

15

From fairways to staffing

Amy Foundation Fundraiser at the Khayelithsha Golf Driving Range built by Peter Biehl. Left to right: Yvonne Lungcuzo, businesswoman; Whitey Mziwonke Jacobs, then Western Cape MEC for Cultural Affairs and Sport; Kevin; Ebrahim Rasool, then Western Cape Premier; Rashieda Rasool, wife and their son; Vuyani Ngcuka, businessman; Bandi Biko, businesswoman and sister of Steve Biko.

At this point I had to shift my focus to fund-raising initiatives and staffing concerns. I was the fundraiser and MD, while Afiefa Behardien was the accounting officer. As part of the process of structuring the organisation, I let the staff know that I was looking for two in-house people to fill the roles of programme manager and chief operations officer (COO). Whilst writing proposal after proposal in a desperate search for funds, I observed them with an eagle eye, seeking signs of potential leadership. It was Afiefa whose administrative skills initially impressed me, and she was duly promoted to COO.

CAN DO! ✓

Next up was to appoint a programme manager, a position I wanted to fill from within. Ntobeko Peni (discussed earlier) soon emerged as the obvious choice. It did not take long for Ntobeko to distinguish himself as a natural leader. So impressed was I with his maturity, wisdom, intellect, and insight, that I offered him the role of programme manager. He was initially reluctant, believing that he didn't have the experience or confidence. Despite his concerns and after much encouragement, he took up the challenge. I was delighted – and what a phenomenal journey it has been! I explained to him that I didn't have the time to train him up myself, however, I managed to source an outside coach, who trained him at no cost, and we sent him on several empowering leadership and management courses. (By this time, I'd mastered the art of asking for things for free!) We saw this as a unique opportunity for Ntobeko to leverage his leadership skills with the youth. As if born to the cause, he rose steadily like a full moon on a dark night, playing host to the sunrise of tomorrow – but more about him later!

Clearing the mind and driving any negative thoughts away at the Amy Foundation Khayelitsha Golf Driving Range – Vuyani Ngcuka, Bandi Biko, Kevin and Yvonne Lungcuzo.

Although many people were familiar with the Amy Biehl story, few were aware that there was a foundation in her name, working to change township children's lives. It therefore became imperative to create a PR, marketing, events, and fundraising position as soon as possible, since there are so many non-profits competing for a slice of the same funding pie. Clearly, we needed to distinguish ourselves professionally in order to obtain the necessary donor support.

Although I needed someone to take on this role, initially we couldn't afford it. A year later, we were more established and able to create the post. Ilchen Retief, my brilliant PA at FNB, agreed to join us for a drop in her salary and she remained with me for a decade, until her personal circumstances changed. Upon losing her to Johannesburg in 2010, the naysayers again emerged to suggest that I would never cope without her. Within a week of Ilchen's resignation, Alison McCutcheon sent me Michelle Bagley's CV, and what a godsend she proved to be! Michelle slotted right in immediately and today, nine years later, she remains an exceptional asset.

> *Kevin is brilliant at surrounding himself with competent people who buy into and share his vision – this is an absolute gift! He is truly blessed that these people catch the balls that he so cleverly throws high in the air – making sure that his grand visions are realised. But very often, he leaves a wake of exhaustion, as everyone battles to keep up with his vast resources of energy! If you could bottle Kevin's energy you would find a new source of light. He truly is a remarkable leader.*
> ALISON McCUTCHEON

As things have turned out, Ilchen's personal life changed yet again, such that she was able to return to Cape Town. However, with her having been replaced by Michelle as PR, marketing, events and fundraising manager, I could not afford to employ her. For about a year, she worked for her father. We stayed in

CAN DO!

touch, hoping that somehow I would be able to find the means to incorporate her again. This became possible in 2015, when the renamed Amy Foundation had mushroomed to an entity which operated six centres accommodating the needs of over 2 000 children and youth. As expected, within a short time she proved invaluable. Capitalising on Ilchen's vast experience lifted a huge weight off the shoulders of both the management team and myself: She was able to take on many of the high-profile meetings and logistical issues – freeing me up for other strategic managerial tasks. Women play a critical role in my personal and professional life! I am so fortunate to be surrounded by such wise, level-headed, strong women. As the saying goes, 'You strike a woman, you strike a rock.'

As the organisation grew, so did the structure to accommodate our vision, mission, and objectives. It quickly dawned on me that the next important post in my team should be a volunteers and HR manager. Again, God blessed us, initially with Isabel Kerr, who had just retired and, recommended by my friend Bryan Bernfield, was willing to volunteer temporarily in this role for a few years. We were even more delighted when Joanna Barry agreed to manage our human resources and volunteers when she joined in 2008. Today, eleven years later, this remarkable woman still provides this critical service three days a week in the office and more from home, without any form of payment.

Team building – no easy feat

During my first year of running the foundation, I learned that the staff wanted a party or team-building exercise, so I invited them to a *braai* (barbeque) at my house. They were all delighted to attend, and the atmosphere was warm and relaxed. During the course of the afternoon it emerged that Easy Nofemela (mentioned earlier) was terrified of water and had never learnt to swim. For over an hour, staff collectively pleaded with him to set foot in the pool. Eventually, after much coercion, they persuaded him to submerge himself in the shallow end. By the end of the afternoon, to our amazement, he was staying comfortably afloat and 'swimming' like a duck!

> **Never underestimate the power of positive thinking, determination, and intense mentoring.**

Talk about peer pressure! I won't forget the sight of Masixole Dudulu floating in the pool as if it was something he did every day, and Themba Diniso provoking him with a reality check, saying, 'Masi – you won't be able to afford a place like this.' Masi replied, 'Eish, but I can still dream!' And can't we all! Never stop dreaming.

A few weeks later, I took them all on another team-building afternoon to Hout Bay beach. To everyone's astonishment, Easy dived into the water, swam out to sea and returned quite comfortably, having completely overcome his fear. I can only attribute this courageous achievement to what I teach about 'surrounding yourself with the right, optimistic people' – whose collective spirit had egged him on.

The gift of a second chance

Ever since they were gifted with a second chance at life, Ntobeko and Easy have made it their goal to change children's lives for the better. I must also add that in a country where our men are notorious for being abusive husbands and partners, or dysfunctional fathers, Ntobeko and Easy are shining examples of what it is to be the opposite. Easy is also an impressive individual, with a different set of skills, and a great guy to have had on the team. I feel truly blessed to have worked with both of them, and we've shared some wonderful times together.

From year to year, Ntobeko surged in confidence and stature, earning the respect of the team and the respective communities in which he functions. It's been a privilege to work with him and watch him grow to ultimately manage five centres, over 80 staff, and thousands of children on a day-to-day basis. It has been immensely

CAN DO!

gratifying for me, as his employer, to have played an active role in his trajectory. I find the process of sharing my experience and knowledge both exciting and infinitely rewarding.

Besides the work Ntobeko does for us, he's also a superb entrepreneur who runs several of his own successful ventures in the township, including a meat supply business, a laundrette, ice cream, tarpaulin, and transport businesses. I even offered him the role of CEO of the Amy Foundation, hoping to groom him for it before I retire (while I remain on the board as an active member). However, he unfortunately declined, for he doesn't see himself in this role. In 2017 Ntobeko approached me to say that his laundrette was growing and needed more of his time. His passion for his businesses and being an entrepreneur was now drawing him. I respected this and we agreed he would step down as programme manager in 2018 but still work with us in other roles and capacities.

When Kevin appointed me, he knew all my limitations, and yet he took a personal interest in my well-being and developed my career within the organisation. By helping people to work out what they want to become, Kevin motivates people to be ambitious. Over the ten years I have worked for him, I've watched him create openings for many people. But it does not stop there – because he works out what training would be required to make each person more functional and effective, and then raises the necessary funds to up-skill them. He starts with the basic things, like offering them the opportunity to learn to drive if they join without a driver's license. He would say, "You may not want to be a driver, but in the end, we all have to have a driver's license. Don't you want to own your own car? So how do you get to have a car if you don't have a license?" I can honestly say that he's changed all our lives for the better!

NTOBEKO PENI

Although Ntobeko has been approached to tell his remarkable story many times, he refused until a few years ago when he signed the rights for a film to be produced.

A strong executive team

Having a strong executive team 'in my corner' has undoubtedly become one of the four pillars of strength in running the Amy Foundation – the COO, programme manager, PR, marketing, events and fundraising manager, and HR and volunteers manager. As things stand at the time of writing, nobody within the organisation wishes to take over from me, so I plan to recruit and groom a new CEO within the next few years. I hope to formally retire at the appropriate time, but to remain an active member of the board, coming in once or twice a week initially, then monthly. I will gradually reduce my level of involvement to being only a board member.

From a succession planning point of view, it's reassuring to think that if something unforeseen were to happen to me, my management team could keep the wheels in motion until a replacement is found. Like any business, if there is no internal successor, we would then advertise for the best external candidate.

> **Make sure you have a strong executive team around you. No one is indispensable, including the CEO or MD of any organisation!**

Whilst I have high expectations of my staff, I'm comfortable with the fact that people sometimes find me tough and demanding, since it's all for the right reasons. In return, I'll always treat them with respect, and show that I value them greatly. Some years after I left FNB, I bumped into the then-manager of Sea Point branch, Michel Leroy, and he said, 'Kevin, I must tell you that at one stage, my stomach would knot up whenever I saw you coming, and I would literally feel sick. But when you left, I really missed you – in fact, in hindsight, you were the best boss I've ever had!'

CAN DO!

Yes we can!

Most of us are familiar with the oft-used slogan made famous by former US President Barack Obama in his 2008 presidential campaign: 'Yes we can!' While today it may be regarded as something of a cliché, it still holds enormous value. I am always gratified to see how previously disadvantaged people, who lived under the degradation and deprivation of apartheid, have through ambition, positive thinking, and simple hard work, successfully turned their lives around to replace an 'I can't' mentality, with 'I can'.

> **CAN'T usually means WON'T. The fact is that we all CAN – if we believe in ourselves and don't give up!**

South Africa and the world need more cases like Ntobeko's. Much more positive, lateral, and proactive thinking is needed if we as a nation are to change the cycle of impoverishment that appears to be ingrained in the lives of the historically disadvantaged. While we know that our education system is still sorely lacking, there is ample opportunity for entrepreneurship, especially amidst the new generation of 'born-frees'.

I've no doubt that Ntobeko's ascent from an angry, desperately disillusioned youngster, to clerk, driver, community leader, programme manager, and pioneering businessman, is one of this country's most phenomenal success stories. Determined to put the past behind him, he managed to turn his life around, and shape it into one that is profoundly inspirational. ∎

> People are always blaming their circumstances for what they are. The people who get on in the world are those who get up and look for the circumstances they want and if they can't find them – make them!
>
> GEORGE BERNARD SHAW

16

Hosting Ubuntu festivals

Ubuntu Festival 2015, Jimmy Nevis wowing the crowd.

By the end of 2008, I realised that I was spending so much time growing and managing the Amy Biehl Foundation, that if I did not run the Ubuntu Festival, I should delete 'part four' from my business plan. I still believed that the Ubuntu Festival had a role to play in breaking down 'cultural divides' through the joy of sharing music and food together.

I prayed, 'Lord if I am to do the Ubuntu Festival and it is part of your plan, I must do it this year or not at all but then I need help.' Prayer is a powerful process and it struck me that I could do the festival by pulling in the right people.

Given my time constraints, if I was to hold the festival, I needed lots of help. Drawing on what had always worked for me, I believed that I could call on the expertise of others and utilise the strong team I had nurtured and built. I could do it by bringing in someone like Alison

CAN DO! ✓

McCutcheon of Rainbow Experiential Marketing, who had seamlessly run the Table of Peace and Unity so successfully for years. When I shared my vision of the festival with her, she loved it. So, we held the first Ubuntu Festival in St Georges Mall on Mandela Day, 2009.

Kevin loves nothing better than seeing people from all races, religions, creeds and cultures getting along together and sharing their stories. It was through multiple endeavours on a smaller scale that Kevin decided there should be a festival to truly bring Capetonians together. At the time I was wearing two hats – being 'executive director of Mandela Rhodes Place' and 'event producer/co-owner of Rainbow Experiential Marketing' – so when Kevin approached me to stage a festival it resonated immediately. I saw his vision in technicolour and found a solution for staging the event in St George's Mall in the centre of Cape Town.

We birthed the first Ubuntu Festival on Mandela Day, and what a wonderful weekend it was, since we achieved all our objectives and truly celebrated Mr Mandela, the icon of 'Ubuntu', in a way that was accessible to all. Going forward, the need seems to be greater to cultivate the spirit of Ubuntu, the philosophy of humankind, the magical thread that unifies people. The Ubuntu Festival provides a necessary platform where through music, song, dance, and food, people can engage with one another with respect, understanding, compassion, and congeniality in a heartfelt celebration of diversity. The festival is an important annual event to engender a culture of Ubuntu amongst citizens of South Africa. It takes someone like Kevin with his passion, determination, and tenacity to make it happen. He personifies Ubuntu and walks his talk every single day – so who better to lead the way?
ALISON McCUTCHEON

Kevin and performers Jimmy Nevis, J'Something of Mi Casa, Chad Saaiman and Emcee Siv Ngesi.

The festival was attended by 20 000 people and it proved to be an absolute winner. This became the successful blueprint for subsequent festivals. Given that most events of this nature usually run at a huge loss, people were amazed that we managed to break even.

Running those festivals was never easy. If I could find the money, Alison and her team would coordinate and arrange the whole event for us, but fundraising is always our biggest challenge. Alison proposed using the services of Beryl Eichenberger of Hippo Communication – in my view, one of the best marketing and PR professionals in Cape Town, and an icon of the communications industry. Despite the fact that most people thought I was nuts to take this on, particularly since I'd never organised something like this, by surrounding myself with the right people, my dream was ultimately realised.

With the downturn in the economy in 2012, after three successful festivals, I foresaw that we could ill-afford the risk, and I canned the idea for that year and the next.

> **Never be afraid to make a decision not to proceed with something if you have weighed up all the pros and cons. If there is a high chance of making a loss, then be bold enough to stop the train.**

CAN DO!

My team understood this decision, even though they were disappointed. In 2014, however, I was approached by Sunlight, Unilever, who had seen my website and wanted to be involved. They offered to give us R500 000 to put a festival together, which we did on Human Rights Day, 2015. It opened with an International Cultural Festival featuring performances from schools around the globe, including Na Sumskom from Moscow and Milton Academy jazz from Boston, followed by a well-attended concert featuring the popular comedian and actor Siv Ngesi as Emcee and headline artists Mi Casa, Jimmy Nevis, Chad Saaiman, and Toya Delazy. And what a smashing success it was! ■

I have worked with Kevin on the Ubuntu Festival as publicist since inception, and while some of his ideas have been a little ambitious, the end result has seen an event that gets people together, showcases talent, and creates awareness for the foundation. Not a lot of money is raised, but the primary objective is to build a brand for the foundation, which is happening. Working with Kevin is exhilarating to say the least ... sometimes it feels like one has boarded a bullet train that does not stop until the end of the line and one is swept along with it! He does tend to be a 'lastminute.com' guy but everything falls into place, exactly as he wants it, because we all end up working as a team – but not without stress!

Kevin never takes no for an answer. Because he is so passionate, you get carried away by his enthusiasm and you know that the end result will be making a better life for so many young people. He can be very stubborn and he has 'nagging' in his genes! He is a networker of note and knows how to connect people, but he always maintains a friendly ambience. Maybe the famous NIKE slogan should be his – Just do it! And you do! The difference is that Kevin always adds a please.
BERYL EICHENBERGER

17

Creating sustainability by diversifying income

The race to the end – Cape Town Cycle Tour – son-in-law Keith Watkins and Kevin.

When I first took over the Amy Biehl Foundation, my fundraising proposals were met with an endless wall of rejections, which was a shock, given that I hadn't bargained for this much of a struggle. The general perception was that we were being funded by the US, and that Amy's parents were very wealthy. Neither was true at that stage. While everyone knew the Amy Biehl story, few were familiar with the important nature of the work being done at the foundation. Clearly, we needed to hold fundraising events, and embark on a well-targeted PR campaign, so I structured our SA Ubuntu Foundation events to

CAN DO!

also be a source of revenue for Amy Biehl Foundation. However, when I am asked to speak as 'Kevin Chaplin' on how to run a business or how to maximise your potential, or making the impossible possible etc, the fee is mine, although I always use these engagements as an opportunity to raise awareness and funds for the Amy Foundation. Conversely, if I'm asked to speak about the Amy Foundation, then the proceeds obviously go directly to the foundation.

Accountability and transparency

As a staunch businessman, I chose to run the foundation like a business, placing emphasis on clearly defined goals and strategies to ensure that we operate in an efficient, practical, businesslike manner with sustainable outcomes and good governance. When one is dealing with people's lives and other people's money, one has an onerous responsibility to ensure that all donated funds are not only well controlled and used cost effectively, but spent within the context of stated aims. We send regular reports to thank donors, stating clearly how their money has been spent. The relationship with donors is vital to ensure that they stay on board and remain sustainable. I must emphasise that every NPO should be aware that donors want to know who is behind the entity, therefore the credibility of the MD/CEO, COO, as well as board members is critical to its success. From a corporate governance point of view, an NPO should be run by principled, strong leaders who remain accountable to one's donors through regular contact and transparency. The aim of the project should always be clear, viable, and goal directed. Like any business, donors are one's lifeblood and they need to be appreciated in order for trusting and strong relationships to develop.

I believe that any organisation that aspires to hold a high profile, be sustainable, and build a reputation of impeccable credibility, needs highly esteemed brand ambassadors. This is exactly what we have done, and Amy Foundation today has great ambassadors – some official and many unofficial – who tirelessly spread the word of our work and help us to raise much-needed funds for the organisation. Indeed, it has been my privilege and good fortune to have met and worked with a broad spectrum of some of the most noteworthy achievers from South Africa, UK, Northern Ireland, USA, Netherlands and Belgium – ranging from top businessmen and women, politicians, performers, athletes, and religious leaders to many generous, socially-minded private citizens.

An extremely important part of running any organisation is to have a strong board that supports the MD or CEO, also from a corporate governance point of view. Earlier I mentioned the support of SA Ubuntu Foundation's board. A huge debt of gratitude is owed to Amy Foundation's board, especially, in the early years, Linda Biehl; Cyril Prisman, an attorney at Cliffe Dekker Hofmeyr; and then Carol Bouwer, television producer and CEO of Carol Bouwer Productions; Sindiwe Magona, author; Siya Mapoko, entrepreneur, speaker and author of *The best advice I ever got* and *Conversations with JSE AltX entrepreneurs*; Rob Williams, Group CEO of Savoy Hotels; Shabnam Sablay-Parker, a Risk and Compliance Manager; Lele Mehlomakulu, MD of mPower People Solutions; and Phephelaphi Dube, a lawyer. In particular, I would like to thank the Chairman of Amy Foundation, Rob Williams – a remarkable businessman – for his unfailing support.

As a banker, I saw too many NPOs close down because the management was either seriously inefficient, ineffective, or greedy. One of my biggest bugbears has been the massive salaries drawn by CEOs and management of some non-profit and welfare organisations. One of the reasons the Amy Foundation has functioned and thrived financially, is because we have always worked to a tightly controlled, conservative expense budget in order to get the job done effectively and ensure the foundation is sustainable. The fact that certain CEOs of NPOs are happy to plunder donor money for personal gain is appalling. Many people start out with noble intentions to make a difference, but they lose perspective along the way. When you're dealing with donor money, it's vital to remember the important connection between what you are hoping to achieve and who should be benefiting along the way in terms of your overall goals.

CAN DO!

On a macro-economic level in South Africa, the millions of destitute, unemployed, and uneducated people in this country, owe their sorry fate to the widespread corruption, looting of state-owned enterprises, and gross inefficiency that has prevailed in the previously Zuma-led government. In short, the combination of greed and ineptitude is lethal, for it ultimately will lead to the failure of any organisation! Despite the terrible losses the nation suffered under ex-President Jacob Zuma's kleptocracy, it is not helpful or useful for people to become depressed, as I strongly believe in the saying, 'This too will pass.' And so it started with the forcing of Jacob Zuma to resign in February 2018, and Cyril Ramaphosa being elected the new President. The people of this beautiful country, and countries all over the world, deserve leaders who are ethical and who genuinely have our best interests at heart. It's widely hoped that President Ramaphosa will bring prosperity and a sense of patriotism back to our beleaguered nation. I remain positive that justice will be done. The fact that the ANC lost major support in the 2016 local elections is a sign that people are voting for change and are much more circumspect regarding where they place their mark on the ballot paper. The outcome of the 2019 national elections has sent a clear signal that change needs to occur to ensure South Africa can overcome the serious challenges it faces. There is an air of optimism that Cyril Ramaphosa is the right man for the job as president but also nervousness and concern as to whether he will be able to overcome the factionalism evident in government and also the remanant left behind from the Jacob Zuma era, especially those members infected by corruption and greed re-appointed in the new government. The daunting task of reducing unemployment, crime, and poverty – and creating a home for all – is a mammoth task that cannot be undertaken by one man alone. And so it will be up to government, civil society, individuals, and the business sector to be part of the solution.

Cape Town Cycle Tour ride to raise funds

> There's no such thing as impossible. The word itself is: I'm possible.
> AUDREY HEPBURN

Over the years, Cape Town's internationally famous cycle race, the Cape Town Cycle Tour (previously the Argus Pick n Pay Cycle Tour), has become a popular vehicle for raising funds. In 2012, my friends and Amy Foundation Ambassadors – Amanda Cromhout and Tony Romer-Lee, along with Alison MacFarlane – decided to ride the Argus in support of the Amy Foundation, collectively raising a tidy sum. The following year, the inevitable happened, when they asked me, 'Why can't the MD participate in the drive?' I was challenged to join in, a moment I dreaded, for the last time I'd cycled was at the age of 14 (although I do keep reasonably fit by jogging)! Despite my misgivings, I felt morally obliged to make the effort. Having only trained three times, I had the chutzpah to set myself the ambitious target of raising R150 000 from my first cycle tour. I recall two members of my team, Michelle and Afiefa, saying 'Kevin, don't be ridiculous. Rather set a realistic target. Without training, you'll never finish and you can't possibly manage to raise anything near *that*!' As the reader will have gathered by now, nothing mobilises me faster than hearing the words 'you can't'. Undaunted, in the upcoming weeks, I emailed, and messaged virtually everyone I'd met since birth to sponsor me. In my mind, there was absolutely no way I was not going to meet my target!

Ultimately, I was on the saddle for a gruelling six hours and 20 minutes of pain – and somehow made the eight-hour cut-off time by just one hour and 40 minutes. From a physical point of view, this was undoubtedly the toughest thing I've ever done, but every agonising push of the pedals, I was lured by the tantalising prospect of R150 000 for the township kids, as if it were looming just ahead! It was well worth the virtual collapse that night from sheer exhaustion!

So, now I have done five Cape Town Cycle Tours to raise funds for Amy Foundation, along with many other inspiring riders who cycled to raise funds for the foundation. Special mention must be made of my fellow cyclist James Fernie of Uthando, who singlehandedly raised large sums for the foundation through his network. He is a wonderful Amy Foundation

> The person who says
> it cannot be done,
> should not interrupt
> the person doing it.
> CHINESE PROVERB

Ambassador. In the latter rides, my son-in-law Keith Watkins (also not a cyclist) kindly decided to ride with me out of concern for my wellbeing, which was a rare privilege.

> *Kevin's spiritual radiance propels everyone around him to reach out to others and make the world a better place – by building the lives of youth at risk. With a clear vision of what he wishes to achieve, he does everything with tremendous energy, and is always upbeat. Kevin never gives up!*
> HELEN LIEBERMAN

Building Eluthandweni homes for Aids orphans

While I'm not known for succumbing to or fading under pressure, there have been times I've had to restrain myself in order to cope with existing commitments. While I was working at FNB, my friend Bandi Biko introduced me to Dr Mamphela Ramphele – the well-known politician, political activist, medical doctor, academic, and businesswoman. I was most impressed with her wisdom, intellect, and insight. About twelve years ago, during one of our many discussions, Mamphela asked me to help build a home for Aids orphans in Gugulethu. The aim was to provide them with a safe, loving, child-friendly environment. I agreed to do this, provided that she obtained the funding from a corporate or private funder, which she duly did. Building an Eluthandweni home turned out to be a huge amount of work, which put me under immense pressure, given that I was running both the Amy Biehl and SA Ubuntu Foundations by this time. Upon its successful completion, she requested that we build another, but I declined, explaining that I had to focus on my own projects and could not stretch myself so far as to under-deliver, possibly all round. While Mamphela was very upset, she of course had to come to terms with my decision. Focus is just as important as not taking on more than one can handle – particularly if, like me, you believe that if you commit to doing something you must give it your all. In the journey of life, remember to check your own itinerary.

> Learning when to say 'no' is just as important as knowing when to say 'yes'. Sometimes you have to step back, take stock of your commitments, and say 'no'. Rather focus on doing a few things well than a lot of things badly.

Rotary International

This is why, despite having been invited to join Rotary International many times, I have thus far declined – because I don't have the time. One must be careful not to overcommit oneself, or just be a member of something in name only. One day, when my schedule is not as busy, I will reconsider this proposal. I have so much respect for Rotary, what it stands for and their members, who work so hard to make a difference. I have spoken at many Rotary Clubs and was privileged in 2017 to be presented with a Paul Harris Fellow Award. Trevor Wilkinson, Farhat Danyal, Gavin Shachat, Eldred Polikoff, and Rodney Mazinter from Sea Point Rotary have always supported the Amy Foundation where they can. Farhat Danyal, who personifies the concept of dynamite coming in small packages, has been instrumental in working with youngsters in our sewing programme and securing opportunities for Amy Foundation. Thanks to Rotary Sea Point and Roermond Maas en Roer Netherlands, Amy Foundation received a much needed 23-seater bus. We look forward to doing more with Rotary in the future.

I like the Rotary Four-Way Test, which is a non-partisan and non-sectarian ethical guide for Rotarians to use for their personal and

CAN DO!

professional relationships. Besides being recited at every club meeting, in my view, the words to this test, which have been translated into more than 100 languages, should be a guide for everyone in everyday life.

Of the things we think, say or do:

Is it the TRUTH?

Is it FAIR to all concerned?

Will it build GOODWILL and BETTER FRIENDSHIPS?

Will it be BENEFICIAL to all concerned?

Lions International

Another organisation I have a great deal of respect for is Lions International, who also do exemplary service work. In 2004, I was privileged to be awarded a Melvin Jones International Fellow Award for Dedicated Humanitarian Service – a very special honour, given that other recipients include Raymond Ackerman and Archbishop Desmond Tutu. I have spoken at several Lions Clubs in Cape Town and have always been impressed by the dedication of their members. Whilst at FNB, I learnt that one of the Lions Projects was in urgent need of a vehicle to collect and distribute food from retail stores that was at sell by date but still good for consumption. Together with my good friend Suzanne Ackerman-Berman, who was at that time GM Corporate Affairs at Pick n Pay, I was able to get FNB to co-sponsor a vehicle with Pick n Pay, have it branded with both their logos and donate it to the Lions' feeding project.

Gala fundraisers

In my corporate years I gleaned experience in bringing clients to 'gala dinners' as an effective mechanism for both PR and fundraising. The first gala dinner I arranged took place in 2003 during my time at FNB, held at the Cape Town International Convention Centre. It brought together FNB Cape Town's high net-worth clients at an amazing evening. The spectacular event was co-ordinated by my own staff and it raised money for three non-profits. The staff rose to the occasion and loved doing it as something they had not been involved in before. The customers enjoyed

MASK AFFAIR

Celebrating a good cause

South Africa's cream of the crop gathered for the Amy
Biehl Foundation Trust Dinner at the Arabella Sheraton
Grand Hotel on 26 August, with the honourable
Archbishop Tutu as guest of honour and Idols presenter,
Colin Moss, as the MC. It was an exuberant evening of
radiant colours and fanfare, with a festive banquet and a
décor theme of a masked-ball dinner. The kaleidoscope of
revellers, anonymous in their masks, danced to the
soulful sounds of our very own Diva of Song, Yvonne
Chaka Chaka.

The Amy Biehl Foundation is dedicated to the
development and upliftment of the youth in the
townships around Cape Town. The Foundation's creative
arts programme administers various projects to over
4 500 children, up to the age of 16. This is a holistic
educational project that includes after-school care, sports
development, performing arts, HIV/AIDS peer education
and environmental awareness.

Guests were treated to scrumptious dishes, from slow-
roasted leg of lamb with lemon to Mediterranean
dauphinoise potatoes. Staying true to the spirit of giving,
all celebrities providing the entertainment did so

SOCIETY

One of the many colourful masks...

Pearl Nel, Ilchen Retief,
Marlon Crow

Amy Biehl Foundation kids

Gwen Gill, Kevin and Robyn Chaplin, Robin Fryer,
Nicky Greenwall, Christoph Maier, Noki Dube

Herschel Gibbs and Juliet Notley

Ahmed Kathrada, Kevin Chaplin, Tho
Ntshinga, Farida Omar

Tamarin Kaplan and Joey Burke
(auctioneer for the evening)

Kevin Chaplin, Archbishop Desmond Tutu,
Linda Biehl

Yvonne Chaka Chaka

Hilda Ndude, Pat Gorvalla, Kevin Chaplin, Shado Twala

Kevin Chaplin, Dr Mamphela Ramphele, Yvonne Chaka Chaka

it and their loyalty to the bank grew tenfold through the event. Over the years, as my passion for the Amy Biehl Foundation grew, I held these gala evenings exclusively for the foundation, inviting all our corporate and business contacts and their clients, loyal donors, high profile personalities, employees, and numerous friends of the foundation. These memorable evenings offer an excellent dinner and superb entertainment, along with a short auction of highly desirable donated items like overseas air tickets, accommodation, extreme adventures, jewellery, and art.

October 2015 saw us hosting a glittering Amy Foundation fundraiser for 320 people that surpassed anything we had ever held previously – in terms of its slickness, scale, attendance, and professionalism. We raised R750 000. My heart melted when the children sang an amazing song composed for me by the choir, thanking me for everything I was doing for them and everyone at Amy Foundation. The song's narrative tells of a man who works hard to provide for his family. He would like to do right by his wife's family, pay *lobola* for her, and honour his commitment to support the family. (*Lobola* is an African custom in which a bridegroom makes a payment in cattle or cash to the bride's family shortly before the marriage.) He leaves them to work on the mines far away and make enough money to provide for them. Here are the exact words: *Darly thathumthwalo uyosebenza uzondilobola ngani.* Translated: Darling, pack your bags and go and work hard so you are able to provide and support our family and pay *lobola*.

That function set the bar high, leading us to even greater heights in the next two years at the magnificent Century City Conference Centre, with each event raising R1 million. We were lucky enough to have Yvonne Chaka Chaka perform for us again as well as P J Powers at our gala dinner in August 2016; the delightful trio, 'Three Tons of Fun', in September 2017; and Vicki Sampson and Black Ties starring Chad Saaiman, Keeno Lee, and Lloyd Jansen in 2018, always together with our Amy Foundation children. The talented Dr Michael Mol, Colin Moss, comedians Rob van Vuuren and Alan Committie as our Emcee's over the years, as well as Joey Burke as auctioneer, enhance the

Amy Foundation Brass class performing.

Aviva Pelham and the Guguletu Tenors inspiring the guests.

Suzanne Ackerman-Berman, Kevin and Wendy Ackerman.

CAN DO! ✓

success of the evening every time for over 400 guests. The event goes off seamlessly, thanks to the superb organisation of Michelle, our PR, marketing, events, and fundraising manager. Aviva Pelham consistently showcases the children's talent in the best light possible – all of which sends a strong message to our donors that their money is being well spent.

Thanks must also go to Roxy Levy and Paul Johnson, who assist Aviva in dedicating countless hours to choreographing polished performances in which the children give it their all on the dance floor. Our faciltators at Amy Foundation work hard throughout the year and nearer the event to direct the learners, organise all the performances and costumes on the day. As a result, the whole evening is always a success beyond our wildest dreams. People who have attended previous functions say the event just gets better and better – which is important feedback, since we aim to ensure that they leave with heart-warming memories of the evening and wanting to attend again the next year. Theo Essau, former head of communications and PR for the City of Cape Town, who attends many NPO functions, once said that they all pale into insignificance when compared to ours! It's safe to say that as an organisation, we excelled ourselves.

> *I was only prepared to work within a structure – otherwise one wastes so much precious energy and time. Kevin provided the infrastructure that I needed in order to upgrade each group I worked with. I have been able to oversee the consistent improvement in teaching methods, structure, and content of the various groups: traditional dancers, sticks and tins, choir, ballet, brass, marimba, contemporary, strings etc. ... and I have brought in professional companies such as Jazzart who also adopted Amy Foundation as their outreach project.*
>
> AVIVA PELHAM

Yvonne Chaka Chaka

One of our most loyal stalwarts and stellar performers is Yvonne Chaka Chaka, inimitable drawcard and close friend, who has made every effort to perform at many of our gala fundraisers. No less a luminary than Nelson Mandela insisted that she sing at most of his local and overseas star-studded engagements. From the moment she sets foot on stage, she has the pizazz and charisma to win over any audience by creating a vibe that gets everyone rocking.

The fact that Kevin is such a positive thinker and 'go-getter' who always wants to do good for others, enables him to bring out the best in the people around him. This means that he is one person to whom you cannot say 'no'! It has thus been my joy and privilege to sing at many of his fundraisers and functions over the years, and ultimately become a patron of the foundation. We have found an amazing synergy together, in terms of what I do as an entertainer. With our love and friendship being reciprocal, he in turn assists me with my 'Princess of Africa Foundation'. I believe that Kevin is cut from a different cloth. Always mindful of others, he lives the truth of good Christian values. He's a great, humble man who takes nothing for granted, other than the belief that God will make a plan to help him.

YVONNE CHAKA CHAKA

Yvonne Chaka Chaka taking the guests to new heights. Kevin and Gwen Mahlangu-Nkabinde getting into the vibe with Amy Foundation children.

CAN DO! ✓

Cultural township tours

One of the first ideas when I took over Amy Biehl Foundation in 2006, was to introduce cultural township tours to bring in much needed income. I sensed that many tourists in Cape Town would enjoy this and find the encounter meaningful as opposed to other drive-through township tours. And why not introduce a tour that includes performances in music, drama, and dance by the children in the Amy Foundation programmes – as well as seeing them participate in sport, greening and the environment, literacy, and much more. This has proved to be a highlight for many tourists and they leave feeling enriched, whilst providing good income for the foundation. Cape Town Tourism is a great supporter of our work and markets our tours. It is always exciting to welcome international tour groups through African Travel, Lion World Travel, Trafalgar Tours and Thompsons Africa, part of The Travel Corporation group, as well as from Uthando and other private bookings.

> *With a clear sense of the work needing to be done as a nation to create a live spirit of Ubuntu, Kevin has defied the discouragement of many to establish a programme that acts as a call to action for all South Africans to play their part in shaping a caring, cooperative, visionary nation that works for the good of all. His determination makes it impossible for skepticism or fatigue to take over. His example is a great inspiration for all of us.*
> BRETT TOLLMAN

Relating to relate bracelets

I cannot thank Aviva Pelham enough for introducing me to Lauren Gillis, who at the time we met, was looking to give away her childhood piano. Although we clicked immediately, we were not to know what a mutually beneficial friendship and important connection this would be.

> *It was not just about helping unemployed people – I also wanted to create something self-sustaining that would bring self-reliance, dignity and hope to others. In the interests of moving away from the old 'poor me', begging bowl scenario, we subsequently introduced a fundraising mechanism, for other non-profits like the Amy Foundation and Ikamva Labantu. Today, we assist approximately 110 such causes in this way.*
> LAUREN GILLIS

Lauren came to a point in her life where she felt she had been blessed with enough, so with an innate passion for making a difference to the lives of needy people, she thought about how she could implement significant change. Bearing in mind the international success of the 'LiveStrong' bracelet concept as a fundraising mechanism, she wondered whether a similar bracelet could be handmade locally by unemployed people who could earn some income by beading bracelets.

I recall Lauren showing me the contents of her boot, filled to the brim with hundreds of multicoloured bracelets that refugees had strung for her. This was part of her initial drive to offer employment in collaboration with an NGO. Who would have guessed that from this humble beginning would come Relate – the remarkable organisation as we know it today. With no infrastructure, she started off small in 2008 after obtaining her first order from Nando's for 6 000 bracelets in celebration of their twenty-first birthday.

Amy Foundation Relate bracelets.

CAN DO!

Initially, the bracelets were beaded by single mothers of limited education. Other partnerships began in earnest as Lauren put together a strategy to create a part-time employment option for elderly people at Ikamva Labantu's clubs for seniors, which are dotted around the various townships in the Western Cape, giving dignity and income to the elderly.

The venture took on its current form in 2010, when it became the Relate Trust, a registered 'not for profit' and 'public benefit' trust. Lauren introduced me to her husband Arthur Gillis, who at the time was the dynamic CEO of Protea Hotels. Much like Raymond and Philip, Arthur taught me innumerable business and personal life skills. I have huge respect for Arthur and his brother Glenn, who helped grow Relate to achieve the footprint it has today. I joined the board virtually at its inception, with Lauren, Glenn and Sherwin Charles, and feel proud to have played an integral role in its growth. It remains a 100 per cent not-for-profit social enterprise, defined by the vision of helping the less fortunate create better lives for themselves. Having gained enormous traction since it was registered in 2010, Relate has sold an astonishing three million bracelets at the time of writing.

The Relate Trust business model has been perfected over time to offer more opportunities and benefits to several entities involved in the process: From the selling price of each bracelet, approximately a third goes to the people who thread the beads at seniors clubs in the townships – elderly gogos (grandmothers) and tatas (grandfathers) – and upskilling programmes designed to benefit the young adults who finish, close and pack the bracelets, as well as enterprise development initiatives to help grow fledgling black businesses in South Africa.

Lauren and Arthur Gillis with Amy Foundation Relate bracelets in background.

The second third goes towards

funding the project's overall running and material costs, whilst the remaining third goes to the chosen cause or NGO. Any credible non-profit can raise funds by selling their own branded Relate bracelet and in this way, the wearer can connect to his/her chosen cause.

> *Many small actions can lead to big change. If every tax paying South African bought just one Relate bracelet each year, it would raise a quarter of a billion rand towards social upliftment annually. What a great legacy we can leave for our country!*
> LAUREN GILLIS

On a much bigger scale, corporates have the option to select their own beneficiaries and to initiate projects, whilst receiving exposure and a platform for building their brands. The key to this lies in the bracelet's pewter 'connector' closer, on which the selected beneficiary's name or logo can be engraved. Every bracelet bears a signature 'R' bead – an emblem of trust and authenticity representing Relate's commitment to monies reaching their intended beneficiaries. Besides its income-generating capacity, the 'R' holds particular significance for me, and this is something I touch on at every Ubuntu breakfast and at all other opportunities. My dream is for everyone in the world to wear one, to remind them of the many Rs:

- **Respect** people of another religion, culture, colour, language or background.
- Build **Relationships**.
- **Recognise** differences.
- Be **Responsible**.
- Be **Reliable**.
- Not to be forgotten is the **R of Re-invent** yourself.
- We all need to regularly **Renew, Review** and **Reconcile**.
- On a lighter note, Easy, our delightful long-serving employee, says his bracelet reminds him to be **Romantic!**

CAN DO! ✓

This ambitious venture has become so viable, that Relate creates earning opportunities for hundreds of people, and to date, the organisation has donated the staggering sum of over R50 million to social upliftment and other non-profits! Lauren can be immensely proud of her exceptional achievement.

Now these cool, colourful, and attractive fashion items are merchandised at the tills of some of the country's biggest retailers. Hotels like Red Carnation Hotels, Twelve Apostles Hotel and Spa, Protea Hotel Group, Uniworld Boutique River Cruises, and tour operators such as Lion World and African Travel have also come on board by supporting the Amy Foundation Relate bracelet.

Whilst I was always passionate about promoting and growing the Relate venture, Amy Foundation bracelet sales took priority for me over others. Eventually, in order to avoid any potential conflict of interest, I resigned from the Relate board in 2016. In the previous year, I had brought a friend and ex-colleague, Elizabeth Matlakala, on board as a trustee and along with my resignation, I was able to propose that Brett Kaplan (who had just retired) replace me, which he did. But I remain an active partner, friend, and driver of sales.

We of course market the Amy Foundation by selling the bracelet ourselves, and I'm proud to say that our foundation achieved the magical R1 million income target from bracelets in 2015.

> **Start small and dream big. You will see what is possible with a CAN DO! attitude.**

Skills training and development

I reflect with much pride on the achievements of many of the youth who have participated in our Amy Foundation programmes. Relate had a role to play in the success of one of our alumni, Sibusiso Ntisana, who grew up in a single-parent, poor household in Gugulethu. He first participated in our Amy Foundation after-school programmes as a nine-year-old. After some computer and maths training, he completed his Grade 12 and was selected to participate in an overseas exchange programme with one of Amy Foundation's partners. Continuing to show promise, he was employed at Relate Trust, where they gave him the opportunity to attend a butler's course. He went on to participate in the Amy Foundation's first hospitality programme.

> *Through Relate, I completed a butler's course at the South African Butler Academy. We focused on every aspect of the industry. What amazed me is that you as a person are being built as an entrepreneur, and you're taught to think strategically about guests and service. I'm so grateful for this unique opportunity to further my education and up-skill myself. After completing that course, I worked at Relate's bracelet closing and packaging office in Harrison Street, where I learned a lot about running a business.*
> SIBUSISO NTISANA

The Tollmans and The Travel Corporation

The Tollman family, of hospitality industry fame, has been a huge source of support and funding to us. Stanley and Bea Tollman, the famous South African husband and wife partnership, are icons of the international hospitality industry. Through hard work and determination, the Tollmans built a very successful corporation in the travel, tourism, and leisure industries spanning five continents. After leaving South Africa in the early seventies, they established an international travel group, The Travel Corporation (TTC), comprising over 25 award-winning travel brands across the world. TTC has now been trading for over fifty years.

Being strong on philanthropy, the family decided they wanted to give back meaningfully to South Africa, but given their concerns about corruption in the non-profit sector, they weren't sure how to go about doing so. With this in mind, Arthur Gillis thankfully saw fit to introduce them to one Kevin Chaplin! I must confess that our first meeting was quite daunting, since I had to address the legendary Stanley, along

CAN DO! ✓

with his children Brett, Toni, Vicki and nephew Gavin all at the same time! To my immense relief, the family welcomed me warmly and I was made to feel at ease immediately. There and then, they committed to assisting the foundation as donors, and they've remained true to their word. It was not long before I got to meet Stanley's wife, Bea, with whom I had an instant rapport. This was the first of many warm meetings over the years. Never could I have imagined that I would enjoy a sense of trust with the Tollmans that would develop into such an enduring friendship, with Brett Tollman in particular.

I was fascinated to learn that Bea makes a point of visiting every staff member in person over Christmas to present gifts, topped off with handwritten thank-you notes. If you look at how successful the Tollmans have been, one can only assume that this caring gesture would have a distinct role in boosting morale and performance over the years. As the reader will recall, I implemented something similar whilst at FNB, having been initially inspired to do so by Raymond Ackerman.

Horst Frehse, former General Manager of Twelve Apostles Hotel & Spa with Bea Tollman and Kevin.

When The Travel Corporation held its international sales conference in Cape Town and was looking to support worthy causes, the Amy Foundation was selected as a suitable beneficiary. Stanley celebrated his eightieth birthday with his family and TTC employees, during which celebration he made donations to five local charities, one of which was the Amy Foundation. They all had lots of fun on one of the conference days, when their staff built several sturdy wooden wendy-houses as kitchens and libraries for us.

Two Travel Corporation companies, Red Carnation Hotels and Uniworld Boutique River Cruises, became particularly committed to the cause. Every year, Red Carnation Hotels donates a stay at the luxurious Twelve Apostles Hotel & Spa, at Bushmans Kloof Wilderness Reserve & Wellness Retreat, as well as a five-day stay at one of their magnificent London Hotels for auction at our Gala Fundraising Dinner. Uniworld donates the major drawcard prize – one glorious week on a cruise anywhere in Europe! In addition, Trafalgar Tours has in the past donated seven days on one of its family tours in Italy. Red Carnation Hotels, Lion World Travel, and African Travel also generously order their own customised bracelet to give guests and staff. Not to be outdone in terms of generosity, over the years, Uniworld has ordered a customised Amy Foundation Relate bracelet that's given to every guest on their upmarket river cruises, as well as to every crew member. The impact of a single Uniworld order of 31 400 bracelets a few years back was astounding, with Relate being able to deposit R251 200 into the Amy Foundation account – enough to support 50 children in the programme for a full year! This was followed by another Uniworld order of 36 000 and to date the group has bought over 70 000 bracelets.

Thank you must go to Brett Tollman, Chief Executive of The Travel Corporation; Michael Tollman, CEO Cullinan Holdings; Jonathan Raggett, general manager of Red Carnation Hotels; Sherwin Banda president of African Travel; Lucille Sive CEO, Africa Division, The Travel Corporation; Guy Young, past president of Uniworld (now chief engagement officer of The Travel Corporation Group) and Ellen

CAN DO!

Bettridge, President and CEO of Uniworld Boutique River Cruises, who are committed to supporting the Amy Foundation.

Divine donations from Twelve Apostles Hotel & Spa

We are given a further boost and upmarket profile through the small surcharge added to every guest's bill at the luxurious Twelve Apostles Hotel in Camps Bay. The previous general manager, quintessential and distinguished hotelier Horst Frehse, has since retired and his excellent successor, general manager Michael Nel, have both been extremely supportive of the Amy Foundation. I enjoy the privilege of being invited to address staff at their monthly meetings from time to time, at which I explain that by working at the hotel they are also helping township children through the Amy Foundation. I think it's important for one's employees to make a link with the corporate social investment (CSI) commitments of their employers, for it enables them to take pride in having personally contributed to the cause. I'm most grateful to the Twelve Apostles for utilising every opportunity to market Amy Foundation to their guests.

In 2015, GM Michael Nel told Sonja Narcisse, one of the Twelve Apostles hotel guests, about Amy Foundation. It didn't take long for Sonja, a businesswoman, entrepreneur and philanthropist from New York, to become an ardent supporter and friend. She has since launched her own wine label in the US called 'Ardaso', and $1 of every bottle sold is given to the Amy Foundation. Sonja still keeps us foremost in her mind, despite the fact that she's extremely busy conducting business all over the world. We were most appreciative of the fact that she flew out to South Africa on two occasions, to upskill our facilitators in a two-day workshop and conduct workshops for our children, from which they all benefited enormously.

On Mandela Day, the Twelve Apostles Hotel staff come and work at one of our after-school centres. Making a difference through CSI is the heartbeat of their business, and that's exactly how it should be. I feel a part of The Travel Corporation, and hope that they feel equally enmeshed as a part of ours. In the interests of building relationships, it's important to become involved and connected with one's donors.

The approach taken by Kevin towards social upliftment mirrors that taken by The Travel Corporation (TTC). Through our portfolio of businesses and brands, including our Treadright Foundation, TTC proactively works to identify where and how our operations, our people, and our guests may be able to support initiatives around the world focused on social and environmental protection – doing what we can, wherever we can, as frequently and impactfully as we can. This commitment of TTC is what has made our longstanding support of Kevin and the Amy Foundation an unwavering source of pride for TTC.

Within South Africa and across Africa, through a number of our businesses including Thompsons, Trafalgar, Contiki, Uniworld, Red Carnation, Lion World, and African Travel, our employees and guests are able to have a direct experience with the Amy Foundation through Amy's Cultural Township Tours – an experience that never fails to awaken within them a desire to continue to do more for others in need, realising the richness of giving and doing for those needing and deserving a better life.

By working together, the Amy Foundation and TTC have been able to become an important catalyst to inspire others to play a direct role in helping others. Under Kevin's leadership, the foundation has seeded an important call to action within the TTC employee and guest community. The power of one cannot, and should not be underestimated. The Amy Foundation, through the legacy of Amy, the leadership of Kevin, and the support of TTC, works to show that the call to action is a call to invaluable citizen service.

CAN DO!

> *My wife and I give personally every year to the foundation, and we support other activities with in-kind donations and providing Amy bracelets to some of our brands' team members and guests as well.*
>
> *I am humbled to say that this realisation extends beyond our business environment. At a personal level, Kevin has also inspired me and my family to give of our time, energy, influence and financial support, to make an impact within and for the foundation on an annual, ongoing basis and commitment.*
>
> BRETT TOLLMAN

In keeping with Bea Tollman's many remarkable talents, one of the distinguishing features she introduced to the Red Carnation hotels, from their inception, is their world-class cuisine. Bea personally developed many of their recipes and hallmark dishes. Such was the demand, that these recipes have since been published in a beautiful book, with the royalties going to the Amy Foundation. Both as a corporate and as a family, the Tollmans have enhanced my understanding of the importance of giving and making a difference. I cannot thank Brett, Miranda, Stanley, Bea, Vicky, Toni, Gavin, and Michael enough for the exceptional level of personal interest they've taken in our projects, their ongoing friendship and generous financial support – in particular, the wonderful friendship I have forged with Brett.

Amy's bread

The Biehl's had started what is known as 'Amy's bread' – part of a Blue Ribbon Pick n Pay CSI project, which involved baking and selling brown or white Amy's bread at Pick n Pay stores in the Western Cape. Four per cent of the proceeds would go to the Amy Biehl Foundation. When I took over in 2006, I began to market the bread concept more proactively. Having initially yielded roughly R500 per month, this venture picked up, to yield between R3 500 and R4 500 per month by 2013. My appreciation goes to Raymond,

Wendy and Suzanne Ackerman-Berman as well as the management of Blue Ribbon – Terry Lavery, Dave Donovan, Noleen Ballard-Tremeer, and Jerome Wessels – who all had a commendable role to play in growing the partnership with us.

In 2015, they agreed to repackage the bread with an appealing new branding to hopefully attract more people to buy it. They also agreed to sponsor point of sale material on the shelf, which I wanted for a long time, since it would attract the consumer's eye to Amy's bread as opposed to other competitive brands. We are mindful of the fact that there is loads (or rather loaves!) of competition, so we needed to be conspicuous enough for consumers to want to buy our bread. Whenever possible, we would send volunteers to Pick n Pay to promote the bread in-store. With point of sale, our target was to achieve R10 000 per month. Subsequently, however, Premier Foods senior brand manager, Wesley Shunn, approached me in 2016 with a concept that he believed would make us more money, since it eliminated the cost of wrapping a separate bread. He proposed that for one month a year, 25 cents would be donated from Blue Ribbon for every white and brown Blue Ribbon bread sold at Pick n Pay stores and Pick n Pay would match this with another 25 cents per loaf themselves. Besides the fact that the Amy Foundation branding profiled at this annual promotion would give us added exposure, this offer made good financial sense. The Ackermans kindly supported this change, which commenced from August 2016.

Amy's wine

When we came up with the idea of marketing a special wine in Amy's name, I needed to find a wine maker who identified with the cause, since we couldn't take donor money to start producing wine. I had the good fortune to meet Geir Tellefsen, an ex-Norwegian entrepreneur and vintner from Rosendal wines, who liked what we were doing, and agreed to produce a sauvignon blanc and merlot, along with attractive labels. Besides distributing Amy's wine through Pick n Pay stores, the Tollmans sell them via their ships and hotels, so the wine has been a great income generator. Amy's wine is a firm favourite on the wine list

CAN DO!

Amy's wine and Amy Foundation Relate bracelets proudly on display at a Gala Fundraising Dinner.

The new Amy Foundation wine label, a bracelet and the Amy doll in Shweshwe fabric – for use as a keyring or handbag decor – made by the Amy Foundation students.

CAN DO! ✓

at Crystal Towers Hotel and we plan to offer this to many more hotels. Obviously, there's enormous competition and we still need to do lots of marketing. Having started it, however, Geir could not keep up with the demand, so Grant of Vinglo Wines took over production. Besides having the capacity to distribute to Pick n Pay and the ships, Vinglo had facilities to export shipments to places such as the US, France, the UK, and Holland. This venture has proven a great marketing tool in assisting the Amy Foundation to become self-sustainable. Inevitably, challenges come with expansion. By the end of 2017, Vinglo Wines was unable to continue with production due to their own financial challenges, so we have finalised negotiations with one of the highly esteemed wine farms in Stellenbosch to start producing, bottling and labelling Amy's wine under their banner. We are very excited and confident that it will be a bestseller.

The Power of Diversification

As we grew, it was critical to diversify and expand our source of income, away from relying solely on donations and debit orders. Thus the advent of cultural township tours, bread, wine, bracelets, cookbooks, gala dinners, and later handcrafted aprons and dolls as part of our youth-skills development programme. Each of the latter enabled us to make the shift from insolvency to raising the necessary running capital of R3.5m annually at 2009; R4.9m at 2012; R7.1m at 2014; R8.6m at 2016 and R10m by 2017 and 2018.

Thus, through lateral thinking, hard work and a 'can do' approach, we 'canned the can't' expressed by several naysayers, who believed that the foundation could not be salvaged from the grip of insolvency. I must confess that my first year at the helm was unimaginably tough, since I had to work out how to maintain the existing financial infrastructure to pay for food for the youngsters, transport, and of course, salaries for the facilitators and co-ordinators. Now that we have grown it is equally tough on a bigger scale, but manageable through sound business principles, the support of many wonderful people, solid relationships, friendships, and hard work. For me personally, the power of prayer in that year and the ensuing years has been phenomenal. ∎

18

New name, new logo

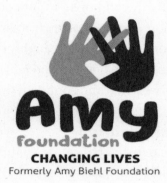

CHANGING LIVES
Formerly Amy Biehl Foundation

Kevin with Ahmed Kathrada, veteran anti-apartheid activist who was jailed for life on 12 June 1964, along with Nelson Mandela, Walter Sisulu, Raymond Mhlaba, Denis Goldberg, Govan Mbeki, Elias Motsoaledi and Andrew Mlangeni.

CAN DO! ✓

From the moment Peter and Linda Biehl founded the Amy Biehl Foundation, Linda took an active interest in the organisation's well-being, but she always maintained that she would retire when she turned 70. As mentioned earlier in this narrative, when the Biehls opted to employ Amy's killers, it shocked the world. Many die-hard Americans were appalled by this seemingly unfathomable decision, and never came to terms with it or accepted the rationale behind this brave act of reconciliation.

Although Linda lives in the United States, she, along with her family, have to this day borne the brunt of vicious, racist hate mail in the US for having pardoned Amy's killers. Linda often told me that she had long ago decided she did not want her children and grandchildren to be subjected to this abuse – which distressed her. Initially, with Linda turning 70 in 2013, we invited one of her children to become a board member of the South African organisation, but they felt this was their parents' mission, not theirs, and opted not to do so. With her family no longer involved in the foundation, Linda was adamant that we should change its name entirely – preferably to a Xhosa word, phrase, or concept.

Our staff and board members expressed serious reservations, raising many valid concerns. After grappling with the implications of this issue for countless hours over many meetings, we could not see our way clear to agreeing with Linda. Eventually, it was unanimously agreed that it would be tantamount to institutional suicide for us to lose the name in its entirety, since we had all worked so hard to build and shape the organisation to the brand it is today. Within the NGO world, we have established a legendary reputation. Besides Amy's significance in terms of our history, the foundation holds immeasurable gravitas and credibility both locally and internationally. Having overcome an onslaught of enormous challenges that took many years to overcome, for us to change the name entirely at this stage would have been like starting all over again. While this was not an easy decision, I feel that it's also about honouring the youngsters in the programmes, maintaining the jobs and salaries of our staff, ensuring ongoing funding for our programmes, and preserving the stature of the sterling organisation that we've collectively built with such drive and passion. Unfortunately, when I explained all this to Linda, she got very upset and in fact, extremely angry with me.

Clearly a broader, less subjective view was necessary to best settle this impasse. I therefore raised all the relevant issues, from both our perspectives, with our board. They were steadfast in the belief that the name should not change. We approached attorneys, Edward Nathan Sonnenbergs, who always gave us pro bono legal guidance, for their input on the best way forward. After viewing the trust deed, the attorneys advised firstly that a name change should only be considered if it was supported by two thirds of the trustees; and secondly, only if such trustees believed that the change would benefit or be in the best interests of the trust. Together with the board, we decided on a compromise that would hopefully avoid causing Linda any further anguish: We approached international branding experts Young and Rubicam (Y&R) to do some research on our behalf. Based on the results, Y&R proposed that we call ourselves the Amy Foundation – with the byline 'Changing Lives'. We all agreed that this was an excellent compromise – for both us and the Biehl family – that would create a fresh, new appeal.

In addition, Y&R suggested that we replace the rather dated orange colour in our logo with a more appealing, fresher shade of green. Personally, I was averse to this, as I always felt that the brilliant orange was an unmissable, distinctive trademark. I was hopelessly outvoted by my management team, who unanimously preferred the green! They were generous enough to suggest that since I am the boss, it could stay if I really wanted it. Fortunately, since I am not caught up in my own sense of self importance, I was more than happy to accept the majority vote and concede to their preference and, of course, the professional advice of Y&R. In hindsight, the green is much nicer than the orange and I really like the new, fresh logo. Thank goodness I listened to my team and especially Michelle Bagley who did an excellent job in designing and implementing the strategy for the name change and new logo.

CAN DO!

No such concession from Linda, unfortunately, who was asked one last time to give her blessing to the new name in the spirit of Ubuntu, but she flatly refused to do so. This has saddened me immensely, since the last thing I want is for anyone to feel such bitterness toward me. I sought input from Ahmed Kathrada, famous ANC struggle fighter and close friend of the late Nelson Mandela, since he is also a long-standing friend of both Linda, myself, and the foundation. He advised me not to choose a Xhosa name. He added that at this point it was not about the Biehls but about Amy's legacy and the good we are doing to change lives. 'Kathy' (as he insisted I call him) visited us numerous times. Until his death in March 2017 he frequently accompanied our staff when they read to the children in the townships. When he last visited the centre, everyone posed for pictures with him, and we all felt so proud to show this great icon what we've achieved and how we're making a difference. ■

The Amy Biehl Foundation, apart from its youth upliftment projects, has an important message on reconciliation, based on the history of the organisation and the story of its namesake. Through its survival, Kevin has ensured that this message continues to resonate in a country where racial tensions have by no means disappeared post 1994. Now officially named 'The Amy Foundation', it must be commended for the work it does. So too, should the likes of Kevin, who keeps the organisation running.
AHMED KATHRADA

19

Making the impossible possible

Before and after.

CAN DO! ✓

Finding premises while teetering on the edge of a precipice

Without a doubt, 2014 proved to be the toughest year of my life. Everything had been going relatively smoothly, until the start of the year, when Themba Ngono, head of premises and facilities at Woolworths, informed me that their premises would no longer be available to us, as their own staff desperately needed more space. He gave me just one month's notice to vacate the building! I was horrified to be given such a short notice period, particularly since we'd maintained a good relationship throughout close to nine years of tenancy. There was no way I could accept this, as it would certainly see us having to close our doors. No donor would be prepared to sponsor rent, and we would not be able to find new premises and move in one month!

I asked to see the MD, then Ian Moir, as Andrew Jennings had retired and gone on to run Karstadt in Germany. Ian explained that they couldn't reverse this decision, as they had builders lined up, who would be working on penalties, although he acknowledged that in fairness, they should have given me much more notice, or warned me that this was coming. I had neither planned for suddenly having to find other premises, nor budgeted for rent. It soon emerged that the cheapest rental we could find for the existing 300 square metres was R35 000 per month or more. Friends and staff feared that this meant the beginning of the end, and that I wouldn't be able to save Amy Foundation this time. Eventually, Ian Moir agreed to extend our lease to four months notice, which would take us through to mid April 2014.

Promises, plans and painting new premises

So where to from here? I was under immense pressure – not only to find something suitable, but also to relocate a complex business that employed 20 full-time and 80 contract facilitators, all within this limited period. Besides the fact that staff livelihoods were dependent on their Amy Foundation jobs, my onerous responsibility to keep things going lay with meeting the daily needs of over 2 000 township children. The number of children we can reach is directly proportionate

> The good news is that bad news can be turned into good news when you change your attitude and resolve to solve the problem. When one door closes, don't assume that it is the only option, for with an open-minded approach, another door will inevitably open.

to the funding we are able to raise: It is through the unfailing support of our generous donors that we're able to provide a brighter future for these children.

I am reminded here of the famous words of William Shakespeare, 'Uneasy lies the head that wears a crown.' (From *Henry IV, Part II*, 1597.) As the deadline loomed closer with each passing day, the pressure gauge seemed to relentlessly slide up a few notches! The naysayers again piped their familiar tune, 'Kevin, you can't save it this time.' Having always had the attitude, when faced with a problem, that I *can* and *will* solve it, I was not to be deterred.

In the ensuing weeks, while praying for an answer and trying to think out the box, it struck me one evening that it would be easier to find people willing to contribute to buying a property – an asset that would become a legacy (as opposed to paying for rent). It would therefore make sense to look for something to buy and renovate to meet our needs. My mind then started racing, thinking even bigger: 'What about housing not only our offices but also some classrooms for training and maybe even some bedrooms to accommodate overseas students who come to us as volunteers? They would then pay us for their accommodation, instead of someone else! Indeed, this could be a more sustainable, excellent source of extra income.'

It had been worrying me – since 2012 – that whilst we did well at keeping 5- to 18-year-olds away from negative influences in the townships, we were not resourced to assist our youngsters once they had completed their schooling. In 2013, we piloted a one-month hospitality training programme, in which a sample group of youngsters were taught sewing, cooking, and waitering skills thanks to Piet Huijbregts (more about this later). We were unable to roll this out, however, owing to lack of resources at the time.

CAN DO!

Inside courtyard with student accommodation upstairs.

If we could buy a property, and build some classrooms, we could introduce skills training of this nature for 18- to 25-year-olds. Besides the fact that these youngsters relished this learning opportunity, it triggered something special for each of them – flicking a switch of opportunity where previously there was no light aglow. I knew at the time that I wanted this project to continue, but had shelved the idea because we lacked permanent access to a kitchen. If I wanted to roll out this hospitality programme on a more permanent, formalised basis, I would also have to find a property on which to build such an infrastructure, along with the necessary office space.

Literally within a day of thinking this would be a good idea, I met with an agent who had come to show me a rental property. In the course of our meeting he casually asked, 'By the way! Would you ever consider buying something?' 'Yes, I would,' came my immediate reply. There was a run-down house on a great property next to the Rondebosch Golf Course, he said. But somebody had already submitted an offer, so I needed to see it immediately... like that afternoon! Wow, was God answering my prayers so fast this time? Thank goodness, despite being so busy that day I agreed to go and look. 'Success occurs when preparation meets opportunity' – another well-known saying that rings loud and true for me. When the opportunity presented itself, I was mentally prepared to take advantage. Given this vision and foresight, I knew exactly how to act on it. This would lay the foundations for what I believe is a remarkable story of success against all odds – made possible with a 'can do' attitude underpinning my every action. After cancelling several appointments, I rushed off to view the property. Located in Golf Course Road, Sybrand Park, Rondebosch East/ Athlone, Cape Town, just off the M5 at the start of Klipfontein Road, between the townships and the centre of town, the site offered great visibility from passing traffic and easy access to buses and taxi ranks. It was the most derelict eyesore imaginable, but I knew immediately that with careful planning and the necessary capital injection, it could be perfect for our needs. As I paced through it, I visualised exactly where we could position the classrooms, the students' residence, the kitchen, even a restaurant, and most importantly, our offices. I clearly remember saying aloud: 'This *must* be part of God's plan!'

Peter Golding of Pam Golding properties was wonderfully supportive, helpful, and a great friend. He sent out an assessor, who advised me that it was a bargain: 'If you can get it, go for it!' He went out of his way to assist me with the offer to purchase, and to find a surveyor and electrician, etcetera. Safe to say, I couldn't have done it on my own!

I ventured that I'd like to put in an offer, but needed a little time to speak to my board in this regard. The agent phoned the seller, who revealed that he had received a good offer from a businessman, who wanted to build a shopping centre there. In response, I asked the agent to pose the following question to the seller: 'Would you like to die one day knowing that you made a businessman rich or that you enriched the lives of thousands of children by making this property available to the Amy Foundation?' This must have touched a nerve, as the seller compromised by giving me exactly one week to submit an equivalent offer to the one he had. Our board agreed to my proposal to purchase the building, provided that I raised the capital myself, stating in no uncertain terms that none of them would be prepared to sign surety and provide guarantees for a bank loan. Again, the naysayers came out saying that it would be impossible for me to raise R2.6 million for the property, as well as the necessary funds to renovate and build what we needed.

Things seemed to swing my way, because the seller agreed not to sign the other offer and gave me three weeks to come up with either a loan or a bank guarantee, so I submitted an offer of R 2.6 million. 'Fantastic! This shouldn't be too difficult,' thought I. 'I'll simply contact 26 private individuals or corporates and ask each of them for R100 000, or 52 people and ask each for R50 000.' But oh boy, did I battle! It wasn't nearly as easy as I'd thought. Never before had the words 'if it's to be, it's up to me,' rung so true, and of course my grandfather's saying: 'Never say die, get up and try.'

Thus began what proved to be the most stressful, daunting three weeks of my life (although to be honest, I had never lost faith that it would somehow work out). Why would God bring us this far, if it wasn't meant to be? Interestingly, some of the people whom I thought would be willing to give me something towards the building, ignored my emails and messages, while others surprised me beyond all expectations.

> **You can rely only on your faith in God, the inherent goodness of certain people, your determination to achieve and lots of hard work!**

God was in control

Determined not to lose the property, I approached First National Bank in the interim to apply for a loan. People questioned my optimism, saying, 'Why are you wasting your time with a bank?' Even Hilary George, one of my ex-branch managers at FNB, was pessimistic, explaining in no uncertain terms that since the economic downturn I should surely know that banks do not lend to NPOs any more. It is ironic for me as an ex-banker to experience how different things are when you sit on the other side of the desk, wanting to borrow money! It's the everyday encounters like this that deepen one's understanding and sense of empathy. Perhaps it's moments like this that have enabled me to 'walk in another person's shoes' – sometimes referred to as an 'awakening experience'.

> When your determination changes, everything will begin to move in the direction you desire. The moment you resolve to be victorious, every nerve and fibre in your being will immediately orient itself toward your success. On the other hand, if you think, 'This is never going to work out,' then at that instant, every cell in your being will be deflated and give up the fight.
>
> DAISAKU IKEDA

Despite the prevailing sense of doom, I remained undeterred. By D-day, I had succeeded in raising only half the required sum. With just one hour to go, I got a call from FNB to say that they were prepared to lend R2.6 million to Amy Foundation, based purely on their trusting relationship with me – with no suretyship or security needed – but for one year only. Whew! What a relief! The provincial head of FNB, Stephan Claassen, was in Hong Kong at the time and had strongly supported this decision. This was absolutely amazing news and another affirmation that God was in control. I won't forget the words of my friend Aviva Pelham, who was overjoyed to hear this, 'OK Kevin, I believe you. There definitely is a God!' At last, I sensed that we were on track. We finally had the loan that would make it all possible!

As already mentioned, credibility is vital and I was determined not to touch the programme money (which required R7 million – $500 000/€450 000/£400 000 – per annum at that time) or dilute that funding for the building. With the new Youth Skills Development Programme, the amount escalated to R10 million – $715 000/

€640 000/£570 000 – per annum. Although it sounds a lot, if you break it down, it works out to only R500/$35/€32/£28 per month, per youngster, or R6 000/$420/€384/£336 per annum, realisable simply because we are so cost efficient. So now we had the new property, but it was far from habitable in its present form. The existing building would take at least nine months to renovate and for us to add on what we wanted. Where to go in the meantime, with only three months left before we had to move out of our existing premises?

Temporary move to Oude Molen, Pinelands

By now, Peter Golding had given me the name of an excellent contact: Sanele Nyoka from the Western Cape Provincial Government. I approached him saying, 'We've never asked for help before, but we are desperate to access an empty building for quite a few months, just to tide us over, but for free please.' In response, from mid-April, we were given rent-free access to an old, government-owned building in a rather derelict complex called Oude Molen in Pinelands.

Entering these filthy, dilapidated premises, it occurred to me that the building was the perfect set for a horror movie, with its salient features being broken windows, shards of broken glass as obstacle course, and shattered toilet seats behind broken doors. Every surface was generously sprinkled with bird poop, interspersed throughout with impressively woven spiderwebs. Our staff set about the huge task of cleaning it up, repaired and freshly painted throughout. Having pulled off a renovation – the likes of which sun king Sol Kerzner would have been proud – we moved in, during April 2014. Our move accorded with the promise I'd made over a handshake with the managing director, our landlord, that I would not come back claiming that we had nowhere to go.

Building to open windows of opportunity

So started the laborious process of getting plans drawn and approved for the new building we had bought – and what a massive undertaking this was! After gutting the entire structure, we needed to replace every window, knock down most of the walls, re-paint the entire roof, and undertake all the new extensions and renovations. We were, however, determined to finish it properly before our scheduled occupation date of June 2015. Luckily, there was no pressure to move in as we had permission to remain in the Oude Molen Provincial Government building for as long as was needed.

However, in order to renovate and build exactly what I had envisioned, we needed another R3.7 million, which by the end of the project became over R5 million. This escalated the required sum to a whopping R7.6 million! In the weeks and months that followed, I embarked on what can only be described as an arduous journey of relentless, gut-wrenching perseverance, in which I targeted virtually every high net-worth individual, corporate, and business I had ever met! Thankfully, some of the latter came to the rescue with exceptional generosity. Unfortunately, space does not allow me to mention them all, and we are mindful of the fact that all in their own way gave what they were able to afford.

When I was group MD of Woolworths South Africa, we loaned Amy Biehl Foundation office space for a number of years. When the agreement came to an end, after I had left the organisation, Kevin advised me that he was going to build a facility that could be used for workshops, teaching facilities, and general gatherings. Without any financial resources, Kevin challenged, persuaded, and endeared sponsors to support this far reaching, mammoth project. To his great credit, he has built a remarkable centre that will serve the foundation for many years to come. In a word, Kevin Chaplin is remarkable!
ANDREW JENNINGS

Fundraising warrior/worrier hammering out a deal

FNB had given me a year to repay the loan of R2.6 million, and by July 2015 I had paid back R 1.35 million. The pressure on me was

CAN DO!

unrelenting. Besides having to raise sufficient funds to pay the builders, I had to raise the remaining R1.25 million to repay the bank by the end of July. Cap in hand, I asked the bank to extend the deadline to December. After tough negotiations, they agreed on a staggered repayment of R250 000 by the end of September 2015, R500 000 by end October, and R500 000 by the end of December. The fact is that in terms of what we had built, the value was evident for all to see. The other R5 million to renovate and build what we now have was funded by generous donors.

While all this was going on, there was absolutely no time for a breather. To my huge relief, a large portion, R1 million, came our way from the National Lottery. In terms of the cost of building materials, we made sure to negotiate the cheapest prices on tiles, fittings, and fixtures.

From a cash flow perspective, it was hugely stressful to be this geared. Besides having to repay this debt, we had to meet all our regular overheads to cover the running costs for five centres, food, transport, and of course our biggest expense, monthly salaries for the facilitators (teachers) – amounting to R450 000 per month at that time for almost 100 staff. A week before payday on 25 September 2015, the foundation had only R100 000 left in the bank, a shortfall which left chief operations officer Afiefa and the team gloomily pondering our fate as we tiptoed at the edge of a precipice again.

It was with deep apprehension and very little sleep that I wondered how on earth I was going to do this, and again prayed hard. A public holiday would intervene on 24 September, which meant that R350 000 had to be in by 23 September for salaries and then another R250 000 by 1 October for the bank. I spent that entire week frantically messaging and emailing one appeal after the next to our longstanding donors, explaining that I had a cash-flow crisis. Slowly but surely, much-needed donations flowed in, including some from my friends in Northern Ireland. Two months earlier, through Arthur Gillis, I had met the new COO of Mariott Hotels, Mark Satterfield, who was blown away by the project when he saw it. At the time, he asked me to send him a proposal, which I duly did. At my nadir of despair, on 23 September, I was relieved to receive an email saying they would give us R100 000. With the public holiday falling on 24 September, any cheques promised from Northern Ireland would only reach us on the twenty-sixth – but I knew they were coming! On the twenty-third, we were still R60 000 short. As an interim measure, I debited my own home loan account to make the payment, knowing that Afiefa could repay me on 26 September when the money from Northern Ireland arrived. Talk about robbing Peter to pay Paul!

The precariousness of our situation certainly took me back to my first 18 months at the Amy Biehl Foundation, when I took over an insolvent organisation and my own money and reputation were both on the line! But this only brought a brief respite, because on 1 October, we had to repay the next instalment of R250 000 to the bank. On 28 September, I prayed with heart-felt desperation, 'Lord, I am exhausted now. I am asking, begging in fact. Please help me. I do not know where to find another R250 000.' In tandem with my pounding heart, Nelson Mandela's famous quote thudded in my ears: 'After climbing a great hill, one only finds that there are many more hills to climb.'

Wendy Ackerman came to my rescue. A few weeks earlier, she had agreed to read to the children (as she often did) on 29 September. That morning, since she'd never been there, I invited her to visit our new centre. She kindly agreed, and despite being under pressure, managed to spend considerable time walking around. She was visibly impressed by what we had achieved, for she repeatedly exclaimed, 'Kevin! This is an absolute miracle! Do you realise that!' She offered to make a contribution to the building, and 'miracle upon miracle', she deposited the much needed R250 000 in the bank on 1 October! (I must add that she was unaware at the time of how much I needed to pay the Bank on 1 October.) Floating with joy – as if being tugged skywards by a string of balloons – I was once again able to enjoy a brief breather. Another instance I will never forget is when Glen Heneck, Director of Melbro Holdings and Crazy Stores came to meet me in

CAN DO!

October at the new centre. I had been trying to see him for a long time and out of the blue he contacted me and said he was able to visit that day. Quickly clearing my diary, we met and he was astounded at what he saw, saying 'wow, there has to be a God to achieve all this', and promptly donated R50 000. This meeting led to a great relationship and increased support over the years from Glen, Melbro Holdings and Crazy Stores. We still, however, had to pay the remaining R500 000 by the end of October and another R500 000 by December to repay the full debt, which we ultimately managed to do, not by December 2015, but March the following year in 2016.

Kitchen, cash, catering and careers

One of the most thrilling aspects of this venture is that it has enabled us to forge new and previously unimagined opportunities for our students. As per my vision outlined earlier, we built a small restaurant adjoining the fully-fitted, functional teaching kitchen, in which the hospitality students would be given the opportunity to gain work experience. As we raise sufficient funding, some learn to become chefs and waiters, while others will be trained to be entrepreneurs in restaurant and catering businesses.

We are constantly thinking big and laterally about how to maximise the use of the kitchen as both a training venue and source of funding. The restaurant facility, called Amy's Bistro, is now geared up to offer a full spectrum of South African cuisine – such as traditional Cape Malay, Xhosa, Jewish, and Afrikaans dishes – to visitors taking Amy's Cultural Township Tours. To introduce an especially heart-warming dimension to the dining experience, our guests are entertained by the students who serve them, since many are good singers. Corporates even bring clients or staff to lunches catered by the students – who are expected to make a starter, main course, and dessert. We've also had a calling from the corporate market to hold fun-filled, team building cook-offs in our kitchen – all of which are slowly starting to provide a viable source of extra income towards the total budget needed annually.

Strategic partners and volunteers

Practising the philosophy of praying for everything and surrounding yourself with the right people, I knew that the only way to ensure the success of the Youth Skills Development programme would be to recruit someone outstanding to implement and run it for us.

With no funding, I believed that the most suitable person to do this was Hilary George (mentioned earlier), who was one of my best branch managers at FNB. Fortunately, she agreed to run the Youth Skills Development programme when I approached her in 2015. I particularly liked the fact that she wouldn't simply accept my view. Instead, she'd occasionally challenge me in a constructive manner (which is important) so that I was always kept me on my toes. Despite the lack of funding, we managed in a short space of time to get 265 learners to become economically active by mid-2017, 402 by March 2018, and 614 by March 2019. This is testament to the impact and success of the project. The abundance emanating from God's blessings has been beyond my wildest dreams. I could see the vast potential for growth, if we could secure long-term financial partners.

At the end of 2015, thanks to Blum Khan, CEO of MMI at the time, we welcomed Stewart Miller, a volunteer from Northern Ireland who came for a year and stayed considerably longer. He was later joined by Anele Nyembezi, a welcome addition to the team. Hilary then reminded me that Tracey Younghusband had run the Eleven Kitchen venue, which had in the interim closed down. Tracey came on board soon thereafter to run the hospitality course. What a blessing she has been in taking this programme to where it is and what it has achieved! Other exceptional volunteers were to follow, like Vina Patel, who was introduced from the UK by Jacques Tredoux (one of our benefactors), Paul Aspeling, who has become a core member of the hospitality team, known to the students as Chef Paul, together with Val Pillay, and not forgetting our wonderful overseas volunteers (too many to mention) who come for two months or longer.

CAN DO!

I'm both proud and hugely relieved to say that by March 2016 we had managed to raise 100 per cent of the much-needed R7.6 million. Most of the money came from individual donors – the most generous emanating from Dutch, UK, US, and South African donors. The teaching kitchen would never have materialised without contributors like Christine Cashmore, Kenwood and Mac Brothers Catering Equipment, which fitted out our entire teaching kitchen with much generosity and vision. I am also deeply indebted to Piet Huijbregts, René Clarijs, Willem Emmens, Harry van Leusden, Uipko Ebbens, Anton van Kooten and Annette Mul from the Netherlands, who all raised funds for this project.

As we source more funding we will grow this programme. A main component of this project involves developing strong 'partnerships' (based on CSI principles), with like-minded individuals, businesses, and corporates, focusing on developing the youth on a sustainable and long-term basis. One of our biggest contributors to experiential training and subsequent employment opportunities for our learners has been the Twelve Apostles Hotel & Spa, followed by Century City Conference Centre, One&Only Cape Town, and the Vineyard Hotel. Today, the strategic partners' list is set to grow exponentially.

In doing so, we secure tangible outcomes by way of actual employment secured, businesses created, or study opportunities. We believe in handups and not handouts: In order for the youth skills development and entrepreneurial programme to be sustainable, it needs to be a win-win 'partnership' for all parties concerned. The learner becomes employed or starts a small enterprise; the Amy Foundation derives actual outcomes; and our 'strategic partner' businesses (who want to grow our country's economy) get to take new, preferred employees from a credible programme rather than 'off the street'.

Amy's Bistro attached to the teaching kitchen.

THERE ARE FIVE MESSAGES HERE:

Out of every challenge comes a greater opportunity. It's been proven time and time again that when one door closes, another opens. (And in my experience, the door that opens usually offers better opportunities and more exciting options.)

Don't be afraid of adversity. Try to think big, dream big, and take on fresh challenges. In most cases, the bigger the challenge, the greater the effort required and the higher the reward or gratification upon achieving success. One only needs to look at the incredible infrastructure that resulted from the challenge I faced upon being given short notice to vacate our offices. Although it was in a sense thrust upon

CAN DO!

me, the whole project proved to be an unimagined, monumental success – a tribute to all that one can achieve if one is 100 per cent committed to taking on a challenge and solving the problem by giving it your all.

Don't allow yourself to be deterred by the negative people who will always find a reason why something cannot be done.

Stay focused on your goal, regardless of the naysayers and the obstacles that may be in your way.

A significant relationship exists between prayer and hard work. While prayer is important, it is not enough on its own. Prayer can never replace diligent effort, because to succeed, you also have to work your butt off. The same applies to achieving any success in life: Once you've put in the hours, done the 'hard yards', and used the tools and abilities you were given, you can pray for the desired outcome – and then thank God.

This remarkable series of events has taught so many people what is possible if you have a clear vision of what you hope to achieve, and doggedly set out to pursue it. Synchronicity is a fascinating phenomenon. Having decided in 2013 to write this book on eliminating negativity with my 'can do' philosophy, I was duly put to the test on every imaginable level in that same year! While it was the toughest year of my life, I came through at the end of it all with a real-life, working example of everything I'd set out to achieve and share in the book. I must add that when faced with the challenge of finding new premises and then building a new centre virtually from scratch, I took the decision to put writing the book on hold in 2014 and 2015. If I had printed the narrative in 2013, without including the gut-wrenching challenges of the past six years, it would not have been nearly as impactful. As an allegory to illustrate my point, I could not have conjured up anything better!

Today, we are infinitely proud of this pristine, fully functional new Amy Foundation Centre, which boasts office space for our core staff of 25, free parking, as well as comfortable accommodation for 15 to 20 international volunteers at a time (two or three beds per bedroom), a lounge and kitchen. It also houses seven well-equipped classrooms for sewing, beauty and technical skills, including a fully fitted teaching kitchen and bistro that enables us to offer youth skills development and training programmes, as well as entrepreneurial and vocational training programmes to township youth. In addition, we currently hold various other interventions and classes in two of the classrooms, which double as a conference venue when required and also bring in income.

I had originally wanted a plaque above our list of building donors on the outside of the building to read: 'To God be the Glory.' But then our COO said she was uncomfortable with this, as it could be offensive to Muslims, who might think this organisation is only for Christians. I certainly wouldn't want that, so after giving it much thought, we decided on: 'Everything is Possible for Those Who Believe.' This has since been widely accepted. So much time, energy, and planning has gone into establishing this centre, that I would like to believe this will leave a legacy for Cape Town for generations to come. How gratifying to be able to add that the centre is now valued at over R10 million! ■

20

Current Amy Foundation programmes

Enthusiastic Amy Foundation soccer class with DHL soccer balls.

CAN DO! ✓

Our mission is to educate, develop, and empower children and youth from challenged and vulnerable communities of the Western Cape, in a safe environment. By unlocking innate creativity and talent, we encourage the youth to make positive life choices that will help them become functional, contributing members of society. In so doing, we aim to create future leaders, entrepreneurs, and emotionally well-rounded citizens in a global society.

Through participation in our activities, these vulnerable teenagers are kept away from gang-related violence and crime, as well as sex and drug abuse. If one looks at the relevant statistics in South Africa, over 50 per cent of children who start Grade One, drop out of school before Grade 12. We have found that the children in our programmes do not drop out of school. Most participants will complete their schooling and find themselves better equipped to deal with the challenges of tomorrow.

Uplifting programmes for scholars

The foundation currently operates after-school care centres for 5- to 18-year-olds in various communities of Cape Town – each hosting over 300 students per day. These programmes, which run Monday to Thursday throughout the school year, as well as weekend activities, are having a positive effect on the youth as well as the communities in which they live. At a cost of R500 per month, per child, they get free tuition, a meal every afternoon, as well as transport to holiday camps and outings. Our programmes aim to make learning enjoyable – so that the children want to learn.

Over the years, we have developed and widened the scope of our work in the townships considerably, such that our offering now includes after-school care, music in choral, marimba, brass, guitar, and violin, drama, and art, various types of dance classes, and HIV/AIDS prevention and peer education. Life skills is a core component throughout these and the programmes mentioned over the page.

Working with children and the community, our greening and environmental programme focuses on beautifying township schools, teaching respect for the environment and growing vegetable gardens. Children are also taught about global-warming issues, pollution, and the need for recycling.

Academically, we have also made a notable impact by boosting their literacy skills through our literacy and academic support programme. We also focus on improving their numeracy skills and have recently included extra mathematics tuition.

Besides these, a wide range of popular extra-mural sports are taught and practised: soccer, hockey, surfing, swimming, diving, chess, cycling, cricket and golf.

The Amy Foundation is a testimony to the fact that the positive development young people experience in community arts and cultural programmes is related to success in other areas of their lives. Youth who participate in our programmes, for example, are less likely than their peers to engage in delinquent and violent behaviour, or exhibit behavioural and emotional problems, and they are more likely to participate in school leadership and have better attendance and higher academic achievement.

Inspirational volunteers

At any time, we have up to 10 international volunteers from all over the world, working at Amy Foundation. They pay their own way to South Africa, along with their own living expenses. There are too many to name individually, but every one of them has made a difference.

Some years ago, it was a great privilege to have Braam Malherbe, the well-known extreme adventurer, conservationist, and motivational speaker, come on board as an ambassador and donor. Giving of his time in running youth development camps for township youngsters, it did not take long for this charismatic explorer to become 'The Man'! What an inspirational figure to children who are so desperately in need of courageous, hardworking male role models – particularly since the absent father syndrome has become an endemic township problem. Over time, we have learnt that one cannot overestimate the value of passionate people like Braam doing their bit to make a difference, since their impact is far-reaching and potentially will last a lifetime.

Talented Amy Foundation Dance youngsters performing.

Amy Foundation gum boot dancers.

> *Kevin has an infectious energy and is one of the most positive people I know. We have a complementary relationship. We feed off one another's optimism and both believe in the power of good intention. As a proud Amy ambassador, I took boys displaying leadership potential on a bush camp. Kevin saw huge value in this and assisted me with the selection process. I enjoy the fact that Kevin is a real 'doer'. He puts his heart and soul into anything he truly believes in.*
>
> *I chose to assist Kevin because of his strong value base and because he cannot do this huge job without support. The support I believe I have to offer him is to motivate him and inspire him in tough times.*
>
> BRAAM MALHERBE

Skills development for school leavers

One of the biggest issues facing our country is the lack of jobs and employment opportunities. My staff and I have embraced this challenge wholeheartedly. I'm particularly proud of the fact that in 2015 we were able to launch the youth skills and entrepreneurial development programme for school leavers and unemployed youth. The programme includes computers, literacy, conversational English, business etiquette, and life skills for 18- to 35-year-olds. (Interestingly, the South African Government defines 'youth' as those younger than 35, while other countries set the upper age limit for youth at 25 to 30.) The theory and interactive classroom programme that all students go through with Corina van der Linde sets them up for success in the workplace, with valuable input from business leaders like Chantal Kading, Phumi Nhlapo, Ruth Kamau and others who have since contributed. We have also piloted a much-needed vocational skills training programme for high school youth (aged 16 to 19), which we plan to roll out further, funding dependent.

CAN DO!

The Amy Foundation Youth Skills Development Team – Stewart Miller (far left), Roxy Marosa and Anele Nyembezi (far right), and Hilary George (kneeling in front row) – with facilitators in one of the workshops covering business etiquette, life skills, conversational english and much more.

Amy Foundation Sewing, Craft and Design Programme – co-ordinator Tessi Bont with volunteer facilitators and students.

Making the impossible possible

Amy Foundation Hospitality Programme – co-ordinator Tracey Younghusband with her students.

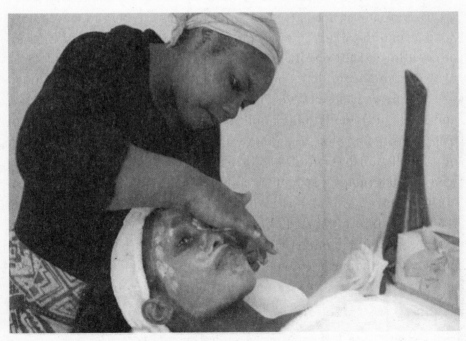

Amy Foundation Beauty and Wellness Training in full practical mode.

CAN DO! ✓

These promising young people are up-skilled through theoretical and practical interventions. The main disciplines are: hospitality, sewing, beading, arts & crafts, beauty and wellness, retail readiness, technical skills, entrepreneurship, and enterprise development. Technical skills was introduced in early 2019 thanks to Orlando Luis and Brights Hardware. The impact of these classes in a short time has been remarkable. In addition to the hospitality programme with Tracey Younghusband mentioned earlier, the sewing and craft class has grown in leaps and bounds under the untiring guidance and mentoring of Tessi Bont, who is ably supported by volunteers Rita Boes, Debbie Slomowitz and Glynis Scott. The students produce the most amazing items that have expanded from dolls and aprons to jackets, waistcoats, and so much more, also earning the students much needed income through sales to our tour groups and visitors. The beauty and wellness class directed by Roxy Marosa and Leigh-Anne Van Wyk, assisted by volunteer Lee-Anne Hodson, has seen rapid growth in the development of learners, leading to successful placements and starting of their own businesses. Members of the public can now even come and have treatments at Amy's beauty and wellness training academy. At the monthly Ubuntu business breakfasts a feature is now some Amy Foundation students sitting at a table massaging guests hands or shoulders for R30 – and the guests love it.

Everything we do in the Youth Skills Development programme is aimed at growing the self-confidence of learners, developing their skills, building their CVs and creating employment. The ultimate objective is for them to become independent, prosperous, and contributing citizens of a non-discriminatory South Africa, of whom we can all feel proud.

Programme facilitators and co-ordinators

By identifying and training potential black and coloured leaders living within these communities, and ultimately employing them as programme facilitators, we've given them an opportunity to improve not only their own lives, but also to impart their skills to their communities. In so doing, the beneficiaries have a dual stake in the

Amy Foundation children enjoying a literacy class.

upliftment process. It is people like our dedicated staff and especially all the amazing movers and shakers: our co-ordinators and facilitators, who continue to spread Amy's legacy. Their transformation represents the powerful legacy of Ubuntu, as well as the transformation she was working for. Amy's dedication and courage continues to inspire so many people throughout the world, and the foundation has gone on to become a source of extraordinary opportunity for thousands of South African youth.

Just two examples of young children who were in the programmes and went on to become facilitators: Masixole Dudula was being negatively influenced as a young boy in the townships until he joined the Amy Foundation programmes at 11 years of age. On completing

Amy Foundation children performing at the Table of Peace and Unity.

CAN DO! ✓

his schooling he became a facilitator, followed eventually by being promoted to run his own after-school centre. Today he is proudly working in the corporate world. Phelisa Ngondzi joined at 11 years old, became a facilitator and then a co-ordinator of her own centre in Gugulethu. This, and many other examples, inspire us to continue doing what we are doing.

I'm often asked why we do not expand our services beyond the confines of the Western Cape. The reader should know that many of the children come to us from other areas like the Eastern Cape, Gauteng, and KwaZulu-Natal. The socio-economic needs in our immediate surrounds are so vast that it makes more sense to focus on the children in the Western Cape than to dilute our offering by expanding to other provinces.

> **Don't spread yourself too thin; bigger is not always better.**

Alumni success stories

Psychologists will tell you that people who believe their lives are meaningless are more prone to commit suicide, whereas people who believe they are making a difference lead more fulfilling, satisfying lives. Our mantra is that the tried and tested recipe of hard work, commitment, focus, and innovation – with heaps of ambition thrown into the mix – will inevitably deliver excellent returns.

I share just two success stories of Amy Foundation alumni who are daily making a difference and who are an inspiration. There are many more.

AKHONA MNGQIBISA

Akhona participated in Amy Foundation after-school classes from the age of 11 in marimba, greening, and later Muay Thai kickboxing, amongst others. After completing Grade 12, he was selected for the six-month exchange programme we'd established with CEMEA in

France (*Centre d'entraînement aux méthodes d'éducation active*) through my board membership of the European Association of Institutions of Non-Formal Education of Children and Youth (EAICY). Three months after participating in our first hospitality programme, we placed him at the Twelve Apostles Hotel & Spa. He loved his job from the beginning and has always been so dedicated and committed. Akhona was justifiably proud to win their 'Employee of the Year' award for 2016 upon which he was flown to London for the Red Carnation Group Awards evening in March 2017.

SIBUSISO NTISANA

From the age of nine, this promising young man participated in several Amy Foundation after-school music programmes (see the section on Relate bracelets). He went on to perform in many of our festivals and events and completed his Grade 12 at Rhodes High School in Mowbray, Western Cape, thanks partly to Sam Montsi, a  successful businessman, who mentored Sibusiso and sponsored his upgrade to a better school. Sibusiso used to come to our offices where staff member Cikizwa Mnyamana would assist him with computers, discuss his marks and give him extra lessons when needed, but it worried me that he lacked self-confidence.

I'm very curious and I like learning. I've always thought that I could do anything. You just have to be at the right place, at the right time, with the right people, and together you can find solutions. I am indebted to the Amy Foundation for taking me off the streets and giving me hope by showing me a different way.

SIBUSISO NTISANA

CAN DO! ✓

In 2014, after returning from a six-month exchange programme in France with CEMEA, I was blown away by his new self-assured persona and well-spoken manner, which oozed nothing but charm and success!

When Suzanne Ackerman-Berman visited the Amy training kitchen in April 2016, she was impressed when Sibusiso approached her, expressing a desire to work for Pick n Pay. She encouraged him to send her his CV, and following a screening process, he was appointed to participate in their Trainee Manager Programme. As the director of transformation at Pick n Pay, Suzanne makes a huge impact on many people's lives, while implementing and overseeing transformation within the group. This is an extraordinary feat, if one considers that Pick n Pay currently employs over 50 000 people at more than 940 stores, nationwide. ■

Amy Foundation students in the Hospitality Programme.

21

When bad things happen to good people – how to not only survive but thrive again

Amy Foundation Management team proudly standing in front of the centre.
Left to right: Afiefa Behardien, COO; Phumi Nhlapo, Programme Manager After-school Programmes; Kevin Chaplin, MD; Hilary George, Programme Manager Youth Skills Development Programme; Michelle Bagley, PR, Marketing, Events and Fundraising Manager. (Absent: Joanna Barry, HR and Volunteers Manager)

CAN DO! ✓

'Life happens to you while you're busy making other plans,' goes the saying. Indeed, when you least expect it, your life can turn in a flash. Things change so suddenly that reality as you know it seems to take on another form, becoming distorted almost beyond recognition.

Never in my wildest dreams did I imagine that my whole world would come crashing down on me in October 2018. Earlier that year, the economy had taken a dramatic downturn, largely owing to widespread corruption and disastrous pilfering of billions from our state coffers during the Zuma era. I had explained to the management team of Amy Foundation that, along with the latter, we had also raised less funding for our after-school programmes, and we could not operate in a bubble.

We had managed to reduce costs slightly by cutting out some camps and outings from the programme, but it soon became clear that this wasn't going to be enough. My good friend Salim Young, for example, readily tried to assist with his own donation and persuaded many of his friends and business associates to donate, raising over R100 000 in a few weeks. We made cost-saving decisions over many months and included the staff in considering all possible options.

From an empowerment perspective, our donors seemed to prefer funding the youth skills development programme. After spending the next eight months trying to balance the needs of the centre with very limited resources and increasing cost restraints, we decided to downsize the Khayelitsha After School Centre. Ultimately, we had run out of options, having reached a point where we could not sustain the centre any longer.

Unfortunately, this entailed having to retrench the co-ordinator of the centre. After the board approved this measure, which would save us over R50 000 per month, we followed all the due labour processes. Little did I dream that a nightmare was to come!

On 23 October 2018 one of our black programme co-ordinators – who had only been with us a few months – stormed into my office with one of our drivers and demanded to talk to me immediately.

I apologised, explaining that I was in the middle of something and would make the time to see him later. He instantly became aggressive, and angrily handed me a letter which came as a bolt from the blue, threatening us with the following, unless we retracted the decision to retrench that one staff member:

1. To discontinue the after-school programmes in our townships;
2. Expose the foundation to the media about its unfair and brutal decisions that are against its philosophy of changing lives;
3. Take protest action against the organisation;
4. Reach out to funders/donors of our programmes regarding the hazardous matters we face in the organisation; and
5. Unionise and mobilise the communities where our after-school programmes operate.

Finding myself in the midst of a tornado

By now in a fury, I exclaimed that I would deal with this as soon as I had finished what I was doing. This young man reacted by brazenly striding into the main office area and rounding up other black staff members, upon which the group marched off site before I had a chance to talk to them. (I have chosen not to name the ringleader, as it would grant him undeserved publicity.)

What a terrible shock it was for me to learn that he had mustered the support of some of our other black staff, each of whom had played key roles, and with whom I had long-established, excellent relationships. I was deeply disappointed in these trusted people, who suddenly, for no logical reason, had been brainwashed. I could not believe what I was seeing, and couldn't help wondering what was really behind their appalling show of disloyalty.

At the time, Babalwa Mongezi, our receptionist and switchboard lady, who had doubled up as my PA for five years, hovered anxiously behind, saying, 'I'm scared, I don't know what to do, because they know where I live.' I assured Babalwa that we would protect her.

It was too late to call the other staff back to reason with them, but then one of them returned and called on Babalwa to join him, which she duly did. In the midst of all this chaos, I remember

CAN DO!

screaming, 'What the hell is going on here!' but the two of them ignored me. There are no words to describe my astonishment and utter disbelief that this was happening.

I immediately contacted our lawyers Webber Wentzel, who have always assisted us pro bono thanks to the ongoing involvement of senior partner Mike Evans. What a blessing it has been to be able to call on them regarding Amy Foundation matters, and never more so than with this latest turn of events. Labour law is a very complex field in South Africa, particularly in dealing with volatile situations of this nature. We owe a huge debt of gratitude to Deon Visagie, partner, and Joani van Vuuren, associate, who readily came to our aid and have stuck with us all the way.

The next day we sent the rebellious group various messages to return to work, which they duly did, without showing any contrition or humility. This led to many discussions, during which I tried to get them to understand that downscaling of the centre and retrenchment of the co-ordinator emanated purely from a business decision, but they were having none of that. They believed that the action was unjustified and racist, alleging that it stemmed from my two coloured managers wanting to get rid of the black co-ordinator from Khayelitsha.

Nothing could have been further from the truth, and I attempted to correct this perception by explaining why it was purely a financially based business decision. My explanation fell on deaf ears, however. I even suggested that we get the Commission for Conciliation, Mediation and Arbitration (CCMA) involved, but the ringleader adamantly refused to consider assistance by the CCMA.

The board also responded to the group, but despite this things came to a head on 14 November. The co-ordinators were attending a session in which they made their annual presentations to the monitoring and evaluation (M&E) officer, who would then present the findings and plans for 2019 to my executive committee (EXCO). Fifteen minutes after I had opened the session, one of my managers came to tell me that the ringleader was shouting and pointing his finger in the face of the M&E officer, so I went to the boardroom to see what was going on. Then the ringleader and the driver (who had originally joined him in presenting me with the petition) both went beserk – becoming riotous and violent, angrily banging their fists on the table and accusing me of racism. Coming from nowhere, I suddenly had a race war on my hands.

They were both screaming, 'You are a white supremacist! Kevin must fall! No longer will black people be ruled by white people!' I immediately informed them that they were to be suspended, along with another staff member, but they refused to leave the room and continued yelling.

I managed to call the police, who came to our assistance and escorted the three suspended members off the premises after I had issued them with suspension letters. I stood there in total shock, incredulous that this could have happened. My sense of logic about the way things are supposed to work in the world had suddenly been turned on its head. My knees were shaking, but I knew I had to remain calm: there was no time to dwell on the loss of trust or to become angry.

I now needed to settle the remaining black staff, and especially the coloured staff, who by this time were nothing short of terrified. I appealed to everyone to remain calm and return to work, which they duly did.

That afternoon Michelle, my PR, marketing, events, and fundraising manager picked up that the ringleader was posting terrible things on his Facebook page – accusing me of being a corrupt, white supremacist, and referring to the two coloured managers on my EXCO as 'my Guptas' (Jacob Zuma's henchmen). Later that night, Michelle picked up that he had called for a strike and was also inviting the media and public to participate in their so called 'important fight'.

To give some context to these events, I quote from an article, featured in the *Daily Maverick* of 12 December 2018, by Ferial Haffajee:

'In the past six months, the EFF [Economic Freedom Fighters] has emerged as the key merchants of political disinformation campaigns in South Africa... At both Eskom and Transnet, the epicentres of investigations and a clean-out of the patronage groups

CAN DO! ✓

which milked them dry, the party has taken up arms, deploying a race narrative that Minister of Public Enterprises Pravin Gordhan is exorcising black executives. The effectiveness of the EFF campaigns has, in 2018, ushered South Africa into an era of disinformation where social media is weaponised to spread campaigns often built on falsehood. There is no doubt that the EFF in some instances participates in spreading disinformation. It is clear that many of their officials spread the messages and retweet, spreading disinformation, said William Bird, director of Media Monitoring Africa, the think tank building up a database on disinformation and misinformation ahead of the 2019 national and provincial elections. Disinformation is generally used to refer to deliberate (often orchestrated) attempts to confuse or manipulate people through delivering dishonest information to them. Since June 2018, the EFF has sown four impactful but false narratives into the national news agenda and migrated them from social media disinformation to the top of the mainstream news media's agenda where they were given serious and prominent airing.'

Lo and behold, on 15 November 2018, the day after the ringleader's Facebook post, ten black members of our 29 permanent staff and 16 of our 80 part-time facilitators embarked on a strike. They were all told to return to work or face disciplinary action (besides the others who by this time had been suspended for unacceptable behaviour). It was quite astounding to see them strolling in to work on 16 November at 9 am, as though nothing had happened, although they were being very noisy. My chief operations officer had not yet arrived, which necessitated asking them to please quieten down and get to work until we had a chance to talk things over. Before I had a chance to address the issue, events overtook us yet again.

Rather naively, I thought the remaining black staff would be able to listen to reason and be sensible, without realising how easily and effectively they'd been brainwashed by the ringleader.

We subsequently found out that he uses anti-white and anti-coloured propaganda to exploit and influence black people, using blatant intimidation along with making false promises. An ex-staff member from the township cautioned me: he had heard that the ringleader was vying for a position in the EFF (a radical political party), and this was his way of proving himself. He apparently wanted to take over our lovely building in Rondebosch and convert it into a dance centre! It was hard to understand why they blindly followed the instructions of someone they barely knew. We would, however, see a dramatic turnaround in just a few months.

Living in the country's fiery crucible of change

In hindsight, I realise this type of environment provides fertile soil for charismatic, populist leaders to take root, rise to power, and flourish. They divide and lead by turning the status quo into an 'us' against 'them' situation. In so doing, they simplify a complex problem by arriving at ill-founded solutions, most often using intimidating, fear-mongering tactics. Bold and convincing, they make all sorts of promises via social media to a gullible, vulnerable group of people who are seeking a quick-fix solution to a given problem.

History has shown us how dangerous such populist leaders can be: one only needs to look north across South Africa's borders to see the havoc wreaked on human lives by leaders like Robert Mugabe, or look back in time to leaders like Adolph Hitler, whose philosophies were responsible for committing unimaginable atrocities in the name of achieving racial purity. Other modern-day examples are of course Brexit and Trumpism, which have become popular largely through propaganda – based on half-truths – circulated on social media about the wave of immigration into the United Kingdom, Europe, and the United States.

The events at the Amy Foundation formed a microcosm of the very disturbing political events occurring at the macro level in South Africa at the time. (In his testimony before the Zondo Commission our much-respected Public Enterprises Minister, Pravin Gordhan, referred repeatedly to social media campaigns. 'The onslaught continues. It is to manipulate public opinion. Fake news undermines democracy,' he told Judge Zondo.)

CAN DO!

Later on the morning of 16 November, Michelle picked up that the ringleader was again calling for a strike on social media. I quickly called all the remaining staff together and spelled out the consequences of embarking on an illegal strike. I appealed to them to think carefully for themselves and urged them to refrain from striking. At this point, co-ordinator Vusumsi Ntoni promptly went out to join them. I was surprised: we had done so much to assist him during a prolonged illness, and he had always worked so well – with us and for us. The remaining black staff asked me to meet with them, and I duly did so in another attempt to resolve the situation.

All they were interested in, however, was getting rid of my two coloured managers, claiming once again that the two were racist and had too much influence. They also demanded that I reinstate the four suspended staff members and appoint as programme manager the co-ordinator from Khayelitsha who was to be retrenched.

I emphasised that the two managers were not racist: they had in fact played a key role in building the Amy Foundation, but this fell on deaf ears. I explained that none of their demands were possible to meet and that the four suspended staff members would be subjected to a disciplinary enquiry – chaired by an independent person – where they would be given a fair chance to put their case. But the black staff would not listen. Things came to a head when one of the co-ordinators, Lindiswa Mavavana, started screaming hysterically at me that this was 'like apartheid all over again'. The screaming got louder and increasingly hysterical, and despite my efforts to calm Lindiswa down, explaining that we could not talk if she was like this, she ultimately lost it completely, which set off another employee, Ayanda Mazwi.

Ayanda's involvement shocked me to the core, as she had been with us for ten years. In a Bosses' Day card a few months previously she had commended me for inspiring her and thanked me for all I had done, both for her and the foundation. I had also taken her to France with me about five years earlier, when I was sponsored to take a staff member with me for a training course. We had recently earmarked her to become an assistant programme manager. To see Ayanda later holding up a placard saying, 'Kevin – stop abusing black people', was both extremely hurtful and bizarre to say the least! How was my life's work, my entire proven track record, so readily cast aside and simply obliterated in a matter of days?

The process of trying to reason with these staff members now felt like feeding steak to a crocodile about to close its jaws on you – in the hope that it would become a vegetarian. By this time the suspended four, along with the 16 facilitators, were outside banging fiercely on the windows.

Our meeting ended when the black staff followed Lindiswa Mavavana out of the boardroom to join the other striking workers, who by now had fired up one another into a total frenzy. Since the gates were closed, our logistics co-ordinator, Baden Samuels, had to go out and unlock the gates to let them out. Suddenly the striking workers stormed through the gates and Baden ran for his life to lock himself in the student accommodation upstairs. The strikers yelled and banged on the front door, which luckily has a security gate. Frenzied beyond all reason, the striking workers would not listen and held us hostage, basically under siege inside the building, for about three terrifying, interminable hours. We made frantic calls to the South African Police Service to come to our rescue, to which they replied unashamedly that they were too afraid to do so! My coloured staff and I eventually escaped out the back of the building, tumbling into cars waiting to whisk us to safety.

In the interim, the ringleader was revelling in the sense of power he had over the staff, having been buoyed by other people on social media who encouraged him to pursue his attack. By now, he was totally out of control, having been ignited into an adrenalin-fuelled frenzy, and people had posted death threats to me on his Facebook page.

For the first time, I sensed that my life was truly in danger. Understandably, my family became increasingly distressed, and was particularly traumatised when a photo of me with my daughters was posted amidst the terrible tirade of racist, hate-infected postings. Many of the strikers had been to our home and some had in fact been to the wedding of my daughter Sarah to Keith, so the whole thing made no sense at all. The fact that they knew where we lived was more cause for concern. At one point, Keith, my son in law, commented that he'd heard me worrying about the kids and the future of Amy Foundation, but what about the security and safety of my family? This was understandably a wake-up call. Family members also started questioning whether there was a future for white and coloured people in South Africa, reasoning that if this could happen to someone like me, then anything was possible.

Did I begin to question my commitment to bringing about change in this country? No, but this betrayal and willingness to risk everything we had worked to achieve, made me very angry. How was it possible that certain people could so easily be brainwashed into actively undoing all the good and causing so much damage? The very future of the Amy Foundation hung tenuously in the balance. How did their commitment and passion to support an important cause so suddenly turn to hate?

Media causing more damage

The reader might well be wondering where the media were throughout this debacle. After things began to go wrong (just before the strike) we had informed the media that the Amy Foundation was having to downsize one of its centres owing to the poor economy. We believed that being proactive would get the media on our side, but we soon learned that they only want to publish controversial, inflammatory content that sells.

The ringleader was strategic and shrewd in making immediate personal contact with certain journalists who were clearly not interested in hearing our side of the story.

To our immense dismay, the media played a big role in fanning the flames of this seemingly unquenchable fire. Long-established newspapers like the *Cape Times, Cape Argus*, and community newspapers would happily publish detailed, exaggerated accounts of only the ringleader's side of the story, followed by a one-liner which simply said, 'Kevin Chaplin, MD of the Amy Foundation, refutes this.' When I objected, one of them printed my letter to the editor, but not on the front pages where they had featured all the negative articles. Michelle and I, along with a communications expert, Neeran Naidoo, were writing daily replies and sending the facts to all the media. Michelle arranged for me to be interviewed on many radio stations like Heart FM, Cape Talk, Smile FM, and Voice of the Cape. The response we got from listeners was uplifting and very positive, for they could hear that I was genuine and that our story made sense.

The ringleader continued posting the most horrendous things on Facebook, announcing on Sunday 18 November that the strike was continuing. Many of our other black facilitators, who had not joined the strike, told us that they had been threatened and were hiding in their shacks in fear.

Things went from bad to worse when the ringleader began to personally target me and my other five highly respected board members, who voluntarily, on an ongoing basis, give up so much of their time to assist us. It was cold comfort to know that I was not alone.

Helen Lieberman, the highly respected, much-loved founder of Ikamva Labantu, found us a mediator, but the court ruled at the first hearing that the CCMA had to take over the mediation process. Suzanne Ackerman put me in touch with Alan Winde, former Provincial Government MEC of Community Safety (currently serving as Premier of the Western Cape) to help address the safety issue at our building as well as that of my remaining staff, my family, and board members.

I laid a charge with the police against two staff members for threatening my life and for racially based hate speech. I also opened a case with the Equality Court against the ringleader for racial discrimination, hate speech, and harassment. The Equality Court hearing proved a disaster, as the judge ignored all the ringleader's lies and the damaging PR he had inflicted on our organisation, simply pronouncing that I should have understood where the ringleader was coming from due to our apartheid history. She was not even interested in the fact that he had posted a picture of Hitler together with

CAN DO!

unacceptable wording a few days earlier. All she asked of him was to refrain from posting any more hate speech on social media. I wanted him to make a public apology and pay a fine to Amy Foundation, which he was not prepared to do, so we had to leave it at that.

Owing to the events that took place on Friday 16 November 2018 and the unlawful conduct of those employees, we had to close our Sybrand Park offices until we felt it was safe to return. The board and I decided to safeguard the lives of those employees who had been willing to perform their normal duties and to protect the property of the foundation. A huge thank you to Lee-Anne Singer and Leigh Morrison of the Singer Group and Luvuyo Mveleli of the Island Club Hotel in Century City, who were kind enough to give us access to a boardroom, every day, to use as temporary offices whilst this process took place. We also had no choice but to suspend the after-school programmes from 15 November instead of early December, when schools officially closed.

I have often been asked whether, after all this was over, I had lost the heart to continue running the project, and the answer is a definite 'no', as I knew these troublemakers were in the minority, and the success of our students kept me focused on the good we had achieved. Needless to say, the damage they caused the organisation was extremely worrying and frustrating.

On 23 November 2018 our case went to the Labour Court, but Judge Hilary Rabkin-Naicker would not rule, insisting that we first get mediation by the CCMA, which deals with labour disputes. If that failed, we would return to court on 21 December. What an overwhelming experience. I obviously insisted that our lawyers represent us at the CCMA, which then gave them the right to also have a lawyer, which was fair.

So racist was the ringleader himself, that he declined the CCMA's offer of a top lawyer, saying that he didn't want a white or coloured lawyer and would bring his own black lawyer!

Throughout this process, Deon Visagie and Joani van Vuuren from Webber Wentzel gave up so much of their time, giving us guidance and instructions and preparing papers. They proved to be a godsend – along with two advocates, Brenton Joseph and Veronique Bartus, who were appointed and readily came on board, offering their services pro bono as well. Thirty-nine hours later, the last day until 2 am, mediation had failed!

Just six hours later, these remarkable advocates began to prepare for court on 21 December. The new judge was President of the Labour Court, Bashier Wagley, who lambasted the striking workers. He also did not want to rule and insisted on mediation again. If that failed we would need to be in court on 31 January 2019, as the courts were going into recess. One more attempt would be made at mediation, but we were certain it would fail. We realised that the judges were trying to avoid ruling, because once they did so, all the striking workers would have to be dismissed.

The CCMA commissioners, who spent many exasperating hours with the striking workers, asked the advocate to advise me to be very careful, as they feared for my life. My family reacted to this very badly, imploring me to sell our home and move, but I was not prepared to hurriedly sell in a panic. The CCMA commissioners asked for permission to use our experience as a case study – to show that it is not always the employer who is at fault. As they pointed out, we had tried everything to reach a solution, but the striking workers' thinking was irrational.

The end of January seemed far away, and the next few weeks proved emotionally gruelling. Particularly vexing to me were the ongoing attacks on our board members, and in particular, our supportive chairperson, Rob Williams, who is an amazing businessman and humanitarian. Somehow, the ringleader found out that I was due to attend a conference in the UK at the end of November (with all flights and accommodation fully sponsored). Unbeknown to him, I had decided on the day of departure that it would not be appropriate for me to go abroad with this matter hanging in the balance, very much unresolved. Somehow, the ringleader found out the date and time of my flight and arranged for the entire striking group to block all the entrances to the airport. Once again, he was very proficient at

CAN DO!

getting the media to do his bidding, and the allegation was broadcast on national television and radio that Kevin Chaplin was leaving the country under suspicious circumstances!

My wife was furious when she heard this broadcast on radio news and she contacted the radio station to inform them that the report was not true: I was most definitely still in the country. When my chief operations officer, Afiefa Behardien, and I collected our computers to work offsite at the hotel, the ringleader saw no shame in informing the media that we had secretly stolen all the computers in the night! I was appalled to see this lie widely publicised without anyone bothering to check the facts.

The ringleader even went to Albert Fritz, then Western Cape Provincial Minister of Social Development, to allege corruption and maladministration at the Amy Foundation. Without bothering to check the facts, Albert Fritz stupidly confirmed to the media that this appeared to be the case, and he would seek to formally investigate. Naturally, this was like handing ice cream to a toddler, for they lapped it up. Donors by now were understandably concerned and confused. Despite our explanations, quite a few contacted me to say they would have to withdraw their funding. This was devastating to say the least. Many stood by us, but the damage inflicted by withdrawal of funding was far-reaching.

Minister Fritz was considerably embarrassed when his department head pointed out that we had emerged squeaky clean from an annual external audit, along with a mid-year audit done as a matter of routine, by the Department of Social Development. Although we were able to then rectify this matter with the media, all the venomous Facebook shares and widely spread media allegations did us unimaginable harm – particularly as we're a non-governmental organisation that is funded by donor money.

Good work at risk

The sad reality is that it takes years to build trust and a good reputation, and only one bad report to lose it. Besides Facebook, reporters like

Melvin Charles, a reporter from Independent Media, have much to account for in this regard. Two interesting TED talks on this subject – one by Scott Galloway on how Amazon, Apple, Facebook, and Google manipulate our emotions, and another by Carole Cadwalladr on Facebook's role in Brexit and the threat to democracy – prove how dangerous the media, journalists, and social media can be.

Within a small space of time, we'd tumbled from the sky, losing about R3 million in support, which was understandable given the pall of negative publicity hovering over us (despite all the allegations being false). The organisation was already financially strapped, so this was a massive setback that we could ill afford.

The onslaught of death threats on Facebook was the worst. One evening, I was due to be on radio and Michelle sent me the latest Facebook post from someone in Daveyton saying, 'Don't worry. We will come and burn Kevin Chaplin to death – that is how we deal with people like him!' I felt ill when I read that and cancelled the radio interview until the next morning. Throughout this period, my board was concerned for my life, along with their reputations and careers. They believed that the ringleader was so radical he would stop at nothing until I'd been killed, my managers and board removed, and he'd taken control of the building. Horrific to say the least!

This is unfortunately the dark side of the post-apartheid era – a world in which innocent, proactive, patriotic South Africans – who are striving for the greater good – now find themselves. It is a world in which one gets caught up in a madness – where the mere allegation of racism (regardless of the facts) is an excuse to vent your anger, somehow offering a plausible reason to recruit your peers for mayhem and destruction, regardless of the consequences. In most cases, it serves the personal agenda of a select few, as opposed to that of the majority, or the greater good. This is part of a raging, collective anger that has become contagious, often socially acceptable, and infinitely destructive. Usually, there are no winners, only losers, and the price to pay is inevitably heartbreaking.

The board insisted that we close down the foundation: it's fair to say that never before in my life had I felt so challenged, bewildered, and uncertain of what to do. I was torn between agreeing with them yet not wanting to give up everything we had fought so long and hard to achieve. 'Should we close down or continue?' This became a never-ending question looping over and over in my mind, like an irritating song that's stuck in your head. My whole life seemed to be in disarray. I spent many sleepless nights tossing and turning, but it was ultimately faith and prayer that helped me as I searched for an answer.

Most friends were adamant that I was crazy to keep the foundation going, stating that it wasn't worth the risk to my life and those of my family. While my family members were very supportive, they were terrified, and agreed with the board that Amy Foundation should be closed down. I cannot begin to tell the reader how difficult it is to ignore all the messages that come from the people who love you most!

Uplifting messages

During this tumultuous period many people sent messages of support, and many supported me by sharing their own similar stories. Malcolm Westmore, owner and founder of Westcor, one of the biggest suppliers of sunglasses, reading glasses, and costume jewellery to the retail market in South Africa, helped by praying for me. He also shared the major industrial action he had experienced a few years back, which had also come like a bolt of lightning from the blue. Jeff Rosenberg, GM of Southern Sun Waterfront in Cape Town, called to tell me of the terrible experiences he had when his workforce went on strike. Raymond Ackerman took me back to the ordeal he experienced when his staff at Pick n Pay went on strike some years ago. Michael Tollman, CEO of Cullinan Holdings (South Africa's leading travel services group, comprising 25 travel-related businesses, and part of the global travel and leisure group The Travel Corporation), called to lend support by sharing how the media had spread lies about their new acquisition in Africa. He gave me much valuable advice on how to deal with things. Rhoda Kadalie, mentioned earlier, recollected the awful experience her father went through in the township when he built an orphanage.

As human beings who are living and thriving as part of a community, we are inherently wired to seek comfort and reassurance in knowing that we are not alone.

Shay O'Brien, highly successful businessman and a director of Bray Capital, was most generous in offering to pay for a personal bodyguard as well as security at my home and at the Amy Foundation centre – none of which I took up – but it was nevertheless reassuring to know that the offer was there. Many discussions were held in the early morning walks I took with Andrew Jennings, former MD of Woolworths, during January 2019. He believed that I was faced with a dilemma, where both options had equally undesirable outcomes: 'If you close he will try to kill you, if you downsize and continue he will still try to kill you.' Quite disconcerting, but that did put matters into perspective in assisting me to make a decision!

Brett and Miranda Tollman, on a fleeting visit to Cape Town, spent a morning talking with me and committed their wholehearted support and friendship to me and the Amy Foundation.

Philip Krawitz, executive chairman of the Cape Union Mart Group and my long-time mentor, shared some very valuable insights with me: Use every negative incident to strengthen yourself. He used Rachel in the Bible as an example: she didn't live 120 good years but 120 years for good. So important.

There are three great lessons in life from the Jewish Talmud:

1. Who is wise? The one who is wise is the one who learns from others.
2. Who is honourable? The one who is honourable is the one who honours others.
3. Who is rich? The one who is rich is the one who is satisfied with his portion.

Still firm in my faith, I knew that God wouldn't bring us this far, only to bring it all to nought. This was reinforced in a sympathetic and

CAN DO!

encouraging SMS I received from my long-standing friend, Archbishop Desmond Tutu.

An email from Nita Luis, the founder and owner of Brights Hardware Stores, was really heartwarming and I have read it many times. I cannot share all the messages I received but I will do so with this one.

'Dear Kevin, This is sad and concerning news and I don't have words to console. But this I know that God is the ultimate judge and avenger. He sees and knows everything. He is Alpha and Omega – the beginning and the end of everything. Our function is to stand firm in faith and trust that He will come through no matter how bad it looks now. He takes us through the storms. We walk by faith and not by what our eyes see or what we feel. The battle is not with flesh and blood but the battle is against spiritual principalities and powers and rulers of darkness of this age, against spiritual hosts of wickedness in heavenly places (Ephesians 5:12). Evil always attacks the purposes of God and God's purpose is for the good of His creation to glorify Him. His purpose will never fail.

'Let's pray: Abba Father, you are the God of all creation, worthy of all praise and worship and thanksgiving and you know Kevin by name. All the good in him has come from You and is You in him. Oh Holy Spirit, you are our Comforter and our Helper. Please comfort Kevin and give him peace in the storm. Replace the sadness with joy in You. The joy of the Lord is his strength. Help him to stay focused on Jesus, the author and finisher of our faith. Help him to surrender all to Jesus so that the Lord can fight the battles for him. Give him Godly wisdom to make solid decisions. Guard his heart against any offence and un-forgiveness. All things are possible with You. I pray, Holy Spirit that you speak to the hearts of all donors, and I cut off all negativity and lies spoken about Kevin and the Amy Foundation, and I take authority that everything that the enemy has stolen or attempted to destroy will be returned and restored double fold – in Jesus' Name.

'I also pray for [the ringleader] and others with him. You created them and love them too. I don't know the circumstances in their lives that have led to this situation but I do know that You are a merciful God, full of love and grace, and your faithfulness is forever. Please remove the hurts and bitterness, soften their hearts. I cut off every evil curse spoken over their lives, every thought, word and deed of rejection spoken over them. Please draw them to you. Thank You that You always hear my prayers. Your Name be exalted and praised to the Glory of God. Amen.

'This too will pass. I look forward to seeing God at work! Regards and God's blessings, Nita.'

Hilton Saven, former chairman of Mazars, currently of Truworths International and Lewis Group, and board member of various companies, has always been a great support to me. He told me to hang in there as the truth will always prevail. It was Roy Fine, prominent businessman, entrepreneur and president of the Cape Town Progressive Jewish Congregation, who shared with me that problems are opportunities. Problems enable us to grow and change. The outcome can be better than before. Little did I realise that this was to prove true.

Moving forward

I again asked myself this question: Why should one individual who is misguided and destructive, cause something so good to close down – to the detriment of the lives and futures of the many children and youth who depended on us? So, in early January 2019 I called my management team together (who thought they were going to be retrenched) to tell them I had decided we must not close down and that I was determined to continue. Fortunately, the management team were in agreement and the board agreed to support my decision. So, it was with determination (and a little trepidation) that we re-opened the offices in January, having decided that big is not always best and downsizing would mean we could be more focused and have a greater impact. Due to the damage that resulted in loss of funding, we would rebuild, but downsize accordingly. Our vision, mission, goals and objectives would remain, but we would shift our focus.

CAN DO!

Instead of the ratio being 70 per cent 'after-school programmes' (which had seen such a steady decline in funding over the years) and 30 per cent 'youth skills development' (which funders preferred) we would now swing this ratio around. In response to the current 27 per cent unemployment rate and 55 per cent youth unemployment rate in South Africa, we would now run three after-school centres for schoolgoers instead of five centres and increase the numbers in youth skills development and training for 18- to 35-year-olds. As funding permitted, we would introduce vocational training for Grades 10 to 12, which we had always wanted, but for which we had never had the capacity.

Emboldened with a new lease on life, a 24-hour security guard and dog at the centre and other robust security measures, my management team and I got going again. As scheduled, the court hearing took place on 31 January 2019, presided over by Madam Justice Nkuta-Nkontwana, who was excellent. After listening to Advocate Brenton Joseph, who presented our case for many hours, she ruled that this was clearly an unlawful and unprotected strike and stated that the employer must deal with the employees accordingly. As if the giant balloon that had kept them afloat had been popped, all the air and bravado seemed to suddenly burst from the striking workers. They were visibly shocked at this dramatic turn of events, especially since they had followed the ringleader so blindly, only to find that all his promises had come to nought.

In terms of labour law, the next step involved holding individual disciplinary enquires with an external and independent chairperson. Thanks to guidance from Joani van Vuuren at Webber Wentzel, this process was duly completed by the end of April 2019.

Much as I had expected, their spineless ringleader suddenly disappeared off the radar with no concern for the rest of the group who had now lost their source of income. Some of the striking workers came rather sheepishly to apologise, pleading for their jobs back, but unfortunately this was not possible. The trust relationship had been irreparably broken. Although I felt a deep sense of disappointment that long-standing, valued members of staff had so readily turned on me and my management team and were now losing their jobs with a resulting impact on their families, there are consequences in life to your actions. You therefore need to make choices based on an understanding of the risks, and your willingness to accept the consequences. Everything about the way in which these rebels conducted themselves and the damage they caused was totally unacceptable.

Sadly, when the chairperson of the disciplinary enquiries asked one of them whether he actually believed what the ringleader had said about me, he replied, 'Absolutely not, I have worked with Kevin a long time.' When the chairperson asked him why he went along with the ringleader, he shrugged his shoulders dejectedly, completely unable to provide an answer.

Before Easy Nofemela's disciplinary enquiry, he tried to convince me that all this had happened because of my coloured managers Michelle and Afiefa, and that we should talk to work things out. Besides this being a ludicrous notion, the time for talking had long since passed. Others tried to justify their actions on the basis that they had been intimidated, to which we replied: 'The others hid away and didn't participate, and you had the option to do this, but chose to come out and strike, often behaving aggressively, waving placards, knowing full well that you were causing untold damage to the foundation.'

Thanks must go to Joanna Barry, our HR Manager and Warren Johannes, HR Officer, for their important role in undergoing many long hours of preparation to present the foundation's side in over 20 disciplinary enquiries.

The striking full-time staff members were duly dismissed, and the part-time facilitators could never work for us again. Some of my team held the view that it was still too dangerous for us to re-open in a black township, but I felt that we could not hold back. After a meeting with the headmistress and deputy head of Siyazingisa school in Gugulethu – during which they pleaded with us to re-open the after-school care centre, saying that the community was devastated that the

CAN DO!

children were losing out on the excellent impact of Amy Foundation – we resolved to re-open in April 2019, having already re-opened the Bontehuwel centre.

The non-striking workers were able to apply for the positions that had now become available, which enabled us to take back some of the best facilitators, such as Yonda Banjwa, Sanele Noji, Tony Mhayi and others. We set our sights on reconfiguring and re-building our infrastructure, along with the equally important task of wooing back our donors. By the middle of 2019, we were very pleased to be back in full swing, with double our previous intake of numbers in youth skills development, along with this, our Bonteheuwel and Gugulethu centres back in full operation and a greater focus on quality. We're now forging ahead to make a difference where it's so badly needed, changing lives.

I'm especially pleased that our experience has been an inspiration to others. Rhoda Kadalie wrote, 'Wow, Kevin you are indefatigable. I would have given up long ago. Respect! You've been through a lot, and still continue. Amazing!'

This expresses, in a nutshell, the contents of many similar messages from people around the world who have remained unfailingly supportive as donors, mentors and friends, with some adding the sentiment that they would have long since run a mile.

So what stopped me from running a mile?

The role of good leadership requires a strong sense of responsibility, and an appreciation of the onerous duty one has to overcome adversity. As I've said throughout this memoir, one should never give up when faced with seemingly insurmountable challenges. I believe that God puts us all on earth for a purpose. I want to inspire others and try to shine for God, to let others see God through me – even though I fail dismally many times.

In the Bible, Matthew Chapter 5 verses 14 and 16, Jesus said: 'You are the light of the world. Let your light so shine before men that they may see your good works and glorify your Father in heaven.'

Knowing that there was so much that needed to be done, I was determined to prevent something as important to this country as the Amy Foundation from falling prey to racial hatred and being discontinued. I truly believe that this was God's way of making the foundation smaller and less stressful for me to manage, whilst ensuring that we could make an even bigger impact and be more focused. Good will always overcome evil. Romans 12 verse 21 says: 'Do not be overcome by evil but overcome evil with good.' Proverbs 24 verses 19 and 20 say: 'Do not fret because of evildoers nor be envious of the wicked, for there will be no prospect for the evil man, the lamp of the wicked will be put out.'

20 IMPORTANT LESSONS FROM THIS EXPERIENCE:

1. Never underestimate the damage that one or two bad apples can cause, but know that they do not necessarily represent the majority.
2. Never be arrogant or complacent enough to assume that everything you've worked for is indestructible. However, with the right mindset, a problematic situation can be turned around.
3. Remember that people can easily be brainwashed by a charismatic leader, against everything they know to be true, and everything their heart is telling them.
4. Bear in mind that the media will always chase a story that sells, often at the cost of fair, balanced reporting, and factual accuracy.
5. Keep all your accounts and books in order, with honesty, transparency, and accountability remaining paramount to your business ethic.
6. With the correct support structure in place, you can stare adversity in the face and handle all the challenges that may come your way. It helps to share the burden.
7. Faith and prayer will hold your hand and see you through difficult times.
8. Surround yourself with strong, clear-thinking, courageous people who will build you up and support you through both good times and bad times.

9. Ensure that your management team and your board are always fully behind you. Collectively work towards a common goal.

10. Listen to the opinions of others, but then be confident enough to weigh up the facts and make your own intuitive decisions.

11. Don't beat yourself up when things go wrong that were never your fault in the first place. Instead, believe in yourself and the fact that your integrity will prevail. Truth is one, paths are many — Mahatma Gandhi.

12. Don't feel guilty if certain decisions don't benefit everyone or make everyone happy. It's not possible to please all the people, all the time.

13. There are always consequences to our actions.

14. Trust in your colleagues is paramount during a crisis, but remember that sometimes trust can be broken. A crisis will reveal very quickly who you can trust.

15. Even when you think all is lost, it's possible to win people back and rebuild.

16. Find your own coping mechanisms, make time to relax, reflect, and learn.

17. Exercise is invaluable in coping with stress.

18. Don't give up hope, be tenacious enough to get back on your feet.

19. Have the courage of your convictions. The only thing necessary for the triumph of evil is for good men and women to do nothing.

20. Not all storms come to disrupt your life, as some come to clear your path. Try to look for the positive in terms of the ultimate outcome.

As the old song goes, this was my turn to 'take a deep breath, pick yourself up, dust yourself off, and start all over again'. ■

22

Ukuhamba kukubona –
Travel opens a window to the world

My trip to Israel, life on the Dead Sea.

CAN DO! ✓

My love for travel dates back to the early 1980s, when I decided that it was time to broaden my perspective on the world, since I had led a very sheltered life growing up in South Africa. In 1984, after painstakingly saving up my earnings, I embarked on my first overseas trip, together with three lifelong friends – Lance and Paul Mindry, and Ronald Basel (my next-door neighbour since birth). We decided that the cheapest way to 'see the world' would be to drive through Europe in a hired camper van. It was a momentous day for us all, with many family members and friends coming to see us off on what would become an epic adventure, and a venture into the vast unknown.

Amsterdam and Austria

So naive were we when we reached Amsterdam that we had no idea what to expect. One day, we parked our van, only to find out that we were in the heart of the red-light district when we returned to it that night. As we meandered through the streets, our eyes nearly popped out of our heads at the flagrant, brazen sexuality – especially since we'd all been reared in fairly conservative homes. The fun and frivolity continued when we went skiing in Austria, however the journey proved challenging, to say the least. As I was not used to driving on snow, tensions were obviously high, and Paul lashed out at me when I skidded our camper van on a curve. After recovering from those terrifying moments, we went on to have the best of fun for six weeks, especially during the Oktoberfest in München, Germany! These are the ups and downs of travel that one somehow never forgets!

Israel

Two years later, we were again struck by wanderlust, so Paul and I decided to do all the things we had neither time nor money for on our previous visit. Our friend Tim joined us for part of the trip. This meant having to take long leave from the bank. In those days, the rand was on parity with the dollar (scary to think that it is now R14 to $1 on 09:09:19), which meant that we were able to backpack on the cheap, sleeping in hostels and eating very simply.

While relishing the sights of Greece, breaking plates to the strains of Zorba the Greek, island hopping and sleeping on a beach on the island of Crete, we bumped into a few people who had just visited Israel and raved about it. Besides our ignorance in not knowing what a great country it would be to visit, we didn't even realise that Israel was a relatively short boat trip away. So, with our money rapidly running out, we decided to visit Israel. Having heard about the kibbutz system being a utopian, socialistic, farming collective, we decided that the experience would be fun and inexpensive. It's fair to say that my time on kibbutz Hulda, located between Jerusalem and Tel Aviv, was life-changing. Interestingly, Kibbutz Hulda played an important role in the War of Independence. Since the village was at the easternmost point of Jewish communities, Hulda became a transit point of convoys to the besieged capital. In May 1948, Hulda was bombed by enemy aircraft, which caused the death of two members, and this led to the evacuation of all women and children to Tel Aviv for three months, to protect them and restore the kibbutz.

I was in awe of the alternative concept of working and eating together with the community and living a minimalistic, unmaterialistic lifestyle where everything is shared. I so enjoyed the warmth of the people, in particular our wonderful kibbutz volunteer mother Vicki Gidron. Picking grapes and onions all day was hard work, but we loved it, although I must add that I didn't enjoy the boring, laborious job of working in their little factory making small transformers! We particularly enjoyed meeting many other volunteers from all over the world. This was where I learned about a 'P' party (mentioned earlier) and ended up introducing this fancy dress concept wherever I worked in years to come. For this purpose, it's the best letter of the alphabet, since it offers the most options, and creates so much fun and laughter at an event, especially seeing who has been the most creative. Even the not-so-adventurous get to enjoy the event.

Weekends were perfect for exploring: on one memorable occasion Paul and I slept comfortably in the lifeguard tower positioned on the soft, warm, sandy beach in Eilat on the Red Sea! Not forgetting

CAN DO! ✓

our visits to the Dead Sea, Jerusalem, Tel Aviv and Masada. How wonderful to be so young and free of onerous responsibilities. After Israel, we returned to exploring the UK and Europe, this time skiing in Andorra, a tiny, independent principality situated between France and Spain in the Pyrenees mountains. At one point on our trip we travelled with two fun-loving Australians named Basil and Pago. I recall a night when we all thought we would 'score' with some attractive French girls – but no such luck! In hindsight, we stood as much chance as a novice gambler in a casino, for besides not having the faintest clue how to chat them up, they failed to understand our foreign sense of humour!

France

It is strange how the travel experiences that linger most vividly in one's memory are those where things went seriously wrong. One such recollection involves an overnight train ride we took in Europe with our two new Australian friends, having bought second-class Eurail Pass tickets. Upon boarding, we found that the second-class section was full, so we moved into the first-class section. When the conductor came around, he started shouting at us in French. We could not understand a word he was saying, nor could he make head or tail of our attempts to explain what had happened. Clearly, this was never going to be a two-way conversation!

Eventually, we found a spare compartment in second class, and moved across accordingly. In the middle of the night, the train suddenly stopped and several policemen leapt aboard, flashing their torches as they stormed through the train, their blue car lights whirring in the background. The next thing, we found ourselves being hauled off and taken to a nearby jail, where we spent the night – our emotions hovering between disbelief, confusion, fear, and laughter (the latter only for some of us)! We wondered how on earth we had ended up in this situation, and more importantly, how the hell we would get out of there – particularly since we were in a foreign country, with no local contacts to call for help. Despite making every effort to get some sort of explanation, no one would speak to us. However, at 02h00 the next morning, one policeman explained that we were accused of boarding the train with no tickets. We showed them our tickets, and they eventually let us out, but into the darkest, bleakest and iciest of nights. Shivering and huddling together in our bitterly cold sleeping bags, we lay like refrigerated tinned sardines on the station platform and spent a sleepless night waiting for dawn and the next train out. Tough as it was, this was one of many adventures that sparked my interest in travel. It was these early trips that ignited my passion for understanding people in the wider context of their backgrounds.

> **Seek every opportunity to become less insular and more experienced. Broaden your perspective through travel. It's a great way to explore and interact with the wider world.**

Cairo, Egypt.

CAN DO! ✓

Every year, for the past fifteen years, through my work, family holidays and EAICY (the European Association of Institutions of Non-formal Education of Children and Youth), I've been blessed to be able to travel to many interesting countries in Europe, as well as the US and UK. I'm mindful of the fact that if I'd stayed with the bank, it's highly unlikely that this would have been possible. Some of the most memorable, beautiful or interesting cities and areas I have had the privilege and pleasure to explore are Moscow, Dijon, Paris, Aix-en-Provence, Prague, Český Krumlov, Munich, Vilnius, Riga, Kraków, Bratislava, Tbilisi, Lviv, Rivne, Kiev, Brussels, Antwerp, Bruges, Amsterdam, Hilvarenbeek, Vienna, Salzburg, Turin, Florence, Rome, Assisi, the Amalfi Coast and its little towns, Pompei, Palermo, Dubrovnik, Venice, Madrid, Granada, Malaga, Zurich, Geneva, Cairo, Corfu, Athens, Los Cristianos, Astana, London, Berkshire, Surrey, York, the Costwolds, Belfast and various surrounding towns, New York, Los Angeles, Orlando and Miami. ■

23

EAICY board adventures

Moscow, Russia.

CAN DO! ✓

After leaving the bank in 2006, I became better known for my work as a motivational speaker. After I did a talk for Tias Nimbas Business School at the University of Tilburg in the Netherlands, René Clarijs of Hilvarenbeek approached me about a European organisation for children and youth. When René invited me to make a presentation at one of the presidium (board) meetings of EAICY (European Association of Institutions of Non-Formal Education of Children and Youth) in the Ukraine in 2010, I jumped at this opportunity. I was most impressed with the organisation, which organises activities throughout Europe, essentially focusing on children and youth-related issues and the importance and relevance of non-formal education. It was so exciting to learn of their existence, given the enormous synergy between their work and my own goals back home in South Africa. Every country is entitled to have one representative on the presidium, with the exception of Russia, which has two. The policy is that one member from each European country represents the association in his or her country, but it was subsequently decided to open up presidium membership to one non-European member – a position for which I was nominated by René, seconded, and approved by the rest of the members. Naturally, I didn't hesitate to accept this prestigious nomination in 2011, which opened up a whole new world for me, and what a phenomenal experience it has been!

EAICY holds two presidium meetings a year, in different European countries, with the general assembly (AGM) being held in Prague or Vilnius, every second year. Let me share some of the more interesting anecdotes and significant memories of my EAICY travels which come to mind.

Kiev, Ukraine

In 2012, I needed a visa for the Ukraine, for which I submitted an application in good time, at least 15 days before my intended date of departure, as stated in the rules. The purpose of my visit was to attend the presidium meeting of the EAICY. According to the Ukraine Consulate regulations, if your application is submitted in under five days, one must apply for an urgent visa. Five days before, I still had not received the visa, and called the embassy. I was blithely informed that I would have to pay R1 700 for a special visa. I replied that this was unreasonable, given that the cost of a normal visa was R700. Undeterred, the embassy official insisted that I had to apply for a special visa. When I explained that I had applied within the given 15-day period, he eventually agreed to process it immediately if I paid the R700, which I duly did. After two days of hearing nothing I phoned the Ukraine Embassy, which once again tried to elicit R1 700 from me, insisting that there was no other way to do it. I reminded him that he had spoken to me two days earlier, when he had told me all that was required was the R700. 'Ah, I speak to many people,' he retorted. I explained that I was representing South Africa and it was important that I get there as planned, within budget. He retorted rather irritably, 'Then collect it in five minutes.' (In reality, that's all the time that such a visa should actually take to process!)

My next problem was how the hell to collect it from Pretoria 'in five minutes'! I was supposed to fly on the Sunday of that week, and this was the Thursday afternoon. I phoned Jan Mutton, the Belgian Ambassador in Pretoria, to ask whether he could perhaps collect it on my behalf. My heart sank when he told me that he was undergoing surgery the following morning. He then phoned the Ukraine Embassy and arranged for the visa to be collected on Friday morning. We contacted DHL, who duly collected it, but said they could only deliver it on Monday, which would have been too late. A phone call later to Steve Burd, the CEO of DHL (who had helped me when I first took over Amy Biehl Foundation), and he stepped in to facilitate, enabling me to collect the visa at the airport on Saturday morning. It's fair to say that no one was more astounded than I, to find myself lifting off the runway in good time, on the Sunday, thanks to Jan Mutton, Steve Burd, and DHL!

> **Never stop pursuing something you've set your mind to:**
> **give it your all, without breaking any rules or being rude.**
> **THERE IS ALWAYS A WAY.**

CAN DO!

Dijon, France

My French counterpart on the presidium of EAICY, Jean Francois Magnin, introduced me to his organisation called CEMEA, which trains pedagogues (teachers) in Europe. This started a partnership which has seen them send six volunteers annually from Dijon in the Province of Burgundy to Amy Foundation for six months. In turn, we sent three of our youth annually to them – until CEMEA Burgundy's financial situation changed in 2017 and the exchange could not continue in 2018 or 2019. Whilst it was sad it had to cease, agreement has been reached to recommence in 2020. The exchange has changed the lives of many South African youth. Just some of the beneficiaries of this exchange programme from Amy Foundation were Akhona, Sibusiso and Phelisa, mentioned earlier.

Cairo, Egypt

In June 2013 the province of Burgundy in France kindly sponsored me and Ayanda Mazwi, an Amy Foundation co-ordinator, to visit Dijon for a week to workshop with CEMEA. When we got the tickets, I noticed that they had booked us to fly via Egypt. I called the travel agent to request a much later connecting flight from Egypt to France, to enable me to explore Cairo, which they managed to do. With only a few days to go before our departure, it was brought to my attention that in order to do this, I would need a visa to leave the airport in Cairo. Everyone I spoke to said that it would be impossible to arrange this at such short notice, but believing that 'where there is a will, there is a way', or as my Grandpa Tram always said, 'Never say die, get up and try,' I nevertheless made the journey, determined to find a way to exit the airport and visit the pyramids. When we arrived in Egypt, I was not surprised to be told that they would not let us exit the airport.

> Stay focused on the vision, if the vision is inspired from within. Start with what you know, and let what you know grow. Read this every day and refine it.
>
> DR JOHN DE MARTINI

Undeterred, I begged the relevant official (or should I say, grovelled!). I guess he took pity on me, for he finally acquiesced, saying, 'OK – just six hours.' We went on to spend the day exploring the pyramids, which are steeped in thousands of years of fascinating archaeological history, and even squeezed in a boat trip on the Nile!

Moscow, Russia

Moscow is undoubtedly one of the most fascinating places I've visited. I had the privilege of visiting the city no less than three times as part of EAICY. Elena Abramova, a most elegant and special lady, is the Director of the Na Sumskom, Russian Palace of Children and Youth – and the perfect host. There is so much to see and experience and the people are wonderful, creative, and fun. On one such visit, our hosts played a prank on us while the EAICY presidium was seated around the table. We were all taken aback and somewhat mystified when several

We are here to check your brain is functioning.

CAN DO! ✓

people, all posing as doctors, walked in and pretended to listen to our heartbeats and take our blood pressures. This set the tone for a very creative and fun experience during the next few days.

Elena Abramova and Kevin.

In 2012, Elena Abramova, Valdas Jankauskas, Lithuanian; and Irena Maskalonoka, Latvian; all three presidium members, visited South Africa for the first time, each bringing two team members with them. Thereafter they paid for me to take eight of the Amy Foundation team, Ntobeko and myself to visit all three countries, and what a trip that was. In 2015 and 2016 Elena brought 15 teenage dancers and four other team members to South Africa to participate in the Ubuntu Festival and to run workshops with the Amy Foundation children. In return, they have requested that I take 15 girls to Moscow, which promises to be a phenomenal experience for the selected participants. However, this will only be possible once we have managed to raise the money for the airfares and visas. Elena has generously undertaken to cover all the other expenses.

Tbilisi, Georgia

On one of my early EAICY trips, I went to Tbilisi in Georgia, a small gem of a country located between Europe and Asia – technically Eurasia. Its people describe it in a charming way: the balcony of Europe. Indeed, wherever you go, it overlooks panoramas of stunning countryside. Upon arrival, I found myself embroiled in some sort of scuffle with the media, some of whom were attempting to film or take photos of us. As if we were paparazzi, flashbulbs popped incessantly, while TV crews jostled for position to get closer

Valdas Jankauskas, Lithuania; Kevin Chaplin, South Africa; René Clarijs, Netherlands; Stefano Vitale, Italy; Irena Maskalonoka, Latvia; Monika Stachnik-Czapla, Poland; Michaela Tuzilova, Czech Republic.

to our group. It did not take long for an underlying sense of panic to set in, since we were followed back to our hotel, and found ourselves having to scuttle down side streets to escape the onslaught of crazed photographers. I was shocked to realise that it was *me* they were after, and naturally perplexed as to what I could possibly have done to attract this type of attention. In a matter of moments, my simple expedition had turned into a nail-biting adventure! Surrounded by TV crews who only spoke Georgian, I had absolutely no idea why they wanted to interview me. To my astonishment, I later learned that they had seen the list of invited guests, and assumed that I was a relative of Charlie Chaplin! For some reason, he's extremely popular there, and believing that I was a close relative, I was asked to unveil a statue of him, amidst much fanfare and fuss. Later, I was even interviewed on national television, but at that stage it was way too late and embarrassing to clarify the matter, or to cause such terrible disappointment! The Georgian director who organised the conference couldn't stop laughing when I explained who I really was. I suspect that the real Charlie Chaplin would have been delighted by this effusive groundswell of latter-day fans. He was most likely joining us for a good laugh in spirit!

CAN DO! ✓

SOME OF CHARLIE CHAPLIN'S FAMOUS SAYINGS HOLD MUCH WISDOM

Nothing is permanent in this world, not even your troubles.

The most wasted day in life is the day in which we have not laughed. Keep smiling.

Enjoy some ice cream, chocolates, and cake. Why? Because 'stressed' spelled backwards spells 'desserts'. One food friend is equal to one good medicine.

The six best doctors in the world are sunlight, rest, exercise, diet, self confidence, and friends.

If you see the moon you see the beauty of God. If you see the sun you see the power of God, and if you see the mirror you see the best creation of God. So believe in yourself.

We are all tourists and God is our travel agent, who has already fixed all our routes, reservations, and destinations – so trust God and enjoy the trip called life. Life will never come again – live today.

Kevin unveiling the Charlie Chaplin statue in Tbilisi, Georgia.

Making the impossible possible

In May 2016 I had the opportunity to return to Tlibisi with EAICY. Yet again, I had great fun posing for another set of pictures at the statue – this time, for a new contingent of students at the Youth Centre. I was so taken with the area on my previous visit that I decided to add three days onto my trip to explore the countryside with my colleagues Monika Stachnik-Czapla and Irena Maskalonoka from Poland and Latvia. Georgia is a very poor country, which remains largely undeveloped, but its incredible scenery enhanced my appreciation of nature and the remarkable influence warm-hearted people can have on one's soul. Travelling south, I found myself at the St David Gareji Monastry, which houses a few monks still living there today.

It was a powerful experience to walk down into the bowels of the monastery, into a little church, which houses a massive painting depicting the slaying of the 6 000 martyrs of the St David Gareji Monastery in 1616. When Persian Shah Abbas 1 invaded Georgia, his enormous army found 6 000 monks in the Gare Valley. They were told that if they denounced their Christianity and converted to Islam, they would not be beheaded. How sad I was to learn that all 6 000 brothers in Christ were massacred without mercy. To pay such a heavy price is an extraordinary commitment to one's faith!

St David Gareji Monastery in Georgia.

CAN DO! ✓

A one kilometre daily walk to her life-sustaining potato patch and graves of her husband and son.

The following day, we decided to take advantage of the beautiful weather and hike up to a little church located far above in the soaring mountains. While some people opted to go on horseback, the walk took my Polish colleague and me about three hours. On the way up, I found a stooped old lady, visibly burdened by the weight of a rake and broom as she painstakingly slogged her way to the gravesides of her husband and son – and her life-sustaining potato patch – more than a kilometre uphill.

Although unable to communicate linguistically, we were astonished to establish that she went through this painstaking ordeal, day after day. It never ceases to amaze me how the unlikeliest of people seem to cope with adversity with such

The monks rooms and courtyard inside the monastery.

bravery and fortitude. In fact, it took much persuasion (in the form of improvised sign language) before she allowed me to relieve her of this weighty load! 'If only I could help her like this every day,' I thought. I could not help comparing her dignified, seemingly contented composure with people who complain about having to walk or even drive a few kilometres to the shops in Cape Town – which felt like a lifetime away! As I reached the pinnacle of the mountain, the joy of drinking the pure, crystal-clear elixir of life, not to mention the panoramic view before us, proved an awe inspiring, transcendent experience.

Vilnius, Lithuania

Despite 2016 and 2017 being busy years of travel, I could not resist accepting an invitation to attend the final presidium meeting of the year early in November 2016 in Vilnius, Lithuania (situated in the heart of Europe). While it is a beautiful city to explore, Vilnius carries the scars of a tragic history steeped in genocide. Many are the museums and memorials depicting places where hundreds of thousands of Lithuanians were brutally tortured and murdered, either by the Soviets, or Nazi Germany. This included a large share of the Vilnius Jewish community during World War II. (In 1931 Jews made up 27.8 per cent of Vilnius inhabitants and the city was nicknamed the Jerusalem of the North.) I was horrified to learn that before World War II there were 100 synagogues in Vilnius, but such was the loss of life and devastation, that the one I visited in 2016 was the only surviving shul. Interestingly, many of the Lithuanians who managed to escape made their way to South Africa, and today a major portion of South African Jews can trace their heritage back to Lithuania.

Occasionally, one has to make tough choices. It wasn't easy for me to go to Lithuania in early November 2016, as Sarah, then 25, was to get married on 26 November, but being such an organised young lady, all the arrangements were already made and I returned two weeks before the big day. Robyn and I feel so blessed that she chose a man of Keith Watkins' calibre and character to be her husband and partner for life.

CAN DO!

Left to right: Kirsty, Sarah, Kevin, Robyn and new son-in-law Keith.

Istanbul, Turkey

In May 2016, on my way to the EAICY presidium meeting in Georgia, I stopped off in Istanbul. I flew Turkish Airlines: Not only would the flights be cheaper, but I could also take a free tour in Istanbul, so I jumped at this opportunity. As I sat down to lunch, a stranger, who introduced himself as Mohamed Bashar Arafat, asked if he could sit opposite me, in the only vacant chair left in the restaurant. We immediately struck up a conversation, and he asked me what I did. When I told him about the SA Ubuntu Foundation and my work at Amy Foundation, a warm, animated smile crossed his face as he replied, 'God clearly had a plan today, for he sent me to sit opposite you – and as we can see, this was the only chair available! I am an imam in Washington DC, US, originally from Syria, now appointed by the US government as an emissary to travel the world, with the primary objective of breaking down barriers to encourage Jews, Christians, and Muslims to embrace one another – despite our religious differences. This is exactly what your mission is!' My hair stood on end as we looked at one another, saying, virtually simultaneously, 'This is absolutely unbelievable! We need to work together!'

What are the odds of such a staggering coincidence occurring? Again, it was a reminder of the remarkable way that God creates opportunities. It just blew me away! How amazing that we not only found one another, but immediately struck up a connection and found commonality of such strategic relevance and importance to our purpose. There and then, we both agreed to seize the opportunity to maximise on this serendipitous occurrence. I've always maintained that when you are well poised and ready for something, God will open the door to help you reach it. Furthermore, nothing happens by accident, since God has a plan and everything happens for a reason.

When I returned from this trip, I sent him a follow-up email, but was disappointed not to hear back from him for quite some time. Undaunted, I followed up a few weeks later – like I always do when I fail to get a response initially. (As an aside, it's always advisable to do this, as there is often a personal or perhaps technical reason for the lack of a much-wanted response.) Yet again, no response. Seven weeks later, however, I was delighted to receive the following WhatsApp from him:

Dear Kevin, Salaam and good evening from Baltimore, Maryland. Do not ever think that I've forgotten about you. You were in my heart because I felt that almighty Allah made me sit next to you in Istanbul, for a reason that we will all know about. I have sent you an email and look forward to your kind reply. My Ramadan and the weeks since I met you in mid-May were extremely hectic. Forgive me for not coming back to you. I've always been fascinated with your story, and I shared it with my entire team for the up-coming conference we are planning to hold in July, 2016. Even if we were out of touch physically, we were not spiritually.

This warm exchange resulted in him inviting me to talk at a Leadership, Intercultural and Interfaith Conference being held in

Kyrgyzstan under the auspices of the Civilizations Exchange and Cooperation Foundation, of which Imam Bashar Arafat is the president and founder. The theme of the five-day conference was '2016 – Better understanding for a better world (BUBW) – Promoting Peace and Prosperity through Understanding in Central Asia.'

Unfortunately, since I had travelled extensively at the time, and only recently returned from Los Angeles (kindly sponsored by Delta Air Lines), I was not able to address the delegates in person, so they arranged for me to speak virtually via Skype. What a wonderful opportunity to share the powerful message of Ubuntu with over 100 delegates hailing from countries all over the world! I believe this was the start of what promises to be an ongoing collaboration. For some time, God has been using the imam to liaise with government officials in Europe, with the objective of finding ways to handle the refugee crisis.

Prague, Czech Republic

As mentioned earlier, every second year an EAICY presidium meeting is held in Prague, thanks to our delightful host, Michaela Tužilová. This has afforded me unique opportunities to explore this exquisite part of Eastern Europe. The beautiful city of Prague is the capital of the Czech Republic – formerly known as Czechoslovakia. It was one of the only cities in Europe to be spared an onslaught by the Nazi Wehrmacht, as opposed to many others that were bombed to rubble during WWII. Ironically, it was bombed accidentally towards the end of the war by US Air Force pilots, owing to a navigation error! While exploring the streets of Prague, I took some great photos of this fascinating city, which is particularly famous for its mix of Romanesque, Baroque, Rococo, Renaissance, and modern architecture. I strolled across the famous Charles Bridge, lined with statues of saints, which is one of the oldest (due to most of the others being bombed in WWII) and most beautiful bridges in Europe. Having walked for hours, I found it particularly interesting to explore the old Jewish Cemetery. It was most meaningful to chat to the locals, who shared stories about the country and its culture. One can only imagine what destruction of those buildings and their inhabitants would have meant. What a bitter price would have been paid for discrimination as a means to domination!

Bratislava, Slovakia

With its old town, cobbled streets, and beautiful castle, this city is definitely worth a visit. Slovakia is a country on its own now, which I also had the privilege of visiting whilst attending a presidium meeting. It is bordered by Poland to the north, Ukraine to the east, the Czech Republic to the west and Hungary to the south.

Riga, Latvia

I particularly enjoyed Riga's Art Nouveau architecture, also known as Jugendstil, friendly people, beautiful old town, and lovely cuisine. Thanks to the perfect host, Irena Maskalonoka, and her youth centre, Annas 2.

Torino, Italy

With my great-grandfather Valentino Tramontino coming from Udine in Northern Italy, I was delighted when Stefano Vitale hosted a presidium in Turin (Torino). Such a vibrant city.

Auschwitz and Krakow, Poland

In 2013, a presidium meeting was held in Poland. When I looked at the map, I realised that Auschwitz was just 30 minutes away from Krakow. Given the historical importance of these concentration camps in terms of the Holocaust, Monika Stachnik-Czapla, our gracious Polish presidium member, kindly arranged that I stay an extra day to visit Krakow, Auschwitz, and Bergen-Belsen. Nothing could have prepared me for the horrors of this visit, which proved one of the most humbling and emotionally moving experiences of my life. Despite the eerie silence, I could almost hear the cries of insufferable hunger and despair of the countless people who lost their lives in those notorious death camps. This was made all the more real by the vivid photographs

CAN DO!

depicting starving people, the well-preserved bunks and the barracks, along with displays of innumerable personal belongings of victims – such as human hair, pitiful pairs of children's shoes, and hundreds of spectacles piled several metres high, each item representing the senseless murder of someone's beloved mother, father, child or siblings.

While most of us have heard about the Holocaust, I don't believe one can grasp the scale of the atrocities committed by the Nazis until one makes such a visit. Many messages emanate from this experience.

> **Everyone should seek to learn from the horrors inflicted by racial prejudice and senseless hatred. Humanity needs to be constantly reminded to never again plumb the depths of such brutality.**

An equally important message comes from the pen of Viktor Frankl, a famous psychiatrist who, together with his wife, was initially deported to the infamous Theresienstadt ghetto, and then to Auschwitz concentration camp in 1944, where he remained until the inmates were liberated in 1945. During this period, his mother, brother, and wife all perished in the Holocaust. Frankl chronicles his experiences as a concentration camp inmate, which led him to discover the importance of finding meaning in all forms of existence, even the most brutal ones, and thus, a reason to continue living. In his famous book, *Man's Search for Meaning*, Victor Frankl wrote the following:

> *Everything can be taken from a man but one thing, the last of the human freedoms: The way I choose to respond to what you do to me. The last of one's freedoms is to choose one's attitude in any given circumstance. When we are no longer able to change a situation, we are challenged to change ourselves.*

Eva Schloss – Holocaust survivor

It is quite amazing how one thing leads to another and another. When I was in Auschwitz, there were countless books for sale pertaining to the Holocaust. For reasons I cannot recall, I zeroed in on a particular autobiography called *Eva's Story: A Survivor's Tale*. I read it in 2015. It was written by Eva Schloss, who described what happened to her family after they fled the Nazis in Vienna and went into hiding in Amsterdam in 1938, where they were ultimately betrayed.

On 11 May 1944, Eva heard her father and brother being tortured in the next room. Next, two men attacked her, beating her with truncheons. She was just 15 years old when she was sent to Auschwitz – the same age as Anne Frank. Along with her mother, Eva endured and somehow survived the horrors of this death camp, which sadly robbed both her father and brother of their lives. In 1953, when Eva's mother Elfriede (known as Fritzi) married Anne Frank's father, Otto, the two girls' became stepsisters (albeit posthumously), and their names would be forever interlinked. The diary of Anne Frank, who died in Bergen-Belsen in 1945, continues to bring the Holocaust story to life for millions of readers around the world. But for Eva, it would take 40 years to tell her story.

A few years after my visit and purchase of the book, I received an invitation from the Cape Town Holocaust Centre, inviting me to a talk by Eva Schloss. I was most humbled, whilst at the same time excited, that this invitation also offered me a private session with this well-known survivor prior to the event. Never dreaming that I would ever get to meet her, let alone chat to her one-on-one, I was of course astounded by the extraordinary coincidence that hers was the very book I'd selected to purchase in Auschwitz! She wanted to know more about my work, and praised me for my contribution to 'balancing the scales' in this country. She duly signed my copy of her book. I also had the privilege of meeting another survivor on that day, Cape Town resident Miriam Lichterman, whom I was blessed to see again in 2017, when she was sitting in the front row of my address to the Union of Jewish Women. What a remarkable lady, whom I was blessed to chat to and hug. I must point out that my connection with the Union of Jewish Women goes back to 2002 when Nilly Baruch introduced me, and I have always been so impressed with their work.

CAN DO!

Despite the fact that the massive Gardens Synagogue was virtually packed to capacity for Eva's address, one could have heard a pin drop as she shared her story. Now in her eighties, Eva shares the lessons we can all learn from the Holocaust, in terms of her horrific ordeal at the hands of the Nazis, and what transpired after she was released at the end of World War II in 1945. She is committed to sharing the artwork her brother did whilst in hiding, which she found hidden under the floorboards of their home in Amsterdam after the war ended. Eva is deeply concerned about the way Europe is treating the desperate refugees who (if they are lucky enough to have reached Europe without drowning) have trudged across their borders in search of safety and a better lifestyle. She explained that if, in the late 1940s, all those countries had not closed their borders to Jewish Holocaust survivors, many more desperate Jews seeking a home or a place of refuge would have stood a better chance of survival. Instead, the world effectively 'closed its doors', causing thousands of people to die needlessly at a time when they were crying for help. (One must remember that this all took place before the State of Israel was established in 1948.) By drawing this parallel, Eva posits important words of caution to all who choose to listen. These are the kind of stories which show the ongoing relevance of Holocaust narratives to the harsh, largely xenophobic world as we know it today. ■

24

Combating racism and anti-Semitism

By examining and illustrating the history of what transpired 70 years ago, the Cape Town Holocaust Centre teaches us how racism was (and still is) at the root of anti-Semitism and examines its relationship to the institutionalised racism of apartheid in South Africa. It is a sobering reminder of the disastrous consequences of prejudice and cultural or religious discrimination.

While still working at FNB during the height of the apartheid era, I was deeply cognisant of this, so I invited all my managers to join me on a visit to the Holocaust Centre, where they were taken through in groups, under the much-valued guidance of Marlene Silbert – founding education director of the Cape Town Holocaust Centre. Marlene is a most impressive woman whose acuity of mind and youthful appearance belies her age. As part of her life-long commitment to human rights activism, she has run numerous educational programmes and developed invaluable learning material on the subject.

When I took over the running of Amy Foundation, I arranged for my staff to undergo the same exercise. More recently, we sent some facilitators and students to the Holocaust Centre as well. To quote from Marlene, the centre 'serves as a place where lessons for humanity can be learned and compassion awakened'. I believe that by exposing employees to something so powerful and significant to the world, organisations can enable their staff to get in touch with the wholeness of their being, helping them to bring their fully conscious, mindful selves to work.

CAN DO!

Further to this, I quote from famous Holocaust survivor Elie Wiesel, who has come to be regarded as 'a messenger to mankind'. His words still ring true, at a time when the world is forced to confront the realities of racism, oppression, and other injustices against humanity. In accepting his Nobel Peace Prize in 1986, Wiesel delivered an unforgettable speech on justice and our individual responsibility to our shared freedom, during which he said the following:

There may be times when we are powerless to prevent injustice, but there must never be a time when we fail to protest. We must always take sides. Neutrality helps the oppressor, never the victim. Silence encourages the tormentor, never the tormented.

Indeed – the importance of protesting against any form of injustice is inestimable and this has been made all the more simple and accessible through social media today.

Interfaith, intercultural youth programmes

Throughout history, religion has been used and misused, mostly as a destructive force. We draw on religion both for our defence, and as a motivation for attack – the ongoing Middle East conflict being a prime example. According to the well-known interfaith proponent Rabbi David Rosen:

The challenge is to ensure that identities, and above all, religious heritages, are vehicles to embrace others and not to reject them. Indeed, the challenge of life is how to use everything in our world, and everything that we are, for a blessing and not for a curse. However, where people live in accordance with the most noble values of their heritage, religion can be a powerful, constructive inspiration and interfaith cooperation can be a blessing – especially in places of conflict and tension.

Besides being a personally enriching experience, interfaith encounters enable people to overcome their prejudices. I believe that all religious belief systems share fundamentally important, good moral values which, besides helping us to find meaning in our lives, promote human dignity, freedom, and well-being.

> A great Swedish theologian, Bishop Krister Stendhal, proposed three rules for interfaith dialogue:
> - Seek to understand the others in the way they understand themselves (and not as others might portray them).
> - View other communities by the best within them – don't judge them by the worst within them. Furthermore, don't compare the best within yours with the worst within theirs.
> - Leave room for 'holy envy'. There is nothing wrong with admiring that which is unique to another culture.

Cape Town interfaith initiative

In 2011, Marlene Silbert initiated an Interfaith Intercultural Youth Programme – forming a partnership with the Amy Foundation with the support of Richard Freedman and Myra Osrin (directors of the Cape Town Holocaust Centre) who have worked tirelessly to create a world-class centre. This programme extends over a period of two years. Each year, 42 Grade 10 learners, from nine schools in different locations within the Cape metropole, are selected to participate in this programme. The pupils come from diverse religious, cultural, and socio-economic backgrounds. They attend monthly sessions that form part of an intensive self-development programme. In the second half of the first year, learners from the different schools begin to work together in community service projects. The Interfaith Intercultural Youth Programme offers an exciting and refreshing opportunity for the pupils to examine their schools as part of a particular community, while exploring what this means to live in a country of such complex cultural diversity. During the second year of the programme, when the learners are in Grade 11, they tutor young pupils one afternoon each week throughout the academic year in maths and literacy. The young primary school pupils who are tutored are in Grades 5 to 8. This component of the programme is organised in partnership with the Amy Foundation. It takes place at Mimosa After School Centre in Bonteheuwel and the Amy Foundation Centre in Sybrand Park.

CAN DO!

Aims and objectives of the Interfaith Intercultural Youth Programme, which we can all learn from are:

- To develop in every pupil the knowledge, values, attitudes, and skills necessary for co-existence in a multireligious and multicultural society.
- To create a greater understanding of self (identity), and respect for people from different religions, faiths, cultures, and backgrounds, within their school environment and the broader community.
- To promote respect, empathy, responsibility, peace, social cohesion, reconciliation, and social activism.
- To understand the dangers and ramifications of prejudice, racism, discrimination, stereotyping, and human rights violations.
- To be aware of the consequences of silence, apathy, and indifference to all forms of injustice.
- To create awareness of contemporary social issues that impact negatively on local and global issues

After participating in the programme, the pupils recognise and understand their role and responsibilities as citizens in a democracy, the importance of social activism, helping people in need, and the imperative of working towards the creation of a society in which the dignity of difference is respected and diversity is valued – thus enabling people to live together in peace and harmony. ■

25

Building international partnerships

From both a personal and career perspective, it has given me infinite pleasure to have been integral to the thrust of Amy Foundation's upward trajectory. However, given the slowdown in the South African economy, very little of this would have materialised without the ongoing support of our generous international donors and several extraordinary partnerships. Over the years, I have acquired and nurtured so many invaluable connections, and these people have often overwhelmed me with their loyalty, warmth, and support. I must qualify this, however: donor support does not occur merely because one's cause is deemed to be worthy. Far from it!

As with any of life's inter-personal relationships, one needs to work at building trust and credibility to ensure loyalty and sustainability. What I like to call the 'courting phase' involves getting the donor to believe in you – just as much as the importance of your cause or the needs of your beneficiaries. You want your donors to buy into your vision and have 100 per cent trust in your credibility. From day one, I made a conscious decision that I was not running a charity but a business, where the profits are wholly directed towards the children. All the business principles I implemented were learnt from the likes of Raymond Ackerman and Philip Krawitz. The best way to assure donors that their monies are being properly spent is through transparency and accountability. Besides sending thank you letters, remember that you owe your donors regular report backs and updates as to your progress. This can be achieved by sending them photographs or arranging visits to your offices or relevant projects.

CAN DO!

GERMANY
Horst and Rita Boes

The contribution made by a German couple, Horst, 89 at the time of his passing in 2017, and Rita Boes, 65, speaks volumes on how one (or in this case, two) can make a notable difference with minimal resources. Having settled in South Africa more than 20 years ago to see out their retirement years, this wonderful pair, who shared the same birthday, have made a generous contribution to Amy Foundation every year since we met. One year, they paid for a 'picnic of peace and unity' for the foundation children, followed by a variety of fun and games. For his eightieth birthday, Horst opted not to have a party, but chose instead to pay for a lunch for 30 of his friends. In lieu of gifts, his friends made donations to the Amy Foundation. On another birthday, they bought us much-needed violins. Performing at their birthday lunch, the children put on a moving musical programme that lasted almost an hour. Interestingly, Horst and Rita had been introduced to me by Aviva Pelham, who followed suit by inviting her own friends to make a donation to Amy Foundation for her sixtieth birthday.

The more times we met with Kevin, the more we grew to like him, and it did not take long for us to trust him completely.
To me, he is one of the best people in South Africa!
HORST BOES

Horst and Rita's most recent contribution involved supervising and paying for the roof of our new premises to be painted, refurbishing tables and chairs donated by the Twelve Apostles Hotel for our outdoor courtyard, and providing shelves for the sewing and craft classroom. The net result looks spanking new and most inviting. Rita is now volunteering weekly and teaching vital sewing skills to learners. Over time, the couple became my close friends, and their sterling work is a great example of the pleasure a donor can derive from making a hands-on contribution.

> *When we arrived at the opening of the new centre, a young man of about 22 approached us and greeted us warmly, asking if we remember him. 'No,' we replied. He went on to say, 'My name is Sibusiso Ntisana. About ten years ago, you bought us musical instruments, and I was determined to learn to play the guitar. I grew up in a violent environment where there were many gangs and drugs. Being able to play that guitar has changed my life.'*
> RITA BOES

The reader should note that Sibusiso is the same person who was mentioned earlier – an Amy Foundation alumnus. Sibusiso added, 'I remembered that they had invited us to perform at Mr Boes' birthday lunch at the Protea Hotel. They are the most amazing people!'

> *As I looked at this boy, with his soft, smiling eyes, my heart felt so happy, and it felt so rewarding to touch his life like that. I believe that we have not only changed his life for the better, but ours as well. The children are so proud to show us what they have achieved. They feel a sense of dignity, and in return one feels one has made a meaningful contribution. Over time, we have developed a special connection with some of them. This means a lot to us, and it's so good to see the direct result of something we have done – which is much more meaningful than just handing over a cheque.*
> RITA BOES

NORTHERN IRELAND

This is a beautiful country that offers the tourist much to see and enjoy in the form of natural and man-made attractions. At my own expense, I've now visited Northern Ireland several times over the years. I have also spoken there at numerous functions. I've made many

CAN DO!

The Northern Irish SA Sports Academy team – Left to right: Kevin, Helen Morrison, Zoe Allen, Eric Jenkinson, Nigel McCann, Alan Webster, Jenny Harvey, Jade Marshall. (Absent: Stuart Baird, Alex Jenkinson, Sarah McCann, Matthew Heaney and Ivor Lennon)

wonderful Northern Irish friends, and visiting the country is always a most rewarding experience. The Northern Irish Youth Justice agency became very interested in the work we are doing at Amy Foundation, because they've had a huge problem with 14- to 15-year-old youth offenders jailed for petty crimes such as shoplifting. Many of these teenagers became repeat offenders after their release. Having visited some of these offenders in jail, I was interested to learn of a TRC type model, in which the victim confronts the offender. This complex process has gone a long way in curbing the high rate of convicted youth who tend to reoffend.

Eric Jenkinson and friends

When Eric Jenkinson from Northern Ireland first toured South Africa, he committed to supporting Amy Foundation when he saw the work we were doing. Starting off with Lurgan Ladies Hockey Club, which involved bringing out 15 young girls from Northern Ireland to Cape Town in 2007 for a life-changing week, Eric went on to form a Northern Irish Sports partnership and programme with us. Upon his return to Northern Ireland, he convinced other businessmen and women to come out for a week to teach soccer, hockey, and golf to a select group of 100 children showing sporting potential. We're so

Eric Jenkinson proudly standing with some of the alumni of the Amy Foundation and the Northern Irish SA Sports academy. Left to right: Nosiviwe Nkitha, Bulelwa Rali, Zimkitha Rubeshe, Sesona Lali, Noloyiso Kebeni, Yamkela Velem.

appreciative that they have continued doing so every year since the partnership was formed.

While Eric proved to be a man of his word, the reality is that loads of people express the desire to return and do something to help, but few of them do so. Every year, for nine jam-packed weeks of sporting tuition and play, he and his wonderful associates and friends – namely Alan Webster, Zoe Allen, Nigel McCann, Helen Morrison, Stuart Baird, Jade Marshall, Jenny Harvey, Alex Jenkinson, Sarah McCann, and Matthew Heaney – have made an impact on the children at many levels. Thanks to their fundraising activities in Northern Ireland, these good people have been able to pay for their airfares and transport costs plus bring the necessary sports equipment to Cape Town, and throw in a generous donation of £2 000 as the cherry on the top!

In addition, Cathy Heaney, Stephanie and Robert Watson, with their daughters Emma and Louise, have been great supporters and become wonderful friends too. Stephanie and Robert came out one year and taught golf, and Emma and Louise taught dance, much to the delight of our youngsters. Cathy Heaney, Matthew's mother, always quietly got on every year with fundraising. One year she even put together an unforgettable event at Hillsborough Castle. A strong woman and cancer survivor, she continues to inspire us and help others at every turn.

CAN DO! ✓

Ray Acheson

In 2008, thanks again to Eric, businessman Ray Acheson fully sponsored a trip that enabled me to take five staff and sixteen Amy Foundation hockey girls from Manenberg and Gugulethu to Northern Ireland. Ray has since become a friend and committed supporter of Amy Foundation. Thanks to all our Northern Irish friends' fundraising efforts, we were able to take girls again in 2014, to spend a week playing hockey. Initially, race proved to be an issue when the coloured girls seemed reluctant to accompany the black girls, but they ultimately formed a wonderful bond.

Some months later, my sports co-ordinator Phumza Magwaza came to see me with some consternation, saying, 'Kevin, you need to talk to these girls. They have fallen back into two separate groups. The coloured girls are only speaking Afrikaans and the black girls are only speaking Xhosa, exclusively within their own groups, and they are not mixing since they cannot understand one other.' To address this, I got them together immediately, and explained, 'This is not how it works. You are showing a lack of respect for one another because you don't understand each other. Since you can all speak English, you must talk English to one another.' They all apologised and agreed, hugging one another. Today, some of those girls have graduated with degrees, and they are a proud testimony to what is possible.

Hendrik Verwoerd

When one hears this name, one immediately thinks of our much reviled former prime minister, the infamous architect of apartheid, whose racist ideologies, when implemented by our then Nationalist Government, led to a crime against humanity. On one of my trips to Northern Ireland, Eric Jenkinson arranged a visit to one of the prisons, where I met someone who said that he'd just met another South African man named Verwoerd. Somewhat astounded by this coincidence, I thought, 'Wow – there can only be one Verwoerd family, and I want to meet him!' He turned out to be Wilhelm Verwoerd, grandson of the infamous Hendrik Verwoerd. We managed to track

Wilhelm down at his home in County Armagh after a one hour drive. What a wonderful guy he turned out to be! He shared some anecdotes about growing up during apartheid, within a white, Afrikaans-speaking family, while living in the shadow of his grandfather (who was later assassinated). He spoke of his marriage to Melanie in 1987, and how the Verwoerd family had ostracised them when they joined the ANC as part of the struggle. The young couple had attracted the attention of the media and were widely acknowledged for their courageous stand and untiring humanitarian work in townships such as Kayamandi – which was very much on the other side of the railway track to pristine Stellenbosch. Apparently, when the conservative Afrikaans community got wind of their cause, all hell broke loose and they were subjected to threatening phone calls, estrangement from the family, and even being spat on in public. Ultimately, they went to Ireland when Melanie was appointed as South African ambassador to Ireland. After her term ended, she became executive director of UNICEF Ireland, while Wilhelm worked with the Glencree Centre for Reconciliation.

Strangely enough, with his deep-seated passion for reconciliation, Wilhelm was hoping to connect with someone from the Amy Foundation. So on his next trip he visited us, bringing some youths from Ireland along as volunteers. I later met Melanie when we arranged for their son, Wian, to come out and work on one of our projects as a volunteer. While he was here, he attended one of our Ubuntu breakfasts featuring the Western Province minister of arts and culture, Ivan Meyer, as our guest speaker. The minister alluded to the fact that Nelson Mandela, in the interests of reconciliation, had broken down barriers when he went to visit Betsie Verwoerd, wife of the late Hendrik Verwoerd. When I rose to thank him, I said: 'You won't believe it, but her great-grandson is sitting with us today, right here, in this audience!' Naturally, this caused a great stir, and everyone wanted to meet Wian, whose presence highlighted the poignancy of the minister's words and made for an unforgettable occasion.

CAN DO!

UNITED KINGDOM AND SWITZERLAND
Andrew Jennings

Although Andrew's contribution has been highlighted earlier, it is important to point out the importance of having ambassadors for your cause. Andrew, previous MD of Woolworths in South Africa and President of Saks Fifth Avenue USA, amongst other positions, is a close friend and has mobilised his network in support of the Amy Foundation, attracting wonderful people like Jacques Tredouw and John Lovering, who are now annual donors. Andrew spoke at a recent SA Ubuntu Foundation Business Breakfast, where he held the audience captive in sharing the concept outlined in his book: 'Almost is not good enough.'

Shay O'Brien

Shay is a successful entrepreneur with worldwide business interests including Bray Capital, The Juice Plus+ Company, The Meatless Farm, Skybike International, Glint, the Body Camp Fitness Retreats and many more. I met Shay at a Juice Plus+ Conference nine years ago and told him all about Amy Foundation. He was clearly most impressed with what he heard, for he subsequently flew out to South

Great excitement as Shay O'Brien opens envelopes from the fundraiser he arranged in Geneva, Switzerland.

Africa to see us and visit our projects. After that we stayed in touch with one another and became friends. He has since given us numerous donations with an annual financial commitment. In June 2016, he decided to arrange a fundraiser for the Amy Foundation in Ibiza, Spain. We were nothing short of delighted to learn that he'd raised a good sum from the evening! Besides matching the amount that we raised at our fundraiser in LA in 2017, Shay sponsored my flights to Geneva in June 2018 and organised a remarkable week of fundraising for Amy Foundation. Jonathan Raggett, GM of Red Carnation Hotels arranged that I stay at their luxurious Hotel d'Angleterre overlooking Lake Geneva.

And what a week that was! As busy as Shay was he organised two fundraisers at which the most amazing people rose to the occasion and made donations to ensure a substantial sum was raised for Amy Foundation. You can imagine the excitement as Shay and I tallied up afterwards. Felix Fein, a previous volunteer in Cape Town travelled all the way from Germany to be there. Anton and Ruth van Kooten from Belgium travelled an entire day from Monaco. They have become friends and supporters. Shay even arranged a radio interview on World Radio Switzerland with Katt Cullen and talks to children at two schools – Geneva English School and International School of Geneva. I thoroughly enjoyed talking to the children. I foresee so much more coming from the trip to Geneva. Shay is another man of honour – true to his word and a committed friend.

Martyn Gowar

Now retired, Martyn Gowar, who was a partner at McDermott Will & Emery, UK, came out to attend a conference in Cape Town some years ago. After his wife Sue did a cultural township tour, she introduced me to Martyn, and we connected immediately. Emanating from the growth of our friendship and his interest in the foundation, Martyn helped facilitate a grant application to one of the big funds that he chairs, which has added the magnificent sum of R1 million per annum over the past few years to our coffers. He and Sue have been kind

CAN DO!

enough to accommodate me at their beautiful home in Surrey, UK, and what a pleasure it has been to stay with such warm and hospitable people. Martyn used to sit on the board of Wellington College, one of the most prestigious independent boarding schools in the UK. I have since visited the school twice and addressed the students, with the school being kind enough to make a donation. Through Martyn, I connected with the headmaster at the time, Sir Anthony Seldon – a historian who has written biographies on several UK prime ministers and is now vice-chancellor of the University of Buckingham. When Sir Seldon delivered a talk in London, he generously diverted his speaker's fee to the Amy Foundation. Talk about the power of networking!

NETHERLANDS
René Clarijs and Piet Huijbregts

Some of the Dutch people I've met have become great friends and an invaluable resource. Over the years, I've given motivational speeches at various corporates and universities in Holland. I was lucky enough to meet a gentleman named René Clarijs of the EAICY board. René's exceptional commitment and energy has opened many doors for Amy Foundation. For three consecutive years, René mobilised virtually the whole town of Hilvarenbeek (two hours south of Amsterdam by train) to hold a massive fundraiser for us, supported by many sponsors. Working in collaboration, René and Piet Huijbregts raised between €5 000 and €10 000 each year – a whopping contribution – until both René and Piet's health made this no longer possible.

Upon René's invitation, I made every possible effort to attend these fundraisers – my proviso initially being that I wanted to use my own money to pay for the ticket, since I was not prepared to take it from Amy Foundation donations. Whilst I paid my own way for the first few years, René since introduced me to some corporates and universities, who were kind enough to sponsor my air tickets, along with paying me a generous sum to speak at various events. At the first fundraiser, René introduced me to Piet Huijbregts, then aged 65, who owns four restaurants in Hilvarenbeek. Piet expressed an interest in up-skilling disadvantaged youth in the hospitality industry so I invited him to come to Cape Town. He jumped at the opportunity and came out in 2013 with much passion and warmth, bringing his wife Loes, his siblings, and their spouses from Australia, who have all been in the restaurant business. They ran a 'pop-up' training school for a whole month, teaching township children sewing and cooking, and the impact on the youngsters and their growth in such a short space of time was phenomenal. I knew then we needed to roll this out but I didn't know how. Before one could say *voila* we had to find new premises for Amy Foundation and would eventually build a dedicated skills training centre. So enthralled and motivated were the youngsters that they suddenly knew exactly what they wanted to do with their lives. What an amazing gift! Piet's sister Truus worked with the foundation phase kids and her class doubled within a day. In 2015, Piet was able to come for only two weeks, after which he held a big fundraiser at a famous horse academy in Holland owned by Joop and Tineke Bartels, from which he raised a tidy sum for Amy Foundation. Talk about a super-successful event!

Willem Emmens, Harry van Leusden, Uipko Ebbens, and Anton van Kooten

Three of Piet's friends, Willem Emmens, Harry van Leusden, and Uipko Ebbens came out to Cape Town in February 2015, and organised a most successful golf fundraiser called the 'Amy Foundation Valentines Cup' for our new building. They have since returned again in February each year to raise money for the hospitality programme. Their lovely wives Erica, Marie-Louise, and Sylvia respectively, get every bit as involved in making the golf day a smashing success and enlisting just about every Dutch golfer staying in Cape Town during our summer! They then enlisted the support of another exceptional gentleman, Anton van Kooten, who spends time between Belgium, Netherlands, Monaco and Cape Town. Many of the players, like Maarten and Linny Seckel, now support us annually – Maarten even requesting donations instead of gifts for his seventieth birthday. Willem did the same for his seventy-fifth birthday and Anton for his eightieth birthday.

CAN DO! ✓

All our donors are given the option to fund either the programmes or the new centre. One has to be transparent with donors about the ultimate beneficiary, as they understandably like to know exactly how their money is to be used. We are immensely appreciative of all the special connections and friendships we've made with these exceptional Dutch people and their unfailing support.

Annette Mul's dream

Annette 'Nobuntu' Mul is a psychotherapist and supervisor, executive coach and trainer of the Ubuntu study programme Intercultural Dialogue and Leadership, and author of several articles and books. Her recent book *Opsoek naar Ubuntu* (Search for Ubuntu) has been a great success and she has donated a percentage of sales to Amy Foundation. Annette described having had the most intriguing, life-changing experience on the night of 10 March 2010:

I had a dream that I will never forget. I saw a bright blue and white light with the letters SAUF written in neon letters, and at the same time I heard a voice saying, 'You have to set up the South African Ubuntu Foundation!' I had never dreamt this before, and did not know what it meant. As a Dutch woman, I had been visiting South Africa for over ten years, and was fascinated by the essence of Ubuntu.

When I awoke the following morning, I went to my computer and googled South African Ubuntu Foundation. To my astonishment, I discovered that SAUF already existed, and was founded in 2006 by a particular Mr Kevin Chaplin!

So who is Kevin Chaplin, I wondered? I searched the Internet further and was totally impressed with what I read. Ubuntu, Kevin Chaplin, Amy Biehl .... I felt a glow in my body, which seemed to call from above. They call this an invocation. I immediately sent him a mail, knowing that I had to meet him!

ANNETTE MUL

I recall how impressed I was to read Annette's email, saying that she and her husband would be coming from Holland for the Ubuntu Festival. Come they did, and she enjoyed every minute, dressed in her beautiful, traditional Xhosa outfit. This has led to a friendship and avid support of my work. It often amazes me to think how much can come from one connection. One of the participants of the study programme, Ron Stevens, worked at Rabobank. Within a few months, this affiliation ensured that Rabobank Roermond-Echt sponsored a documentary for the Amy Foundation. In 2011, Ron arranged that I visit the Netherlands as a motivational speaker, talking about Ubuntu and leadership to the entire management team of Rabobank, and it was an honour to be invited to do so again, a few years later.

In April 2011, with my approval, Annette set up the Stichting Ubuntu Nederland, where they promote awareness about Ubuntu in work, life, and society. She also wanted to raise money for the SA Ubuntu Foundation, but I explained that since Amy Foundation is one of the best examples of Ubuntu, this is where funding was most needed. While their main beneficiary is the Amy Foundation – and Annette and her colleagues work tirelessly to raise funds and awareness for Amy Foundation – they also raise money for various other projects in South Africa. On 10 October 2013, Stichting Ubuntu organised an Ubuntu Symposium in the Netherlands: the first Ubuntu Experience, in which I featured as the keynote speaker.

I never thought I would get a response, but after about three weeks I got a mail saying that Kevin Chaplin would like to meet me and inviting me to come to Cape Town in July 2010. There would be the Ubuntu Festival and the Ubuntu Symposium, in the same week that Madiba would be 92 years old. There were 100 rational reasons why I wouldn't be able to go. But that one reason was the decisive factor – a passion to meet Kevin Chaplin!

Of course every human being is unique, and each encounter is unique, but a meeting with Kevin is extremely unique!

CAN DO!

The combination of the history of South Africa, the story of Amy Biehl, and what Kevin has achieved, has changed my life. I knew for sure that I wanted to be closely involved with Ubuntu, South Africa, Amy Foundation, and Kevin. Inter-connectedness and reconciliation are today the key words in my life. But how does one convert a dream, a vision, into daily practice? I started that same year in October with a study trip, 'Ubuntu, Leadership and Intercultural Dialogue', bringing Dutch managers to South Africa.

None of this would have been possible without Kevin. His unconditional love and belief in what he does, along with his intense involvement in you as a human being, makes one feel appreciated and makes one's contribution seem meaningful. His positive energy causes you to love him and to admire his infinite dedication to the Amy Foundation. He taught me about Ubuntu, and how a dream becomes a reality when you get there but continue to believe in it. Nothing is impossible. His credo is: 'Together we can change children's lives.' Besides Kevin, I also interviewed Easy and Ntobeko. They too changed my life. Baie dankie, thank you, enkosi kakhulu, Kevin. The world has needed you for a long time and I'm so grateful that you are in my life!
ANNETTE MUL

Rob in 't Zand and Willie van Eijs

Rob and Willie are two other people who have supported us both financially and by coming to Cape Town to run a workshop for our staff. Their daughter Enya, accompanied by two friends, Suzanne Vandooren and Merel Veraa, volunteered here for three months and raised funds back home for Amy Foundation, along with other volunteers like Niklas Wiertz, Felix Fein, and Julie De Smedt.

For three years in a row, a delegation from the Netherlands consisting of managers and doctors connected to Tias Nimbas Business School, Tilburg University, asked me to set up a study week for their Masters Degree in Health in South Africa. I successfully organised and hosted them for an unforgettable one-week programme with speakers from South Africa. This experience encouraged me to diversify my skills base, while providing me with a lucrative extra source of income.

The Rotary Club Roermond Maas en Roer, in cooperation with the German Rotary Club Lemgo-Sternberg and the Rotary Club Sea Point, partnered in an international project to support the Amy Foundation with the purchase of a brand new 25-seater bus.

Windesheim University of Applied Science, Zwolle

On one of the annual Ubuntu study programme visits led by Annette to Cape Town I had the pleasure of meeting Marchien Timmerman, leader of the Department of Theology at Windesheim University. This woman of action committed to working with us and supporting the Amy Foundation as much as she could. She has stayed true to her word and every year since then we have welcomed students from the university to volunteer and stay with us. One of her students, Pieter Jan Bos, made a significant impact in his time with Amy Foundation. Marchien has returned many times to Amy Foundation in Cape Town to assist with projects and even produced a book entitled *Weaving barriers against violence – Impressions of the work of Amy Foundation*. Marchien also arranged two amazing speaking trips for me to the university to address groups of students, which I thoroughly enjoyed. On one of my trips to speak at the university a teacher in the Department of Theology, Jan van Dijk, tirelessly sold Amy Relate R bracelets for us. The power of connections leads to partnerships.

Codarts – University of the Arts, Rotterdam

In April 2009, after doing a talk at Tilburg University, Patrick Cramers from Codarts came up to me and that discussion led to a long and exciting partnership, which has seen Codarts send between six and

CAN DO!

ten students in dance every year for two weeks since 2010. Codarts is a Dutch vocational university in Rotterdam that teaches music, dance and circus. The students are led by the talented teacher Hilke Diemers and each student is paired with one of the Amy Foundation teachers for two weeks every year, culminating in a showcase performed by each class to wondrous applause from the audience. What Hilke and her students achieve every year with over 100 children in dance in just two weeks is nothing short of remarkable, including upskilling our own dance teachers. Some of the students have even returned to Amy Foundation as volunteers for two months.

AUSTRIA
Vienna

Eva Aileen Jungwirth-Edelmann, a lecturer at Modul University Vienna, arranged a fundraiser for Amy Foundation at the Mozarthaus Vienna in conjunction with ladies from Juvenilia Vienna, Soroptimist International. This special evening included a performance by Martin Edelmann on viola, and members of the Radio Symphonic Orchestra. We were also able to auction off some beautiful artwork of musical instruments done by our students. All in all a very successful evening.

BELGIUM
Ubuntu Festival

When I initially started the South African Ubuntu Foundation, my aspirations were high. After launching the Ubuntu Festival successfully in South Africa, I hoped to take the concept across the world. However, as mentioned earlier, when I took over the Amy Foundation, I needed to downsize this vision considerably to meet the more pressing, ongoing demands of the Amy Foundation.

Sven Cools

In February 2016 Ilchen got an email out of the blue from Sven Cools in Belgium. Sven had looked at the SA Ubuntu Foundation website and wanted to hold an Ubuntu festival on 18 June in Belgium. He was contacting our organisation primarily to 'shake hands' and broaden their worldly vision. They also wanted to forge links between Ubuntu Festival Belgium and Ubuntu Festival South Africa. They wanted to explain Ubuntu to a wide range of people and bring them in contact with the philosophy, its beliefs, values, and responsibilities.

Ilchen replied that I would be delighted and would also attend if my flight was paid for – to which they duly agreed. As things panned out, I returned from the US on the night of 14 June, spent just one day in the office, and flew on to Brussels the following day, as this was an opportunity too good to miss. Having made my way to the town of Boom, I did a presentation on Ubuntu, met Sven and his family, and spoke at their Ubuntu Festival – and what an outstanding lineup they had over the two days! The following year, it was a privilege to again attend their Ubuntu Festival in an even better location in Boom. This time they cleverly used special plastic cups for the beer and wine, for which people paid a refundable 1 Euro. Many kept their cups or didn't collect their €1 refund which Ubuntu Festival Belgium donated to Amy Foundation – raising €250. This was a great opportunity to introduce people to the Ubuntu concept. In return they introduced me to their beer and some superb performing artists. Besides their exceptional beer, there is much more to Belgium than mussels, chocolates and waffles! Sven Cools, Kyo De Fraeye and their amazing team held Ubuntu Festivals again in 2018 and 2019 and have committed to further annual festivals. I often wonder where the Amy Foundation team would be without fantastic people like this in our lives!

Ida Verlinden

Whenever I can, I stay with my dear friend Ida Verlinden, the previous consul of Belgium to South Africa and other countries like India, Venezuela, Japan, Thailand and Zimbabwe. This courageous lady is an inspiration of survival against extreme odds, having been diagnosed and treated for cancer four times in her life. She has taken me to lovely places like the Grote Markt (Grand Place or Great Market Square) in

Sarah and Keith's wedding. Left to right: Yvonne Chaka Chaka, Hilda Ndude, Robyn Chaplin, Ida Verlinden, Thembi Mtshali-Jones, and Pam Golding (seated).

Antwerp and Brussels, the beautiful cities of Bruges and Ghent, and an old monastry (Abbey Postel) in the town of Mol where the monks still make tasty beer for sale. She also made sure we saw her niece Katrien Verlinden and drove to Hilvarenbeek (which is close to the Dutch border) to visit my old friends and enjoy a meal at Herberg Sint Petrus, one of Piet Huijbregt's outstanding restaurants. Piet always kindly arranged a trip to 'Beekse Bergen' – the most amazing *dierentuin* (zoo) I have ever experienced!

UNITED STATES
University of Miami, Florida

Once a year, I mentor between 9 and 14 students visiting Cape Town from the University of Miami. This is part of an international exchange programme, which offers students the opportunity to study for a semester in any country they wish to visit – South Africa being a particularly popular choice. As a mentor, I believe that the opportunity to experience both the anxiety and thrill of extending themselves beyond their comfort zones can help these students discover more of who they are, and rise to their true potential.

At the start and at the end of their stay, they are accompanied by one of their own lecturers, Richard Grant, Professor of Geography and Urban Studies at the University of Miami. He has written an excellent book called *Africa: Geographies of Change*. Six years ago, Richard suggested that instead of sending out a full-time lecturer, it would be more economical for them to pay me to mentor their students whilst in Cape Town. This new arrangement has proved a win-win situation for all. Besides providing me with a source of extra income, it gives me the opportunity to spend a few hours with the students every two weeks, for four to five months – during which they benefit from a series of meaningful encounters.

I thoroughly enjoy interacting and sharing stories with young people. Besides doing some voluntary work for Amy Foundation and other non profit organisations, these students are given the amazing opportunity to attend our Ubuntu Breakfasts, learn about apartheid (first hand from Ntobeko Peni and Easy Nofemela), and visit the Holocaust Centre under the proficient guidance of Marlene Silbert. They are also given a comprehensive tour of Parliament by Steve Swart of the African Christian Democratic Party. Most of them have listed the Holocaust tour and visit to parliament among the highlights of their Cape Town experience.

This partnership with the University of Miami enabled me to visit that US city in 2017, thanks to Richard Grant and Devika Milner (Director of Study Abroad). Miami is a most fascinating, vibrant city. What a dreamlike experience it was to stay at The Betsy Hotel, South Beach and run along the seemingly endless stretch of palm-tree-lined beaches, gently lapped with a bathtub-warm sea! Richard introduced me to Cuban coffee, which is absolutely delicious. I was also afforded the opportunity to address some classes at their impressive university campus, an honour which was a particular highlight for me. There, I was accompanied by Barbara Gamzu, a talented musician and friend

CAN DO!

who also calmly came to my rescue when – stress of all stresses – my laptop charger failed!

Cynthia Fleischmann, one of the past students, who after leaving the university sadly lost a leg in a motorcycling accident, offered to hold a fundraising event while I was in Miami. I always enjoy reconnecting with our past students and was particularly inspired by Cynthia's story of courage and resilience, continuing with her life as before, but in an improvised manner. Now a body paint artist, she shared her story as part of the fundraiser, ably assisted by another past student, Priscilla Tavares. Although Cynthia is an above the knee amputee, which makes things more difficult, she does not allow her 'disability' to discourage her from working, dancing, travelling, snowboarding, hiking and playing lacrosse. Quite astonishing!

Rollins College, Orlando, Florida

Always ready to pack as much as I can into a trip, I couldn't resist catching a bus to Orlando, Florida, to address students at Rollins College in Winter Park, Orlando. A few months prior to this visit, I had received an email from Jim Johnson, Professor of International Business, Crummer Graduate School of Business, who wanted to make contact. What an opportunity! My visit also allowed me to meet Dr Mary Conway Dato-on, Associate Professor of International Business. Mary introduced the concept behind Amy Foundation Relate bracelets to her MBA Social Entrepreneurship classes. I was fortunate to be able to Skype the students in early 2018 about Amy Foundation, and I presented the idea of starting a social enterprise of their own with our bracelets. We were thrilled to learn that two classes took up the challenge. Jim Johnson was so impressed with the Amy Foundation story, that he went on to bring a group of lecturers out to South Africa, and included a visit to Amy Foundation. Two of their lecturers – Sharon Lusk (Assistant Dean, Rollins College Hamilton Holt School) and Kristin Winet (Assistant Professor, Department of English) – went back home so inspired that they raised funds to buy a whole shipment of children's books for our literacy classes.

Bob Sinicrope and Milton Academy, Boston

A partnership with Bob Sinicrope, Director of Jazz at Milton Academy in Boston, has seen Bob bring a group of 20 students every second year for the past 18 years to the Amy Foundation. They spend a week in Cape Town working with our learners and bring loads of musical instruments and cash donations every time. What a treat to work with Bob. Milton Academy's Jazz Program has enjoyed wonderful and meaningful connections with South African township music programmes since South African musician/composer Abdullah Ibrahim visited their school in 1991. Upon hearing students perform his music he ran on stage and invited them to tour South Africa. Milton Academy jazz students have toured South Africa more than ten times and have delivered over $215 000 worth of donated materials to South African schools and township programs. Bob will tell you that their most significant connection is with the Amy Foundation.

When their students are in Cape Town bi-annually on March 21, the Amy Foundation celebrates Human Rights Day by creating the Amy Foundation Township Jazz Festival, and Milton Academy is one of the featured acts. The Milton students are blessed with many resources and opportunities far beyond those enjoyed by South African township residents. However, when their students play for, and with, South African students all their differences seem to melt away. As Bob says, 'I wish words could capture the joy and love shared by all during performances and jam sessions. The sharing of music levels the "playing field" and forms bonds between musicians who sometimes speak different languages. This is a life-changing experience for many students.'

Given the centrality of self-discovery and self-expression to artistic practice, research finds that community youth arts and cultural programmes help young people develop self-confidence, self-efficacy, and self-awareness. An education rich in the creative arts maximises opportunities for learners to engage with innovative thinkers and leaders, to experience the arts both as audience members and as

CAN DO!

artists, and to endorse the values of cultural understanding and social harmony that the arts can engender.

Involvement in the arts is an unparalleled means for young people to develop the strength, resilience, and self-image that allows them to participate in society on healthy terms. Disadvantaged youth do not have free access to the formally organised and accessible arts and cultural activities that Amy Foundation provides. Youngsters in our music programme become focused, don't drop out of school, do better than their peers, don't fall prey to the negative influences in society. We don't aim to make famous musicians out of them but to create emotionally well-rounded, global citizens. It is wonderful to see the results even after a few days with Bob and the youngsters from Milton Academy.

Bob even came on his sabbatical in 2018 with his wife, Frances, and stayed in Amy's student accommodation whilst working his magic with our brass class.

Brett and Miranda Tollman, Jimmy Eichelgruen, Los Angeles

Earlier on, I discussed my relationship with Brett Tollman, Chief Executive of The Travel Corporation. Some years ago, Brett and his wife Miranda offered to hold a fundraiser for me in Los Angeles, if I could arrange to fly there. Despite my efforts to obtain a donation from various airlines, I somehow couldn't come right, and of course, meeting the deadlines of day-to-day matters took precedence. About five years ago, Arthur Gillis introduced me to Jimmy Eichelgruen, Delta Air Lines' sales director for Africa, Middle East, and India. In mid-2015, Jimmy wanted to give Amy Foundation two Delta Air Line flights. Needless to say, I was delighted. When I met Jimmy a few days later, he specified that the tickets be used for fundraising, as part of a raffle, with the added proviso that the tickets had to be booked one month later. Michelle, my PR, marketing, events, and fundraising manager, felt it wouldn't be possible to put a raffle together in six weeks, because a huge amount of work goes into a drive of this nature, in an effort to reach the maximum number of people. By the same token,

I didn't want to lose this invaluable opportunity to do something useful with this amazing windfall. Being the type who always looks for the opportunity when I 'hit a wall', I remembered Brett Tollman's offer. I explained to Jimmy that given the time constraint, a raffle wouldn't work, and requested instead – perhaps rather cheekily – that he allow me to use the two tickets to fly to Los Angeles for a fundraiser. He agreed to this, provided they were booked by the end of September 2015.

Although Jimmy suggested that I take my wife to LA, I felt that this would be morally wrong, since the tickets were given to me for the primary purpose of promoting the Amy Foundation cause internationally. I saw this as a great opportunity for me to take along our programme manager, Ntobeko Peni, (knowing that this would mean the world to him, since he'd never been to Los Angeles before). Besides the two tickets for Ntobeko and me to fly to LA, Jimmy very kindly agreed to give us an extra two business-class return tickets to raffle from his 2016 allocation (which meant they had to be used that year). We closed the raffle on 27 May 2016 and managed to raise a substantial sum. Jimmy and Delta are so committed to changing lives, that he gave me another four business class tickets to anywhere in the US during 2017 and 2018 – two for me to go and fundraise in the US, and another two to raffle again.

Deemed the entertainment capital of the world, the city of Los Angeles is home to more creative people in the film, TV, and music industries than any other city in the US. Little did we imagine the ongoing pampering and kindness that would be lavished upon us by Brett and his wonderful wife Miranda, who treated us to five glorious summer days at their lovely home in this sprawling Californian city. This area possesses some of the most unique and spectacular terrain in the world – where mountains, ocean, desert, and valley are all in reasonably close proximity.

Brett and Miranda organised a great fundraising and networking opportunity! They welcomed us cordially into their bustling world of business connections, friends, and colleagues – such that we even

CAN DO!

did two presentations a day, to clients and staff of Uniworld Boutique River Cruises and African Travel. This greatly assisted us to increase our overseas donor data base, which is particularly important, since the exchange rate enables the US dollar to go a long way when converted to rand. Miranda put the fundraiser together in their home, where we met many new donors, with whom we will obviously stay in touch. I especially enjoyed meeting Cantor

Brett Tollman and Kevin Chaplin after a scrumptious meal cooked by Brett.

Chayim Frenkel of the Synagogue Kehillat, Israel. Miranda showed us around LA, a highlight being our visit to Universal Studios with their youngest son Max. We also enjoyed some good quality time with their other children – Ella and Jake. On one occasion, we were joined by Brett's cousin Gavin, also a great guy, who runs Trafalgar Tours. Our visit was made all the more memorable by Brett's phenomenal cooking. Undoubtedly a chip off the old block – much like his mother, Bea Tollman, whose exceptional culinary expertise was alluded to earlier. Brett and Miranda's friendship and firm support go a long way in making a difference to me personally and to the Amy Foundation. The reader will remember the contribution of The Travel Corporation Group mentioned earlier.

Thanks to Jimmy's unfailing commitment, Delta Air Lines has now also made a financial contribution to Amy Foundation. Delta has sponsored branded caps, orders custom designed bracelets and dolls, and sponsors two Ubuntu Business Breakfasts a year in Cape Town. The airline sponsored our first ever event in Johannesburg and Durban in 2018 and 2019 respectively – after numerous requests from our database over the years, having always held 12 a year in Cape Town. Delta Air Lines is always the first to book a table for our annual Amy Foundation Gala Fundraising Dinner in September at the luxurious Century City Conference Centre.

Mitch and Linda Weiss

I met Mitch Weiss, who was chairman of Angel City Chorale, a phenomenal choir in Los Angeles (more about them later), when they visited Cape Town in 2011. When Mitch first visited our offices we clicked immediately. He always jokes that we 'hijacked' him to visit some of our township music programmes, which he still loves, being such an accomplished musician himself. I've kept in touch with Mitch and Linda ever since.

On my trips to LA in 2016, 2017 and 2018, I spent time at their beautiful home in Topanga Canyon, Western Los Angeles, California, (located in the Santa Monica Mountains). Mitch and Linda Weiss are generous and committed donors of Amy Foundation. They have also become special friends. For Ntobeko, the highlight of the trip in 2016 was Mitch allowing him to drive his Porsche convertible. Besides his genuine generosity, I must say that Mitch is a particularly brave

Left to right: Ntobeko Peni, Linda Weiss, Kevin Chaplin and Mitch Weiss in Los Angeles.

CAN DO!

man! Again, we were treated to incredible dinners and entertainment, including authentic Mexican food, which we enjoyed at the vibrant Mexican quarter – such fun! Linda, a most accomplished artist, has been kind enough to donate some of her magnificent paintings for auctioning at our gala dinners in Cape Town. I can only express the highest praise and appreciation for these exceptionally warm, magnanimous people, who have become like family.

In May 2017, with Brett and Miranda travelling so much – and the enormous responsibilities of caring for their three busy children – Mitch and Linda offered to do the fundraiser this time, aided by their friends Carole Carpenter and Judy Parker as well as Norman and Marie-Anne Helgeson. What an amazing fundraiser that turned out to be, thanks to the hard work of this exceptional team. Linda's magnificent artwork proved a real hit as well. With our local economy being as depressed as it is, what a godsend that turned out to be! Shay O'Brien, whom I mentioned earlier, was unable to attend, but offered to match whatever we raised that night – turning this hugely successful fundraiser into an epic event.

Norman Helgeson

One of the older members of Angel City Chorale, Norman Helgeson, loved Cape Town so much on the visit in 2011 that he offered to come back to South Africa in 2013 to assist us. The youngsters took to him immediately. In 2015, he came out again, at 78 years of age, and taught the choir at our Bongolethu After School Centre in Philippi for a whole month. Having just remarried, he brought his new wife along to volunteer too – a delightful lady named Marie-Anne. When I told Norman that I would be going to LA, he immediately offered to be at my beck and call as personal chauffeur during the stay – and he remained true to his word. What a joy to be in the company of this remarkable soul and friend, along with Marie-Anne. Wherever I wished to go, no distance was too far, or time too inconvenient. A committed personal donor to Amy Foundation, Norman also works constantly to raise awareness and funds for Amy Foundation. He even proposed to Angel

City Chorale that they bring some children from the Amy Foundation to Los Angeles, a trip that materialised in 2018.

Much more to LA then I had expected

Before I flew to Los Angeles in 2017, in an effort to maximise this foreign funding opportunity, I emailed some churches and the cantor of the local synagogue, without much success. However, shortly before I left, the pastor of Brentwood Presbyterian Church, Dave Carpenter, replied to say that they would give Amy Foundation $500 if I addressed the 08h00 and 10h30 services, to which I immediately agreed. But I was not to know that God had a bigger plan for me at the time. Dave then proposed that if I had enough energy, perhaps I would like to do the 'School of Christian Leadership Talk' they always have for an hour between the two services, for another $250, adding that he'd understand if it was too much. Phew, how could I pass up another $250? So yes! Little did I know I was expected to be the preacher, which meant delivering the sermon at both those services! In a panic, I confided in my wife, Robyn, that I didn't think I could do this, but reminded myself that there is no such thing as can't, besides which, there was no way that I could pass up $500 for the Amy Foundation! I duly committed to this, and just before departing for LA, Dave asked me what my two scripture readings would be, along with the title of my sermon. Oh my, did my stress levels jump! Dave and I came up with the title: 'Be careful what you pray for!' (Check out the sermon on YouTube: www.youtube.com/watch?v=LHh-kt3O_tw)

Robyn helped me choose the two scriptures that follow:
JEREMIAH 29:11 In the Old Testament:
For I know the plans I have for you, declares the Lord,
plans to prosper you and not to harm you, plans to give
you hope and a future.

MARK 9:23 In the New Testament:
Everything is possible for him who believes.

CAN DO!

The morning of the church service, I woke up at 05h00 to work on my sermon, feeling decidedly anxious and unprepared for the challenge that lay ahead. It struck me that since I had chosen an extract from Jeremiah 29, I needed to know who he was and what this chapter was about, so the best place to start would be Jeremiah 1. Lo and behold this is what I read: 'O Lord God,' I said, 'I can't do that, I am far too young, I am only a youth.' 'Don't say that,' He replied, 'for you will go wherever I send you and speak whatever I tell you, and don't be afraid of the people, for I the Lord will be with you and see you through.' Then He touched my mouth and said, 'See, I have put my words in your mouth! Today your work begins.' (Jeremiah 1 vs 6)

And with that, I was overwhelmed with a sense of calm, self-assurance. I went on to confidently deliver a 25-minute sermon, which I felt really good about. While standing at the door to greet all the congregants as they left, I was repeatedly asked whether I plan to become a full-time preacher! I responded, 'No, I believe that God needs me in the workplace. This was a first for me, and I am sure there will be future opportunities, but certainly not full-time. I don't think this is where God needs me.'

Angel City Chorale

Seven years ago, I was contacted by Winifred Neisser, a chorister of Angel City Chorale, and Sue Fink, the founder, director and conductor of the choir, which I'd never heard of. The choir had originally planned to sing at the birthday celebration for South African anti-apartheid and human rights activist Desmond Tutu, but when those plans fell through Winifred suggested a visit and performance for the Amy Foundation after reading about the organization in an LA Times article. Our discussions completed, Winifred and Sue sprung into action, together with Linda Weiss and her hard-working committee, whose members raised the funds to make the trip possible. I must confess to being a little tentative, as I didn't know what to expect. Taking comfort in the fact that the choir sings in various genres, I took the bold step of inviting them to sing at the Cape Town International Convention

Welcome by our host families at Los Angeles International Airport. Front row, far right (L to R): Sue Fink, founder, director and conductor of Angel City Chorale; Leena Matthews, board president; Winifred Neisser, lead trip organiser and choir member. Back row, 3rd from left: Norman Helgeson (page 305); 3rd row, on left: Mitch and Linda Weiss (page 304).

Centre as a fundraiser for the Amy Foundation in 2011. More than 60 people strode onto the stage at the CTICC to create astonishing sound effects and beautiful harmonies, without any backing, in what can only be described as a mind-blowing vocal performance. My hair stood on end! I now promote them at every opportunity. On my visits to LA in 2016, 2017 and 2018, I had the good fortune to attend their annual concert, which was again phenomenal. I suggest that the reader finds Angel City Chorale on YouTube to get a better sense of the choir's prowess. Here's one called Africa – https://youtu.be/-c9-poC5HGw.

From its humble beginnings in 1993 — 18 singers rehearsing in the back room of a Santa Monica guitar shop — Angel City Chorale has grown to more than 160 members under the leadership of artistic director Sue Fink. They've gone from singing in the guitar shop's Christmas show to performing with legends like Stevie Wonder and competing on the 2018 season of the reality show *America's Got Talent*.

CAN DO!

In 2017 Mitch, Winifred and Sue spearheaded a fundraising campaign to bring 15 Amy Foundation youngsters to Los Angeles and perform with Angel City Chorale in June 2018, in celebration of its 25th anniversary. Winifred and her committee worked tirelessly to raise the funds to bring the 15 youngsters, 5 chaperones and myself over for an exhilarating 10-day programme, with host families kindly providing the accommodation. The highlight was the two concerts featuring music from around the world, joined by the young singers from South Africa who, dressed in bright, traditional African outfits, stood out among the adult choir's all-black outfits. Included in the mind-blowing trip were games on Santa Monica beach; a Dodger's baseball game; a visit to the California Science Center, its IMAX and intriguing space shuttles; a tour of University of Southern California; a panel discussion with the Pan African Students Association, a full day at Disneyland with many shrieks of excitement; singing at Holman Methodist Church the first Sunday and Brentwood Presbyterian Church the second Sunday (where I 'preached' again in return for dollars for Amy Foundation, this time my 'sermon' being dual

Amy Foundation choir performing with Angel City Chorale in Los Angeles.

citizenship – check out YouTube: https://youtu.be/1BJHiCXVDK0); a Sony studio tour; and a day engaging and singing with the students at Venice High School, where the iconic film *Grease* with John Travolta and Olivia Newton-John was filmed. This was undoubtedly a life-changing experience for these youngsters and I am certain that they will go on to make a success of their lives, like the girls we took to Northern Ireland in 2008.

Travel is both exhausting and exhilarating. I feel so blessed to have been able to visit so many fascinating places, as far and wide as they are diverse, all the while forging important new connections and reaffirming all those special, long-established relationships. I always return to

CAN DO!

Cape Town invigorated by all the sightseeing, friendships, and unique experiences. Undoubtedly, the best trips are with my family. Throughout this time, I continue to meet all my commitments and responsibilities in running the Amy Foundation and SA Ubuntu Foundation – made possible by the marvel of cellphones via WhatsApp, laptop, and the internet, which thankfully facilitates instant communication across the world, from video conferencing, to phone calls, to emails — albeit often in a haze of long hours and confusing time zones!

For someone infused with wanderlust, I nevertheless always feel good to be home: I miss my wife and daughters terribly and therefore make sure to balance my business travels with lots of quality time with family over the weekends. ■

Making the impossible possible

26

Keeping my dreams alive

A special moment with my grandson, Connor Tramontino Watkins.

CAN DO! ✓

Stepping aside

I believe that the success of any good organisation hinges on its management knowing when to step in and when to step aside. I've already told my staff that I plan to retire in three or four years, although I wish to remain involved as an active board member of the Amy Foundation and assist the new CEO for many years to come. We will obviously need to start looking for the prospective candidate, ensuring that he or she works with me for a few years before I hand over. I've no doubt that somebody dynamic will step in and invigorate the Amy Foundation with fresh ideas and perspectives, whilst ensuring its sustainability.

> So if you feel like there's just too much to be done, it's important to remind yourselves of something our modern culture seems to have forgotten: There are two threads running through our lives. One is pulling us into the world to achieve and make things happen, the other is pulling us back from the world to nourish, replenish, and refuel ourselves.
>
> ARIANNA HUFFINGTON

I will enjoy pursuing other interests and growing the SA Ubuntu Foundation, my motivational, business and leadership talks, and my Juice Plus+ franchise. I have been selling this excellent health supplement part-time – and I can highly recommend it. Juice Plus+ is a branded line of dietary supplements containing the raw nutrients of fruit, berries and vegetable juice extracts in tablet form in exactly the right quantities needed by the body.

Thanks to my friendship with Yvonne Chaka Chaka, I was appointed chairman of the Princess of Africa Foundation, which I will assist in growing. Having been established 12 years ago, it still remains engaged in community upliftment and social charity work. Considered a role model throughout the African continent, Yvonne has demonstrated compassion for others throughout her career.

I will also continue working as a board member of the Western Cape Advisory Council of the National Business Initiative (NBI).

The NBI is a voluntary coalition of South African and multinational companies, working towards growth and development in South Africa to ensure a sustainable future, especially as the voice of business with government. Since its inception in 1995, the NBI has made a distinct impact in the spheres of housing delivery, crime prevention, local economic development, public sector capacity building, further education and training, and other worthy causes.

Besides this important involvement, I also hope to become a paid board member of one or two businesses or corporates, to further utilise my skills and share my experience. Ideally, I'd like to continue running the SA Ubuntu Foundation, and continue giving my talks to corporates, conferences, and universities – all the while taking advantage of other public speaking opportunities that may come my way. As the Ubuntu Breakfasts are still immensely popular, I will continue to run them, maybe in a different format if necessary. To enable me to fully appreciate the bush experience, I intend to book myself on a game guide course in 2021 to further my passion for nature and the bush, which developed late in life.

Ranger Kev

> Connecting with nature is one of the best ways of escaping the everyday pressures of the daily grind – and emphasising that we belong to something much larger than we can ever comprehend. Besides reminding us of the miraculous work of God and the impermanence of life, it also kindles our responsibility for maintaining and appreciating nature, which is all too easily forgotten.

Since I'm most relaxed in the bush, I still fly up to Gauteng with the family to visit the game reserves. Dating back to the time I fell in love with the bush, when Lynne Brown had offered me the job of heading up Cape Nature, it was always my dream to spend time with African wildlife. When we moved down to Cape Town, Robyn

CAN DO! ✓

said that we would have to put that behind us, and focus instead on the different leisure options we could enjoy in Cape Town. In 2015, my daughter Sarah gave me a brochure that was handed to her at a traffic light, which advertised plots for sale at the 7 000 hectare Touwsberg Private Game and Nature Reserve – situated three hours out of Cape Town. I obtained info on the 120 plots that were for sale, 80 of which were already sold. Set against the southern slopes of the spectacular Touwsberg mountain range, it teems with smaller game: klipspringer, steenbok, duiker, and springbok, as well as larger game: Cape mountain zebra, giraffe, red hartebeest, kudu, eland, gemsbok, and black wildebeest. The reserve also hosts natural predators like the leopard, caracal and jackal. Among the more than 160 bird species are black eagle, owl and falcon, kori bustards and Egyptian geese.

When Robyn and I went out there, we knew immediately that the quality of life on offer was exactly what we wanted. We didn't want to be sole owners of the plot, so we approached two friends, Sean Hadskins and Carl Holman, who agreed to come in with us as co-owners, and the deal was signed. They are the perfect partners, as we get on well and enjoy similar interests. For Robyn and me as a couple, it's been so exciting to work on the design together. The only stipulation is that the look and feel of the house should be in keeping with the environment. Plans have been drawn, and we look forward to our dream eventually becoming a reality. I see this as an excellent opportunity for the family to spend countless hours of quality time together, especially as the grandchildren come! By renting it out for some of the time, we hope to get a good return on our investment. It has of course struck me that my enduring vision of spending family holidays together in the bush, has now come full circle – years later.

A choice

You have a choice in how you interpret your life's circumstances. Edward Thorp writes: 'You can choose to focus on the negative by looking at all that is wrong, which leads to more pain and suffering, or you can choose to look for what's right – to find the gifts or the opportunities – which leads to more potential, and more joy, happiness, and fulfillment.' As you shift the way you think about your future, you begin to reimagine and rewrite your past.

We all have a story within us, that is continually reshaped by our struggles and victories, our tests and triumphs. We may not always choose how the plot of our life unfolds, but we can choose whether we see a tragedy as a beginning or an ending. We can choose how we stand up to our villains, and make peace with battles we've lost, and those we continue to fight. We can tell our stories in a way that empowers us, rather than diminishes our strengths. Most of all, we can use our stories for good, to lift ourselves up, and to help those around us who are still learning to stand, and stand again. ∎

CAN DO!

In conclusion

Unwavering commitment

After having been at the helm of the Amy Foundation for a few years, I had a meeting with Michael Louis, CEO of the Louis Group Africa. The group invests in private property and had extended its global reach in property partnerships to South Africa, England, Germany, and Switzerland. Given my background in banking, Michael wanted me to work for the Louis Group in Switzerland. Despite my longstanding interest in working and travelling overseas, I immediately declined his offer. Visibly surprised, Michael asked, 'How can you turn me down so quickly without even giving it some thought?' I replied that since I had taken control of both the SA Ubuntu Foundation and the Amy Biehl Foundation for only a few years at that point, it wouldn't be fair to just drop them. In hindsight, I can say that making the decision was hard in theory, but not hard in practice.

> Even if something better comes up for you, when you've started a project, you can't just drop it at your own convenience – especially when people are dependent on you. Besides, I've always believed that a commitment is exactly that: a commitment.

I had a significant responsibility to the staff and children of Amy Foundation, and therefore would not consider leaving them in the lurch. Furthermore, as a proud South African, I wanted to be part of turning our history around and I don't regret choosing that fork in the road for a second.

Upon reflection, an interesting aspect to this story is how something as simple as timing can change one's entire destiny – in my case, much more than just my own. Had Michael Louis' offer been made to me at the time I was considering leaving the bank, I probably would have snapped it up! Had I done so, this story would never have materialised, this book would not have been written, and my own life – along with the thousands of children I have helped over the years – would have been that much the poorer for it. Had I not said 'yes' to going with Raymond Ackerman, or 'yes' to the US ambassador to meet Peter Biehl, or 'yes' to the estate agent who wished to show me the property for Amy Foundation, how much smaller, less interesting and less productive my life's journey would have been! My intuition guided me to say 'yes', as I was always receptive to a fresh challenge and adventure, with the intention of leading a full life. But even more importantly, I believe that God opens doors and closes doors, and it is up to us to trust when to step inside. The word 'yes' has a certain magic to it, which comes with a promise to open new doors and opportunities. Deep down, I think we all know that 'yes' ignites a spark of opportunity that can often change our lives for the better.

> **Opportunities do not always arise again – or at least, not the same ones: when we take them, we do more, create more, and live life more vibrantly. We all need to pause and take stock of our lives from time to time, and ask ourselves the question, 'In terms of the way I'm leading my life, is this the story I would like to be writing about myself?'**

Interestingly, when I was busy planning the SA Ubuntu Foundation while still at the bank, Archbishop Tutu asked me to take over and run the Desmond Tutu Peace Foundation. Explaining that I had already committed to the Amy Biehl Foundation, I declined. Had I been available, that also would have taken me in a completely different direction.

CAN DO!

How fascinating that timing can affect all the decisions we make, both large and small, such that it has such a profound effect on one's destiny. Michael Louis' offer was just out of sync with where I was at the time, and I shudder to imagine how much I would have lost had I gone to work in a bank in Switzerland. I would like to believe that I have led the highest, fullest version of my life. Having made the choice to stay working for the Amy Foundation, my life has been far more enriched, inspired, and deepened by a cornucopia of unique experiences, relationships with remarkable people, and unforgettable travels. As I reflect thereon, I am so appreciative of all those riches – none of which can ever be bought! I believe firmly that God has a plan for each one of us. Jeremiah 29 says, 'I have a plan for you, a plan to prosper not to harm you.' He never said it would be easy and there would not be difficulties and challenges on the way.

Ubuntu – the way forward

Certain narratives in this country will always stand out as phenomenal examples of Ubuntu. Besides the work of Nelson Mandela, Archbishop Tutu, Martin Luther King, and Mahatma Gandhi, the Amy Biehl story is one of the best examples in the world of Ubuntu in its noblest form. It is an exceptional tale of forgiveness, reconciliation, and restorative justice. Amy's parents reconfigured their potentially devastating loss to change the course of history, and Amy's legacy visibly remains with us in the day-to-day work of the foundation established in her name: an enduring symbol of what is possible by slashing a new pathway through the jungle of prejudice, anger, and fear. If the Biehls could forgive their daughter's killers, we can all look for ways to forgive the people in our own lives who have wronged us. We can also look to Ubuntu to facilitate the healing process in repairing polarised relationships, create a concern for people in the workplace, and create a culture of racial, political, and cultural tolerance based on unconditional respect.

I honestly believe that the Biehls' forgiveness was heartfelt and genuine, and they would have been much the poorer for not having taken the road less travelled. Conversely, it is so tempting to allow bitterness from one's past to define a future steeped in a wretched cocktail of resentment, pain, and sorrow.

When Trevor Manuel (our much respected ex-minister of finance, 1996–2009) was guest speaker at our October 2016 Ubuntu breakfast, he repeatedly congratulated the Amy Foundation for the work we're doing, and stated emphatically that while we should not forget, we must not dwell on the past. Instead, we should seek to learn from it and do something constructive with the lessons we have learnt. 'It is about what we do with the future, given the benefit of hindsight. If the country had simply erected a monument in memory of Amy Biehl and done nothing else, we would have missed an important opportunity to make meaningful sense of this loss in the context of our tragic history. The fact that the Amy Foundation is doing such sterling, life-altering work is testimony to what is possible when we choose to channel our pain into something constructive.' Trevor Manuel went on to draw a parallel between the state of our country and the Amy narrative, explaining the need to ensure that we are all doing the right thing now, to propel us forward in the right direction. I believe that we all have a responsibility to leave the future generations with a valuable legacy.

> The purpose of life is not to win, the purpose of life is to grow and share. When you come to look back at all you have done in your life, you will get more satisfaction from the pleasure you have brought other people's lives than you will from the times that you outdid and defeated them.
>
> HAROLD KUSHNER

The Ubuntu values, if strategically and innovatively adopted, are able to contribute positively to the socio-economic development of both South Africa and the world. We must continue to strive to build a society in which all South Africans and citizens in countries throughout the world, black and white, Christian, Jew and Muslim, walk tall without

CAN DO!

any fear in expressing their inalienable rights to human dignity, with a single shared national cultural vision, and in so doing shape a world of which we can all be proud. We must develop a common South Africa and international community underpinned by Ubuntu-oriented patriotism. ■

Acknowledgements

When I set out to write this motivational memoir, which recollects my personal story, now inextricably linked with the Amy Foundation's history, I wanted to use this as an opportunity to acknowledge the role that so many amazing people have had in determining its trajectory. The fabric of everything I have achieved has been beautifully woven into a complex tapestry by the remarkable people who have worked for me and assisted me over the years. Unfortunately, it's not possible to mention every employee and donor by name, so I ask your forgiveness for this or if your name has been inadvertently omitted.

Without the input and contribution of many friends, supporters, and donors who have helped along the way, none of this would have been possible, and my story would have remained a lifelong fantasy and the book but a work of fiction! It's been an immense privilege to join hands with each and every one of you in reconfiguring the present in order to reshape our collective future, as we participate in the realisation of a sacred grand vision, and hope for reuniting the wonderful people of our beloved country and the entire world.

I wish to give thanks to professional memoir writer Toby Shenker, who agreed to assist me in sharing this narrative, which is intertwined with so much of South Africa's political and socio-economic history. When we embarked on this project a few years ago, little did we imagine how long we would be working together, to cover this expansive story, which seemed to mushroom infinitely

CAN DO!

from year to year, in tandem with the exponential growth of the Amy Foundation and the lessons I learned along the way. Toby spent innumerable hours patiently transcribing and editing the contents of our many interviews, with unfailing determination, to ensure that this book finally came to fruition. Thank you!

Thanks to my publisher, Robin Stuart-Clark of Print Matters, and Beryl Eichenberger, my publicist who believed in me and came on board readily to get this book out far and wide so that every reader can take something away to enrich and grow their lives.

I dedicate this book to humanity and to the memory of my parents, grandparents, uncles and aunts.

Special thanks to my wife Robyn, daughters Sarah and Kirsty, my son-in-law Keith. Thanks also to my brothers, cousins, neighbours, teachers at school, university lecturers, all the friends and mentors mentioned and not mentioned herein, donors big and small, board members, my staff and teams over the years, Amy Foundation ambassadors, and many other people who all had a formative role to play in determining my journey. And most importantly thanks to God, our Creator and Father. ■

Ready or not, some day it will all come to an end.
There will be no more sunrises, no minutes, hours or days.
All the things you collected, whether treasured or forgotten
will pass to someone else.
Your wealth, fame and temporal power will shrivel to irrelevance.
It will not matter what you owned or what you were owed.
Your grudges, resentments, frustrations
and jealousies will finally disappear.
So too, your hopes, ambitions, plans and to-do lists will expire.
The wins and losses that once seemed so important will fade away.
It won't matter where you came from
or what side of the tracks you lived on at the end.
It won't matter whether you were beautiful or brilliant.
Even your gender and skin color will be irrelevant.
So what will matter?
How will the value of your days be measured?
What will matter is not what you bought
but what you built, not what you got but what you gave.
What will matter is not your success but your significance.
What will matter is not what you learned but what you taught.
What will matter is every act of integrity,
compassion, courage, or sacrifice
that enriched, empowered or encouraged others
to emulate your example.
What will matter is not your competence but your character.
What will matter is not how many people you knew,
but how many will feel a lasting loss when you're gone.
What will matter is not your memories
but the memories that live in those who loved you.
What will matter is how long you will be remembered,
by whom and for what.
Living a life that matters doesn't happen by accident.
It's not a matter of circumstance but of choice.
Choose to live a life that matters.

MICHAEL JOSEPHSON – LIVING A LIFE THAT MATTERS

CAN DO! ✓